HAWAII LAWYER
Lessons in Law and Life from a Six Decade Career

HAWAII LAWYER

Lessons in Law and Life from a Six Decade Career

By **JAMES H. CASE**

Copyright © 2017 James H. Case

All rights reserved. No part of this book may be reproduced or utilized in any form or by any electronic or mechanical means, including photocopying, recording or by any information storage and retrieval system, without permission in writing from the publisher, except by a reviewer who may quote brief passages in a review. Inquires should be addressed to hawaiilawyer2017@gmail.com.

Book design: Doug Behrens Design – www.DBDZN.com

Printed in the United States of America

ISBN 978-1977713858

Library of Congress Control Number: 2017916193
CreateSpace Independent Publishing Platform, North Charleston, SC

DEDICATION

I dedicate this remembrance to my clients
throughout my sixty-three year career as
a Hawaii lawyer and to my wife,
Suzanne Espenett Case,
who has been my full partner
throughout our journey.

ACKNOWLEDGMENTS

I could not have had the career I did without the guidance, support and friendship of my fellow lawyers and staff at the Honolulu-based law firm of Carlsmith Ball. They were and are a true partnership in every sense of the word.

My wife, Suzanne Case, a librarian by profession, is an accomplished historian and genealogist. In the early 1980s she meticulously researched the history of Carlsmith Ball's first century, which she published in the firm's weekly internal newsletter over the course of a year-plus. Her account forms the basis for the first chapters of this book.

Suzi's research and account left off when I joined Carlsmith Ball, our understanding being that from then on it was my history also which I would recount myself at some point. That point came after my retirement when daughter Suzanne, a lawyer by profession, offered to take down my stories. We would get together on weekend mornings or family vacations and she would say: "What do you want to talk about today?" Over the course of a few years and with her perseverance we had the draft of this book.

Son Ed, also a lawyer by profession, proved a relentless if not ruthless fact-checker and editor. In this he was assisted by his own two-decade career at Carlsmith Ball where he rose from associate to partner to managing partner before diverting off that track to pursue his first love of politics.

Finally, my career would not have been possible without the support of my family: Suzi and our children Jimmy, Ed, John, Suzanne, Russell, Elisabeth and Brad. They were all a part of it throughout both the good and the difficult, and mostly tolerated my volunteered dinner stories and lessons from work (though I like to think that some of it all rubbed off on them!)

TABLE OF CONTENTS

INTRODUCTION .... *xi*

PART ONE: Path to Law (1896-1951) 1

PART TWO: Birth of a Firm (1800s-1920s)
1. David H. Hitchcock 18
2. Hawaii's First Wahine Loio 19
3. Carl Schurz Carlsmith 20
4. King Sugar and Adherent Planters 23

PART THREE: Setting the Stage (1920s-1940s)
5. The Next Generation: Wendell and Merrill Carlsmith 34
6. The Sugar Act of 1934 37
7. The National Labor Relations Act 39
8. The 1940s 41

PART FOUR: Career Beginnings in Post-War Hawaii (1951-1965)
9. The Dillingham Contingent Fees 48
10. The Fair Price Hearings 53
11. Bank of Hawaii: On Relationships 57
12. Ernest Cameron: On Referrals 59
13. Robert Hind Estate and Aina Haina 61
14. Hawaii Energy Part One: Hilo Electric 64
15. Hawaii Tourism and InterIsland Resorts Part One:
    Beginnings 70
16. The Koehnen Flood 78
17. Ala Moana Shopping Center 82
18. Hawaiian Dredging & Construction in Kuwait 85
19. Sam Chang: On The Unexpected 88
20. Martin Pence: On Confidences and Information 90
21. InterIsland Resorts Part Two: Growth 93
22. Kahekili Highway: On Extortion 101
23. Macadamia Nuts Part One:
    Honomalino Agricultural Company 105
24. Carlsmith Goes Statewide 112

25. Fork in the Road: The Dillingham Offer 119
26. A New Chapter 122

PART FIVE: Full Speed Ahead (1965-1985)
27. Guiding Principles: Taking Stock 134
28. Haleakala: How Much is Too Much 136
29. InterIsland Resorts Part Three: Glory Years 139
30. A Lawyer in London: Dillingham Tries to Buy Davies 150
31. Hawaii Energy Part Two:
    Kauai Electric and Citizens Utilities 158
32. Rapid Expansion for Carlsmith 165
33. The Taiwan Engagement 169
34. The Australian Connection 177
35. Hawaii Energy Part Three: Kahuku Wind Farms 183
36. A Full Service Pacific Law Firm 193
37. On Management 196

PART SIX: Ratoon Career (1985-2012)
38. Taking Stock Again 206
39. InterIsland Resorts Part Four: Final Act 208
40. Tipping Point for King Sugar: Hamakua Sugar 212
41. Family Heritage: Rolling the Boulder Uphill 223
42. Hawaii Land Reform 232
43. Growing Pains for Carlsmith 244
44. Macadamia Nuts Part Two:
    Mauna Loa Macadamia Partners 250
45. Hawaii Energy Part Four: Biofuels 260
46. Just for the Love of It: Waimea Valley 264
47. Full Circle: The Dissolution of C. Brewer 271
48. Closing the Door 275
Index 278

INTRODUCTION

I was born on a Kauai sugar plantation in the Territory of Hawaii in 1920 when Hawaii's population was 250,000 and today's Hawaii barely existed. I was sworn in as a Hawaii lawyer in 1949 when the population had doubled to a whopping 500,000, joined the law firm now known as Carlsmith Ball in 1951, and practiced continuously with Carlsmith for the next six decades until my retirement in 2012 when Hawaii's population had more than doubled again.

The fortunes of Carlsmith have been inextricably tied to the growth of modern Hawaii since the firm's founding in Hilo shortly before the Civil War. When I commenced my practice just years after the Second World War and a decade before Statehood, all of Hawaii, the firm and the firm's clients lay poised for the rapid change that was just ahead and continues to this day.

In all of this I have been most fortunate. For not only did I join a firm with a legacy already deep in Hawaii's history, and whose clients and lawyers had already left their mark on modern Hawaii. But the story was still in its early chapters, and I was able to grow and evolve with Carlsmith, its clients and Hawaii for the next half century-plus. It was quite a ride!

This is partly about Carlsmith, for it offers important lessons to lawyers and the firms in which we have been practicing for centuries. This is partly about one lawyer's career as it may offer professional and life lessons to colleagues, aspirants and others. And this is partly a history of the Hawaii I knew and to which I was privileged to contribute.

But this is mostly about clients, the people and entities who retained me and us to guide them, entrusted with their objectives, confided their hopes and fears, and allowed us to grow with them, celebrate their victories and endure their defeats. Their story was mine and Carlsmith's; they were the real contributors to Hawaii, and theirs are the real lessons.

Just as there have been many good books on Hawaii's history, so are there many other books on lawyers, firms and clients. In my view too many of them follow a well-worn path that does not capture the full flavor of the practice of law.

The real story of any law practice is the story of its clients. If clients grow, then the firm can grow and the firm can help its clients grow.

Here I relate actual stories from my practice and that of others which concentrate on the life of the client in the firm. How and why did the client come to the firm, what were its challenges and objectives, how did the firm grow (or not grow) with the client, and what eventually happened to the client. As any athletic coach knows, it is just as important to understand why something didn't work as it is to celebrate success.

Along the way I hope to shed light on what it's really like to practice law, especially among colleagues in a small and midsized firm. Among the lessons that I hope emerge are that it's ultimately about people and people are problems to be addressed: some all the time, but all at least some of the time. Your clients can be difficult; opposing clients and lawyers are not always cooperative; judges don't always see it your way; your own partners (co-owners of the firm) can be very hard to handle; your own associates (junior lawyers) usually think they know more than their experienced superiors; and your own family and friends don't always understand why you get called back to work on a moment's notice or can't tell them what's really going on. Indeed, contrary to the public perception of lawyers usually arising from a court dispute, the practice of law is much more subtle, complicated, multidimensional and grey than studying statutes and reading applicable court cases.

Perhaps the most important lesson arises from the old lawyer adage that "clients are always right (even when they aren't)". Clients have a great urge to want you to tell them that something they want to do is legal and doable – even when you know it isn't. They want you to win litigations even when they have a very bad case. Good clients will know they have a bad case and will understand if you lose. Bad clients will not accept anything less than a win. You must have enough sense to get rid of a bad client as soon as possible in as pleasant a way as is possible.

No matter: a law firm must have clients who want to engage the lawyers in a firm. Many lawyers are smart, but if clients don't trust their judgment, the law firm will fail. I hope there are lessons in my stories on how lasting client trust and loyalty are earned and retained.

Finally, I hope to shed some light on the Hawaii into which I was born and in which I consider myself lucky to have lived. Through Carlsmith and our clients, I was able to bear witness to the growth of post-war Hawaii, to its economic, political and social evolution, to the rise (and fall) of sugar, the development of tourism, diversified agriculture, alternative energy and much more, and hopefully to contribute positively to its present and future. Perhaps these stories will yield lessons for the opportunities and challenges of the next generations.

I start with a brief telling of my family's history in Hawaii and my own life until I joined Carlsmith in 1951. This is partly to place my family and me in the broader sweep of Hawaii's history, partly to tell the story of how one person became a lawyer, and partly to provide context for the following vignettes on Carlsmith and our clients. But it is also to illustrate another important lesson: the lasting influence of personal relationships, especially those forged early, throughout one's career and life. Looking back, I am amazed at the role relationships I formed in elementary and high school, college, military service, law school and early in my career played throughout my professional and personal life.

These stories are presented in broad chronological groupings to correspond roughly to the periods in Hawaii's history and my own career in which they occurred. In some cases the vignettes are specific to an era, while in others, such as the great Hawaii company C. Brewer, the stories weave in and out throughout the sweep of the last 150-plus years. I hope structuring my story in this way will emphasize one lesson, which is along the lines of the old saying that "the more things change the more they stay the same".

My reflections include many difficult circumstances and choices faced and many quite personal reflections on quite difficult and complex individuals functioning under trying conditions. I have tried to do so fairly and accurately in order to fully impart any lessons to be learned and without depicting unfairly or offending. (And in that, writing these stories at 97 years of age, I have a great advantage, as most of those I write about have now died!) I regret any offence taken and wish my heirs well in addressing any complaints.

Honolulu, Hawaii
October 2017

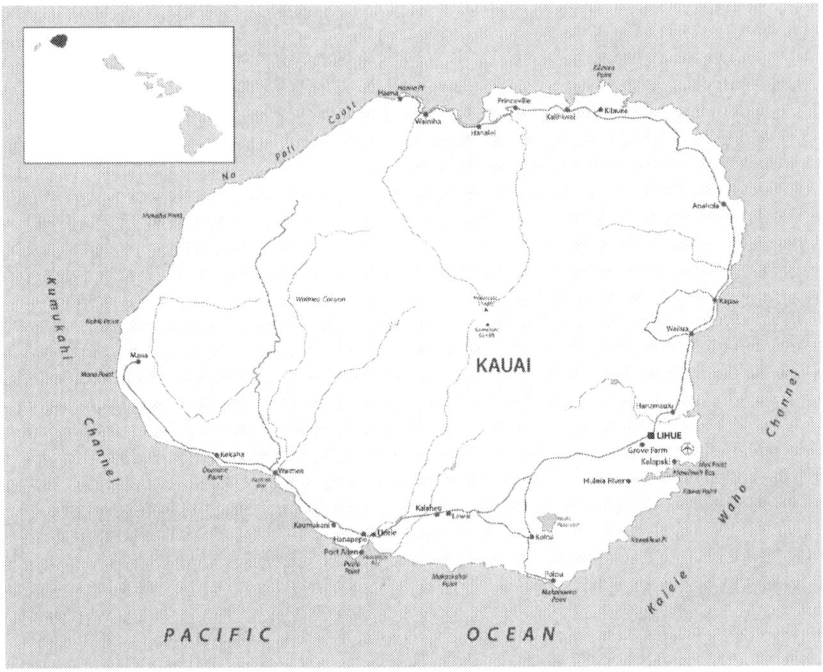
Na Pali Coast
Haena
Wainiha
Hanalei
Princeville
Kalihiwai
Kilauea
Anahola
Kapaa
Wailua
Waimea Canyon
KAUAI
Hanamaulu
LIHUE
Grove Farm
Kalapaki
Huleia River
Kalaheo
Lawai
Koloa
Poipu
Kaumakani
Hanapepe
Eleele
Port Allen
Waimea
Kekaha
Mana
Channel
Waho
Channel
PACIFIC OCEAN

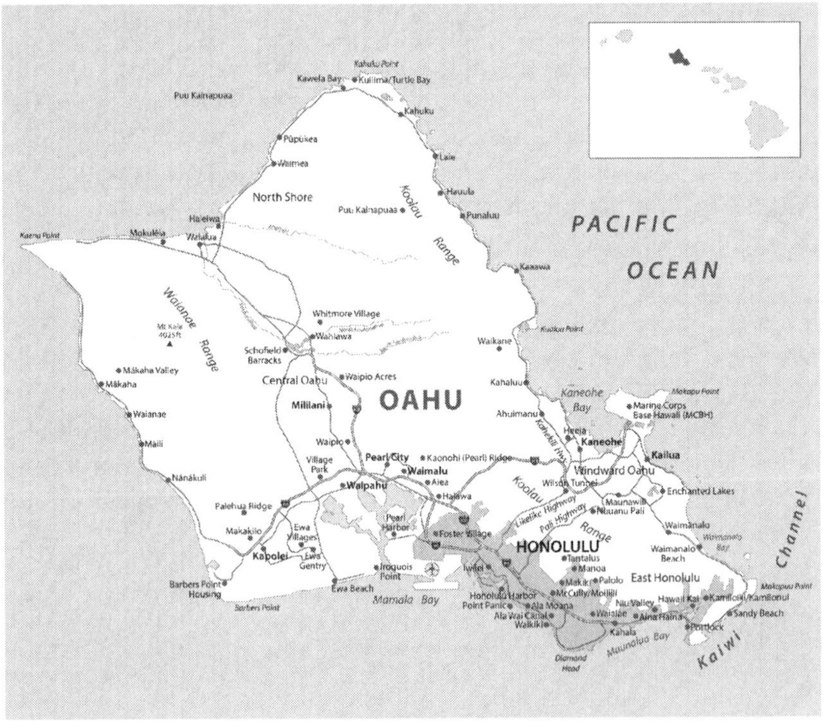
Kawela Bay
Kuilima/Turtle Bay
Puu Kainapuaa
Kahuku
Pupukea
Waimea
Laie
North Shore
Hauula
Puu Kainapuaa
Koolau Range
Punaluu
PACIFIC OCEAN
Haleiwa
Mokuleia
Waialua
Kaaawa
Waianae Range
Whitmore Village
Wahiawa
Waikane
Schofield Barracks
Makaha Valley
Makaha
Waipio Acres
Central Oahu
Kahaluu
Kaneohe Bay
Marine Corps Base Hawaii (MCBH)
OAHU
Mililani
Ahuimanu
Waianae
Heeia
Kaneohe
Waipio
Maili
Pearl City
Kaonohi (Pearl) Ridge
Kailua
Village Park
Waimalu
Windward Oahu
Nanakuli
Waipahu
Aiea
Wilson Tunnel
Enchanted Lakes
Halawa
Palehua Ridge
Likelike Highway
Maunawili
Pali Highway
Nuuanu Pali
Pearl Harbor
Makakilo
Ewa Villages
Foster Village
Waimanalo
HONOLULU
Waimanalo Beach
Kapolei
Ewa Gentry
Tantalus
Iroquois Point
Manoa
Iwilei
Makiki
Palolo
East Honolulu
Barbers Point Housing
Ewa Beach
Honolulu Harbor
McCully/Moiliili
Mamala Bay
Point Panic
Ala Moana
Niu Valley
Hawaii Kai
Kamiloiki/Kamilonui
Ala Wai Canal
Waialae
Aina Haina
Sandy Beach
Waikiki
Portlock
Kahala
Maunalua Bay
Kalwi
Channel

Island Maps xv

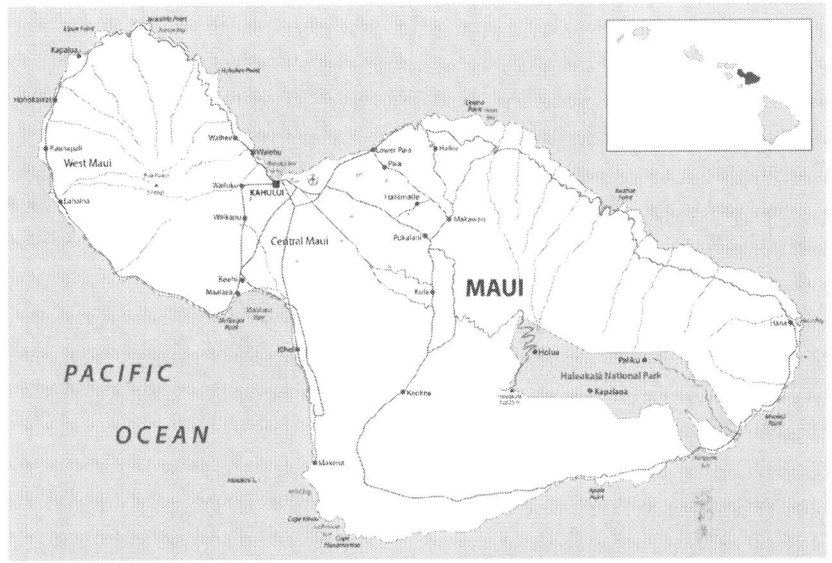

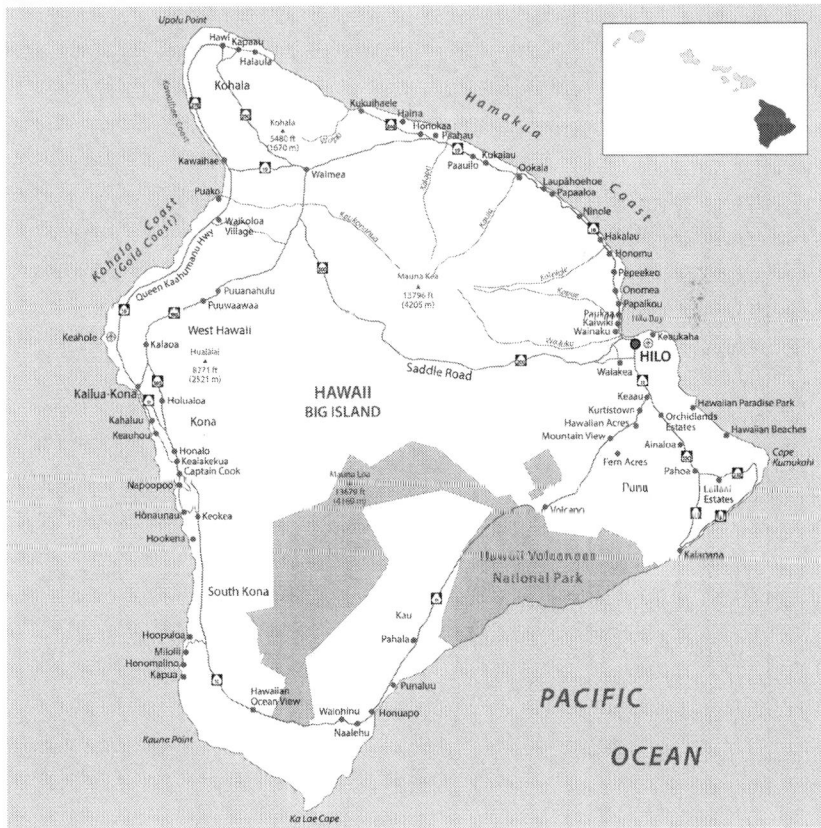

PART ONE

Path to Law
(1896-1951)

I was born at home on Steam Plow Alley, Grove Farm Plantation, Lihue, Kauai on April 10, 1920.

My grandfather, Daniel H. Case, had moved to Honolulu, Republic of Hawaii from Topeka, Kansas in 1896 as an apprentice lawyer. His own parents were pioneer lawyers in Kansas after the Civil War, then practicing under the firm name Case & Case. They would "ride the circuit" around Kansas with a judge, picking up clients and trying cases on the go (whence the term "Circuit Court").

Soon after arriving in Honolulu Daniel Case joined the prominent law firm of Kinney and Ballou as a young associate. (Kinney and Ballou is still one of Hawaii's three largest firms, later to enter my early career as Anderson, Wrenn & Jenks and practicing today as Goodsill Anderson Quinn and Stifel.) In a very odd coincidence to become evident later, he filled a vacancy created by the departure of associate Carl Smith to Hilo, Hawaii to become the junior lawyer in a firm then called Hitchcock and Smith (now Carlsmith Ball). Who could possibly have forecast then that Daniel Case's grandson would later join Carlsmith for a 61 year career to include service as Chair of its Executive Committee.

Daniel's and his wife Kathryn's son and my father, Aderial Hebard ("Hib") Case, was four years old when the family moved to Honolulu. The family lived for about four years in Makiki, right across from Punahou School, which Hib attended.

In 1900 Daniel received an offer from Maui's leading lawyer to move to Maui, become a junior partner, and take over the firm when the older lawyer retired. This Daniel did, later being appointed a Circuit Court judge and serving on the bench on Maui for two decades. His picture still hangs in the old courthouse in Wailuku.

Initially Hib remained behind to continue at Punahou, boarding with his aunt and uncle, Minnie Merriam Atherton and Charles Atherton, but later moved to Maui with his parents where he grew up until high school. He was then sent to Staunton Military Academy in Virginia for high school, and from there to Cornell University, New York to study pre-law. But he was no lawyer-in-waiting, and so transferred to the School of

Tropical Agriculture at the University of Hawaii. His graduation class in 1917 had (astonishing for the time) six men and six women.

These were war years and Hib had joined the Hawaii National Guard, which was mobilized and assigned to Schofield Barracks. There he met his future wife and my mother, Elizabeth (Betty) McConnell, who was then teaching public school in Haleiwa.

Betty was born in Evanston, Illinois in 1895 to Midwest pioneer parents. Her father died when she was just twelve, and her widowed mother moved the family to Long Beach, California where her sister lived. Betty spent her high school years there and then graduated from UCLA with a degree in education, one of the few real career opportunities available to women college graduates at the time.

Her roommate at UCLA was "Babe" Henshaw, who lived in Honolulu where her father was a lawyer. After graduation Babe invited my mother to visit her in Honolulu. When a reasonable visit time had expired, Betty applied to the Department of Education for a teaching job. In the custom of the time, she was hired but to a small remote school in Haleiwa, where she met my father at a Schofield officers social event.

They were married shortly after and moved to Kauai, where my father had taken a job at Grove Farm as a chemist in the Lihue mill. I was their eldest child, followed by my brothers Bill in 1922 and Dan in 1925. Our early years were spent on Grove Farm and all over Kauai.

I went to elementary school at Lihue Grammar School. There were 120 students in the class, divided into four sections of 30 students each. I was the only Caucasian boy in my class; there were two Caucasian girls. A majority of the students spoke Japanese at home. About three fourths of the students needed special training in English. Those who already spoke good English were in a special classroom called the Annex. I spoke good English in the classroom and at home; on the playground I spoke pidgin. I had to remember where I was before I spoke.

George N. ("G.N.") Wilcox, who founded Grove Farm, had set up a scholarship so that Kauai students could go to Punahou. I was valedictorian of my class and received a four-year tuition scholarship at Punahou.

Twenty-five percent of the coed student body at Punahou at the time was from the neighbor islands or rural Oahu and boarded in the dorms. So we saw a lot of each other and formed lifetime relationships that would weave in and out of my career.

I actually enjoyed the school work (and the athletics) at Punahou. I was valedictorian of my Class of 1937 and got a scholarship to Williams College in Massachusetts, one of the oldest colleges in our country.

The majority of the students at Williams were way ahead of me scholastically and I had to work extremely hard to catch up. Luckily, it paid off and my grades were very good (except for the first semester, which seems to be common to island students at mainland colleges). Influenced by my grandfather, Judge Case, with whom I had spent summers on Maui, I had decided on a legal career and was admitted to Yale Law School for the class entering in September 1941.

As I prepared to graduate from Williams in 1941, I and most of my class became convinced that we would soon have to join the war against Germany, and I believed that we would soon be at war with Japan also. As a result, I joined much of my class in applying to Officer Training School and the military rather than go on to graduate school or start careers.

I was declined because I was slightly near-sighted. So I returned to Hawaii and went to work for the U.S. Army Corps of Engineers in Honolulu, building airstrips and otherwise preparing for a Japanese invasion or attack. On December 7, 1941, I awakened at my apartment in Waikiki to the attack and the certainty that the war was on. I continued working for the Corps of Engineers until early 1943, when I applied for and received a commission in the United States Navy (I guess my eyes had improved).

My next three-and-a-half years were spent on active duty as a Naval officer: first at the Naval Officer Training School in Tucson, Arizona; next at San Clemente Island, California where we trained the Navy and Marines for landings in the Pacific; next at the Fleet Training Center in Miami where I received officer training on destroyers; next at the Radar Training Center at Hollywood, Florida where I learned how to be a radar officer at sea; next at the Submarine Training Center at Key West, where I learned how to defend against submarine attacks; next at the Fleet Training Center at Miami for a second time, where I taught radar to newer officers; next at Norfolk, Virginia where the entire crew for a new destroyer escort assembled; next at Brooklyn Navy Yard where our entire crew took over the brand new ship called the USS Heyliger, Destroyer Escort 510; next to Guantanamo Bay, Cuba where we performed shake-down exercises to make sure that the ship was prepared for combat; and next to the Western Pacific for the remainder of the war.

My Navy service "grew me up". At age 23 on San Clemente Island I was in charge of the construction department with a dozen experienced older men under my command; at 24 I was in charge of the radar department on the USS Heyliger with 12 men under my command, and also stood Officer of the Deck watches throughout my service aboard the ship until I was made Executive Officer at age 25. As XO I had all the officers (12 except the Commanding Officer) and all of the crew (200 men) under my command. These early responsibilities readied me to assume executive positions in civilian life early in my career.

After the war ended our ship was sent to Boston, Massachusetts. I still had law school in my sights and an opening at Yale, but I thought it would be more fun to live in Boston for three years than New Haven, Connecticut. So I took the subway over to Harvard Law School and applied for admission. Amazingly, they accepted my verbal report about my grades and admitted me starting September 1946. (My mother thought I had a strange reason to choose Harvard over Yale, but I was 25 and a war veteran and she couldn't do much about it.)

Harvard was exhilarating. Virtually our entire class of 600 students was veterans whose legal careers had been suspended by the war. The average age was 26 (my own age); many were married. Strangely enough, I knew many of them from either college or the Navy. Charles E. Clapp had graduated from Williams (my brother Bill's classmate); another of my classmates was a Williams classmate; another was a Williams graduate with whom I had served in the Navy in Miami. There were many others whom I had met either at Williams or somewhere during my Navy career.

Intrigued with business, I concentrated on corporate law and taxes. During my senior year I took a course on Corporate Finance at the Harvard Business School, in which we studied corporate executive strategies to raise money through equity or debt. My Advanced Corporate Law course studied how to structure transactions to facilitate financing. I also took a course on corporate accounting, which was extremely popular because many classmates contemplated corporate law work. There were 200 in the class, twenty of whom were certified public accountants. The student with the best grade in a class was given an A Plus; I got that A Plus ahead of all the CPAs (and had occasion to tell the story to a troublesome CPA or two during my career).

During my second year at law school I met Suzanne Catherine Espenett of Missouri, a student at Wellesley College just outside Boston. We were engaged in the spring of 1948. She told her parents in St. Louis that she was engaged to a man from Hawaii. They said: "You are not. We would like to meet him." So I dutifully hitchhiked out to St. Louis for the first two weeks of that summer where I passed inspection. We were married on September 18, 1948, and then drove back to Boston to start our life together as almost literally starving students. (Like so many other veterans, I will always be deeply grateful for the GI Bill.)

During my last year at Harvard we had to think seriously about where we wanted to live next. I thought that I could get a good job anywhere in the United States, but where did we want to put down roots? We both liked New England, I had spent good time in New York City but we ruled that out. We ticked through the other places I'd lived in the Navy: Tucson, Arizona (much too hot); San Clemente Island (no trees, no water, no women); San Diego (liked but if there then why not Hawaii instead); Los Angeles/Long Beach (I really didn't like Los Angeles); Miami, Florida and environs (flat, hot, bugs); Norfolk, Virginia (too small).

I went first and said that I liked either New England or Hawaii as my first choices. Suzi, who'd never been west not to mention Hawaii and whose first sight of any ocean was in her teens, answered: "But, what about Missouri?" Frankly, I was shaken. Sometimes you just have to tell the truth, so I said: "There is no water within a thousand miles." She answered: "There is Lake Quivera just a few miles outside of Kansas City". I was getting scared. I tried again. "That's just a small pond. You can't sail on it." "You're right", she said. "I don't think that I would like to go back to Missouri anyway – at least not to live".

So we settled on Hawaii. My wife continues to claim that I had decided on Hawaii before we started discussions; I have always steadfastly denied this.

There was one complication, though: both Suzi and her parents were intent on her getting a college degree and she had one year left at Wellesley. We called them to explain that we were moving to Hawaii (in itself a lot for them to swallow; I'm sure they never envisioned her disappearing for life to the other side of the world) and that we felt we needed to make the move now. Her dad said: "Jim, ok, but promise me you'll make sure she finishes college." I did and so she did and more, though not as and when expected.

Honolulu was by then squarely the center seat of Hawaii and regardless of where one's legal career might lead it was at least the go-to place to start out. Now I began to think about law firms in Honolulu. Where should I apply?

By this time my father, Hib Case, had risen to Chief Financial Officer and Treasurer of Grove Farm and in that capacity had worked closely with the preeminent Honolulu firms then known as (1) Pratt, Tavares & Cassidy (today Case Lombardi & Pettit, after my brother, Daniel Case, who spent his entire half-century career there), (2) Anderson, Wrenn & Jenks (today Goodsill), and (3) Smith Wild Beebe & Cades (today Cades Schutte). Grove Farm's normal attorneys were Pratt. I wrote from Harvard to ask my father what he thought of them and what I should do.

According to him, Grove Farm owner G.N. Wilcox had much earlier told manager Edward Broadbent: "Your son-in-law, C. Dudley Pratt, looks like he will become a very good lawyer. He grew up in Hawaii, went to Punahou, and graduated from Yale, where he was Captain of the Yale swimming team. It looks like he will be very successful. Even more important, that firm is clearly one of the best firms in Honolulu. Therefore, send your legal business to the firm unless there is some good reason to send it elsewhere." This in fact happened and continued for decades.

During that period, though, there had been some changes in corporate management at Grove Farm. Grove Farm had used American Factors (later known as Amfac) as its Honolulu agent to sell its sugar for many years. Gaylord Wilcox, a nephew of owner G. N. Wilcox, had been in the Amfac plantation management division. William P. Alexander had become Manager of Grove Farm in about 1932.

Sometime after G. N. Wilcox died, perhaps around 1933, Gaylord moved to Kauai and took over as president of Grove Farm. He chose to make major corporate decisions, but leave day-to-day operations to two subordinates. Alexander continued as manager for all field operations: sugar, pineapple and ranching. My father assumed all administrative duties, to include chief financial officer, labor and industrial relations, and insurance and legal matters.

In this latter capacity Hib Case followed the policy laid down by G.N. Wilcox; he primarily used Pratt for legal work but worked with

Smith and Anderson when there was a good reason to send it elsewhere. He felt that Pratt had been competent over the years. He did not like working for some of the Anderson lawyers because they were "snooty", and thought moreover that the firm was too busy with major Honolulu clients like Bank of Hawaii, C. Brewer, Castle & Cooke, Hawaiian Electric, and Hawaiian Telephone to pay attention to such a small client as Grove Farm, and that Grove Farm was paying high legal fees considering the experience of the Anderson lawyers who worked on his cases. He had worked with Smith and had been happy with their work.

Somewhere along the way Grove Farm and Amfac (also owner of Koloa Sugar Company) decided to explore the possibility of Grove Farm acquiring Koloa. Both sides needed legal counsel. Either Gaylord Wilcox or my father called go-to Pratt lawyer Dudley Pratt and asked him if he would come to Kauai to discuss a major legal job. In fact, it was Grove Farm's largest legal job in at least a half century.

Much to Grove Farm's surprise, Dudley Pratt did not come personally but instead sent a mid-level corporate partner to Kauai. He seemed staggered by the job and appeared to be floundering and uncertain of how to proceed. My father felt it was a disaster and looked elsewhere.

Grove Farm decided to discuss the matter with Smith, who advised them that they could do the job and put senior partner Urban Wild, who had handled such acquisitions before, on the job. Wild seemed to know what he was doing and laid out his complete plan of attack. Grove Farm was very impressed and retained him; the acquisition closed in 1948.

My father explained to me that the Pratt firm had nearly collapsed in 1947 when senior partner Stanley had retired and senior partners Vitousek and Wynn had died, all within a span of about three months; it would take some superb management to pull the firm back together. He felt my best opportunity was at Smith, though either Pratt or Anderson was still a good opportunity if I could not get a job at Smith. I applied to Smith, who responded some time later that it had just hired Harold Wright, my Harvard classmate, and didn't have room for another lawyer.

I also contacted Page Anderson, my classmate at both Punahou and Harvard Law, who had graduated early and was back in Hawaii, to see what he thought of the Honolulu firms. A short while later (while I was awaiting responses from Smith and Page Anderson), an unexpected notice appeared on the Harvard job search bulletin board that would unknowingly chart the course of my career:

"Mr. C. Wendell Carlsmith, senior partner at the firm of Carlsmith, Carlsmith & Cox in Hilo, Hawaii, would like to interview students interested in practicing law in Hawaii."

Wendell Carlsmith, partner with his brother Merrill in a three-lawyer firm in Hilo I had barely if ever heard of, had decided that he wanted to expand by hiring a competent lawyer from a good law school. I later learned that Wendell believed in hiring the best people possible and paying them more than they could get anywhere else in Hawaii, even though Carlsmith was a small Hilo law firm. He believed in building up his lawyer staff with people he could trust to do the work. He felt that he could bring the work in. And as it turned out he could, as long as he had competent people that he could trust to do the work. He decided to recruit at Harvard, even though his father was a Stanford graduate and both he and Merrill were graduates of Stanford Law School.

The sign-up sheets provided for thirty minute interviews starting at 8:00 A.M. on some date, say, October 15, 1948. There was no way I was going to Hilo; my career lay in the big law firms of the big city of Honolulu. And my wife and I had promised her parents that she would finish college, which she couldn't do in Hilo. I decided to sign up for the 8:00 A.M. spot and see whether Mr. Carlsmith would be kind enough to tell me about the various law firms in Honolulu.

I am surprised today that I had the gall to do this; I could blame it on youth but I'm afraid it was much worse. In any event, it turned into one of the oddest and funniest, and most fortuitous, interviews I was ever party to.

As I walked in to see Mr. Carlsmith, I just decided to take the bull by the horns.

"Look, Mr. Carlsmith, I signed up for an 8:00 interview, because I wanted to ask you for your help."

He asked: "Aren't you interested in a job?"

I said: "Mr. Carlsmith, I can't work for you, but I came here to ask for your help. My wife has to finish college and we have to get a job in Honolulu. I was sure that you could help me."

Taken aback, Wendell said: "So, you don't want a job with me, but you want me to help you? Well look, let's talk about it. You're the grandson of Judge Case, aren't you?" "Yes." "And your father works for Grove Farm." "Yes." Then he said: "Well, I knew Judge Case very well, one of the best judges I ever practiced before."

He thought a moment and then he said: "Okay. Here's the deal. Here's the list of everybody I'm going to interview. I want you to tell me what you know about every single one of them. One of my important criteria is that they're going to stick with me. I don't want to hire them and have them quit."

Then he said further: "I think I can get you a job. I know the law firms down in Honolulu, and I think I can get you the job. I think they will listen to me." So he went down the list.

I said: "Well, the best lawyer on your interview list, Mr. Carlsmith, is a guy called Jack Hoffman. He's one of my best friends here, he grew up in San Francisco, he was in Honolulu during the War, he's a bachelor, and he's your best lawyer. But he won't stay with you. He's not going to go to Hilo and be satisfied there."

(Wendell didn't offer him a job. Jack Hoffman ended up going to Pillsbury Madison & Sutro, the best law firm in California at the time, and was their leading Securities and Exchange Commission (federal securities/stock) lawyer for many years. I worked with him often over the years. If I didn't know the answer to an SEC question, I would call him up.)

Then I said: "Here is a guy that isn't as good a lawyer as Hoffman but ever since he got here, and for three years, he has wanted to go to Hawaii. His name is Luman Nevels."

Then I went through the others. We finished the thirty minutes. I thanked him for helping me. The interview ended with Mr. Carlsmith advising me that he thought he could get a job for me at Pratt.

A very short time later I received a letter from Dudley Pratt advising me that Mr. Carlsmith had applied on my behalf for a job, and that Pratt, Tavares & Cassidy had accepted my application to start in the fall of 1949. I had a job!

Three days later, Page Anderson wrote back and said that the senior partners at Anderson Wrenn & Jenks liked my resume and had authorized him to transmit an offer. However, I had already written Pratt back to accept its offer and could not in good conscience consider the Anderson offer.

Suzi and I returned to Hawaii in September 1949; it had been three years since I was home, and a whole new world for her. We spent that month on Kauai while I studied for my bar exams, and I started work at Pratt, Tavares & Cassidy in October 1949. We were flat broke.

The next two years passed quickly and with mixed results. Our first of seven children, Jimmy, was born in 1950 and we focused increasingly on family. As it turned out, the University of Hawaii only gave Suzi two years of credit for her three years at Wellesley, which made it impossible for her to finish college before the children started coming (for which I still find it difficult to forgive UH).

But I was coming to the difficult conclusion that, if I wanted to realize my goal of rising to the top of my profession as a business lawyer, Pratt, at least as it was then and as it was going, was not my best path. I had been tempted in 1951 by an offer from Hawaiian Pineapple to join as its General Counsel, but had concluded that that was not where I wanted to go.

One day in 1951 Wendell Carlsmith, down from Hilo on a business trip, called me up and said: "Can you have dinner with me down at the Royal Hawaiian Hotel." Of course I said yes, mainly because I wasn't used to having dinner down at the Royal Hawaiian Hotel. He said "Look, two years have gone by, Lu Nevels did come, but he's gone off to the Korean War and we need to replace him right away. Can you come to Hilo now?"

My wife and I struggled with: "What to do?"

I was earning $350 a month at Pratt; Carlsmith offered me $500. So I not only would have a higher salary but I would able to find a much cheaper house to rent in Hilo. I had grown up on a neighbor island and often thought that Hilo would be a great place to raise a family if I had a good legal job. And I believed that, though it was Hilo and not Honolulu, the path Wendell Carlsmith had set the firm upon to grow into the biggest and best in Hawaii was achievable and there was a place in that to realize my goals.

Suzi and I closed our eyes and jumped. I started work at Carlsmith, Carlsmith & Cox in Hilo, a town of 27,000, on November 1, 1951. There were three partners and one associate (me being the associate), one receptionist (also the accounting clerk) and three secretaries. The War was just six years past, the Territory of Hawaii had eight years still to run, and I was to practice law continuously with Carlsmith for over six decades until my retirement on December 31, 2012.

A. H. CASE. MRS. LUCIA O. CASE.

CASE & CASE,
LAWYERS.

119 West Fifth Street,

Law Business Only.
All Courts.

TOPEKA, KANSAS.

Great-grandparents' business card ca. 1880

Grandfather Judge Daniel H. Case, Wailuku, Hawaii, ca. 1930

Part One: *Path to Law* (1896-1951) 13

Case family, Grove Farm, Kauai, 1937 (l.to r.) Dan, Hib, Bill, Betty, Jim

Punahou School graduation, 1937

Aboard USS Heyliger (DE-510), Western Pacific, 1945

With Suzi on return to Honolulu, 1949

Part One: *Path to Law* (1896-1951) 15

Downtown Honolulu, surrender of Japan, 1945 (HAWAII STATE ARCHIVES)

Suzi finally graduates from University of Hawaii, 1958 (with l. to r. John, Suzanne, Ed and Rusty)

PART TWO

Birth of a Firm
(1800s-1920s)

1. David H. Hitchcock

Harvey R. Hitchcock and his wife arrived in Honolulu in 1832 as missionaries. David Hitchcock was born just one month after their arrival. Shortly thereafter the Hitchcocks were sent off to Molokai. They may have been the first non-Hawaiians to live there. David spoke English at home, but in most of his childhood he spoke Hawaiian.

Somehow David's family found the funds to send him to Williams College. He returned to Hawaii and lived for a short while on Molokai. There he "read law" (the path to practicing law for lawyers of that day).

On December 16, 1856 Hitchcock received an appointment as Police Justice in Hilo (judge of the lower court responsible for minor offenses). He moved to Hilo and in April 1857 opened an office for the practice of law (police justices being allowed to practice as well). His office was next to an early park (now called Kalakaua Park) where Carlsmith's Hilo office is still located.

Hitchcock prospered in law, business and politics. He was well educated and benefited from speaking Hawaiian as well as anyone. With court proceedings all conducted in Hawaiian, lawyers who did not speak Hawaiian had a difficult time as they had to work through interpreters. He was an early investor in sugar and served for a quarter century in the Legislature of the Kingdom of Hawaii.

David Hitchcock had two children. Son D. Howard Hitchcock became one of Hawaii's most famous painters.

2. Hawaii's First Wahine Loio

Daughter Almeda Hitchcock grew up in Hilo, also learning fluent Hawaiian before attending Punahou School. She returned to Hilo and was hired by her father to work in his practice. Her job today might be referred to as a paralegal but probably included receptionist, secretary, bookkeeper, and anything else that needed doing and that her father could pass over to her. Just as my own grandparents had done back in Kansas, she rode the circuit with her father all over the Big Island as he tried cases in the various courts.

Soon, however, she met Miss Cora A. Benneson, a graduate of the Class of 1880 at the University of Michigan Law School who was making a journey around the world. Cora energized Almeda and an idea flashed upon this young woman that she might be a lawyer herself. "Why don't I go to law school? Why can't I be a lawyer?" With her father's encouragement, she entered the University of Michigan Law School and graduated in 1888.

In short order, on Almeda's return to Honolulu, the Supreme Court of Hawaii admitted her to practice as Hawaii's first woman lawyer and her father made her his partner practicing under the firm name "Hitchcock & Hitchcock". On their way back to Hilo they stopped off in Waimea where the circuit court was sitting and Almeda won her first appearance in the case of *Apau v. Naaikauna*.

Back in Hilo Almeda settled into the practice with her father, aided as he had been with her command of Hawaiian. ("The natives were all astonished to see a 'Wa-hi-ne-lo-io' (woman lawyer) and the remarks as I passed by were often amusing. They did not realize that I understood their language.") But tragically she died in 1895 at just 32 years of age. Her newspaper obituary observed: "She was a person with great promise."

3. Carl Schurz Carlsmith

In the 1890s David Hitchcock was getting older and was not well. He had developed a notable practice on the Island of Hawaii and was generally known throughout the state, in part from his service in the legislature of the Kingdom of Hawaii. With Almeda's death, he looked for a successor to the firm and practice he had founded.

Carl Schurz Smith (originally Schmidt), a German-American born in Vermont, had grown up in San Jose and graduated in 1893 with the first class at Stanford University, where notable classmates included President Herbert Hoover and longtime Mayor of Honolulu Johnny Wilson. He then attended Northwestern Law School in Chicago, graduating in 1895, and married Nelle Wood, who had been a few classes behind him at Stanford.

How they came to move to Hawaii is unknown, but they arrived in Honolulu, Republic of Hawaii in 1897, where Carl soon landed a job with Kinney & Ballou (in my early years Anderson, Wrenn & Jenks and today Goodsill). But he left within just a few months (replaced by my grandfather Daniel H. Case), prompted by the opportunity to join David Hitchcock in Hilo as his junior partner and take over the firm on Hitchcock's retirement.

Carl and Nelle arrived in Hilo in 1898, just weeks before Hawaii was annexed to the United States as a territory. He commenced practice with Hitchcock under the firm name "Hitchcock & Smith". But on December 12, 1899, as the century turned, Hitchcock died, concluding a four-decade career that had spanned the Kingdom, Republic and Territory of Hawaii.

The law practice was now solely in the hands of Carl Smith, 29 years old. New to Hilo and with better-established competitors, he mostly represented smaller clients in opposition to larger businesses.

One engagement that he remembered later was a criminal case arising out of alleged cruelty by a plantation manager (Scottish, as many were) against his Chinese laborers. The manager had lashed his worker for failing to report to work, and the laborer's cousins had attacked and killed the manager and had been charged with first degree murder. Smith took on the defendants' representation:

"By challenging 12 jurymen out of 24, [I] was able to get a reasonable lot on the jury and so we went to trial. The atmosphere was electric. My argument to the jury in that case was one of the best I ever made. The jury was out for two hours. The verdict: acquittal for one defendant, guilty of third degree murder for the other, who drew a five year sentence and subsequently served only three. How those Scotsmen hated me .... But the case made [me]. Chinese, Japanese, Hawaiians all flocked to [me], and [I] had more business than all the other lawyers in town together."

Another that enhanced his reputation came shortly after he served his one and only term in the Territorial Legislature in 1905, where he focused on establishment of county governments. Retained by the Government of Japan to represent a Japan national whose Onomea store had been washed away because of water diversion by a county road crew, he won a verdict of $7,500 for the store owner as well as the subsequent appeal to the Supreme Court of Hawaii (establishing the principle that counties may be sued for negligence and are not protected by government immunity).

In 1911 Smith successfully petitioned to change his last name (and that of his wife and their by-then four children) to Carlsmith. As the story goes, there were other attorneys in Hilo by the name of Smith, including at least one whose offices were also on Waianuenue Avenue (where the courthouse then stood), and one day a confidential letter to Carl Smith instead went to opposing counsel Smith. That accelerated formalizing the common community referral to the family as the "Carl Smiths" to distinguish them from the other Smiths.

Carl Carlsmith continued his almost exclusively trial practice in Hilo for the next few decades. He sometimes had partners and sometimes practiced alone. But over time, as his reputation and demand for his services grew, his clientele began to switch to broader representation of the businesses and their owners who he had previously opposed. He continued in fulltime practice until his sons Wendell and Merrill joined him in 1928 and 1930, when the firm name was changed to "Carlsmith & Carlsmith", by which it was mostly known until 1959. He gradually phased out as Wendell and Merrill picked up steam. He died in Hilo in 1959, having successfully carried the torch from David Hitchcock to his sons through the changes that would lay the foundation for Carlsmith's growth.

It is sometimes difficult to imagine how Carl Carlsmith and before him David Hitchcock, while they practiced true to the best traditions of the legal profession, did so in such a different time and place. Perhaps this late-life reminiscence of Carlsmith of his early years in Hilo gives some indication of the world in which he lived and worked:

"Out of the old days when native Hawaiians were a majority many things come back. But of all of them I recall most vividly the death wail and the aku song.

"In the quiet of some evening a long drawn wail told of the death of some Hawaiian. As you listened the sound was repeated all night long. It is a long time now since we heard that solemn sound.

"And it is a long time now since we have heard the canoes return from a night's fishing. Before sunrise the fishermen's song would come – It seemed like miles away.

"They stroked the water with even strokes and when they changed sides each gave a resounding blow to the canoe side. They sang the aku song older than Cook or the Spaniards, and at regular intervals they counted in unison the amount of the catch. Ekane, elua, ekolu and so on to tell the folks ashore what generous food the sea had yielded for the day's meal."

4. King Sugar and Adherent Planters

Like so much else of Hawaii present and past, the fortunes of Carlsmith were inextricably tied to sugar in many and varied ways.

Hawaii sugar on a plantation scale dates to 1835 when Ladd & Company started operations at Koloa, Kauai. This was before the Great Mahele of 1848 when the King, who prior thereto owned all of the lands of Hawaii, divided his lands with his chiefs. The ahupuaa system was still in effect, under which the lands of Hawaii were generally divided into pie-shaped slices from the mountains to and into the oceans and the chiefs administered their ahupuaa for the King. The plantation owners occupied the lands of an ahupuaa with the consent of the administering chief and had to ask the chief for native Hawaiian labor to work the fields. The chief would assign labor to do the job, collect all the pay, and split it between the King, chief and laborers, much as in feudal England or Japan.

Ladd & Company had a difficult time until after the Great Mahele, which introduced to Hawaii a "Western" land ownership system that continues to this day with some incorporation of the ancient Hawaiian system. It then acquired a lease from the owner of the ahupuaa, co-signed by the Governor of Kauai who administered the land on behalf of the King. The Hawaiian tenants were now free to work for Ladd & Company on their own account.

Ladd & Company eventually became Koloa Sugar Company, which continued in business until 1948 when it was acquired by Grove Farm Plantation. It closed in 1974 with Grove Farm's suspension of sugar operations and lease of the land to McBryde Sugar Company, which brought in its last sugar crop in 1996, the end of a century and a half of sugar on Kauai.

In the mid-19th century other sugar plantations also started up throughout Hawaii for the same reasons as Ladd & Company on Kauai. They were small plantations in those days, maybe 50-70 of them sprinkled throughout the tillable lands of all the islands.

One of them was Hitchcock & Co. Sugar Plantation. It was started in 1875 by Edward G. Hitchcock (David Hitchcock's brother), David H. Hitchcock, and Dr. C. H. Wetmore at Onomea on the Hamakua Coast just outside Hilo. Edward was the agriculturalist, David was the businessman/lawyer, and Wetmore was the investor.

1875 also marked the beginning of the rapid growth of the Hawaii sugar industry which came to be referred to sometimes as "King Sugar". In that year King Kalakaua negotiated the Reciprocity Treaty with the United States whereby he gave the United States coaling rights at Pearl Harbor, a coaling station being necessary for long-range steam ships. By this time American merchant and naval shipping needed a coaling station somewhere between the United States and the Far East. Every country wanted a coaling station in Hawaii. Pearl Harbor was a very good harbor – certainly the best in Hawaii and arguably in the Pacific. The Reciprocity Treaty provided that Pearl Harbor would be leased to the United States Navy for a coaling station. That was the beginning of the military presence of the United States in Hawaii.

The Reciprocity Treaty gave Hawaii in return the right to export sugar duty-free into the United States. Suddenly Hawaii sugar was very economical and profitable. Hawaii sugar planters could grow their sugar here and send it to the emerging Pacific Coast markets, particularly San Francisco, without import duty. While there were cane sugar plantations in Florida, Louisiana, and Texas and beet sugar operations in Minnesota, Hawaii sugar production was efficient and demand outstripped supply.

An avalanche of further sugar cane plantations started up throughout Hawaii. The shape of King Sugar began to emerge as the Honolulu agents for the plantations acquired and consolidated ownership and operation of the plantations until by the early twentieth century there were just five who owned and operated most of Hawaii sugar. Referred to commonly as the "Big Five", they were C. Brewer & Co., Ltd. (founded 1826), Theo H. Davies & Co. (1845), American Factors (Amfac) (1849), Castle & Cooke (1851) and Alexander & Baldwin (1870).

Hitchcock & Co. Sugar Plantation was part of this evolution. It prospered, changed its name to Papaikou Plantation, and was absorbed into Onomea Sugar Company, which in turn was acquired by C. Brewer. Carlsmith through David Hitchcock represented the plantation, and represented C. Brewer at various points throughout its history. In fact, stories of the Big Five and Brewer in particular weave through this book as they do through so much of Hawaii history.

Aside from Carlsmith's general representation of the sugar industry, one case from the mid-1920s both solidified Carl Carlsmith's position and set son Wendell firmly on course to take Carlsmith statewide. This was the case of the adherent planters, *Correa v. Waiakea Mill*, which went to the Supreme Court of Hawaii a number of times between 1927 and 1932.

The adherent planter system was unique to the plantations of the Island of Hawaii. Adherent planters usually worked for the plantation, but the plantation would separately lease land too difficult for normal cultivation, such as on slopes or in gullies, to the planter to grow and sell back to the plantation.

Correa, an adherent planter and effectively on behalf of all adherent planters, sued Waiakea Mill Company, located just outside Hilo, over a matter relating to the interpretation of the adherent planter contract. Though Waiakea Mill was a Theo. H. Davies company, the outcome of the lawsuit would impact all adherent contracts for all plantations and so all plantations and their owners were keenly interested and involved.

Carl Carlsmith took and won the case for Waiakea Mill, which enhanced both Carlsmith's and his statewide reputation especially with the established businesses of Honolulu. Equally important to Carlsmith in the long run, Wendell Carlsmith was then a student at Stanford Law School. He started working on the case during summer vacations, continued throughout the school year, and started his legal career on the case, in the process becoming an expert on the entire adherent planter system. Not only would this stand him in good stead when related cases arose, as they did, but the movers and shakers of Hawaii knew who this young Hilo lawyer from this small Hilo firm was from the day he started practicing law.

Lesson learned: You can never know when you may get a chance to work on a major case. Wendell Carlsmith gained an invaluable reputation because he got and made the most of that chance very early in his career. Never underestimate the possible importance of a fluke, a piece of luck. The secret lies in making something of it.

David H. Hitchcock (MISSION HOUSES MUSEUM LIBRARY)

Part Two: *Birth of a Firm* (1800s-1920s) 27

Almeda E. Hitchcock (Joan Hitchcock Humme)

City directory for Hitchcock & Hitchcock, 1893-94

Hitchcock & Smith, Waianuenue Avenue, Hilo, 1898

Part Two: *Birth of a Firm* (1800s-1920s)   29

*Waianuenue Avenue, Hilo, date unknown
(Hitchcock law office on left)* (HAWAII STATE ARCHIVES)

*Advertisement by David Hitchcock
in English and Hawaiian
announcing new partner, 1898*

D. H. Hitchcock,
Counselor and Attorney-at-Law,
HILO, HAWAII.

The partnership existing between myself and Mr. W. S. Wise having been dissolved by mutual consent, I would notify my old friends and patrons that "I am still alive" and will still keep up the "Old Hitchcock" law practice on this island.

I am expecting in a short time a "live, wide awake, and up to date" partner who will attend to the business before all the courts of this island, and I hope that my old clients will give me their business as heretofore.   D. H. HITCHCOCK.
Hilo, April 1, 1898.   35-3t

D. H. HITCHCOCK
(HIKIKOKI.)
LOIO,   -   -   -   HILO, HAWAII.

No ka hookaawale ana o'u me kuu hoa hui W. S. Wise, ke hoolaha aku nei au i ko'u mau hoa kanaka Hawaii, e mau ana no ka hamama ana o kuu keena loio ma Hilo nei, no ke kokua ana ia oukou iloko o na Aha apau o keia mokupuni. Iloko o keia mau la e hiki hou mai ana he hoa no'u, he kanaka akamai loa ma ke kanawai.

E lawe mai oukou i ko oukou mau puolo pilikia a kamailio no ko oukou pilikia. Aole uku no na kuka olelo ana a me ka hoolohe ana ia pukou. Ma ka uku haahaa no ka lawelawe ana i na hihia a oukou.

Ko oukou hoaloha imi ka wa kahiko mai.
   D. H. HITCHCOCK.
Hilo, Aperila 1, 1898.

Nelle and Carl Schurz Smith, ca. 1895

Carl Smith office, Waianuenue Avenue, Hilo, ca. 1900

Part Two: *Birth of a Firm* (1800s-1920s)　31

Fishing canoes, Wailoa River, Hilo (Hawaii State Archives)

Carl S. Carlsmith

PART THREE

Setting the Stage
(1920s-1940s)

5. The Next Generation: Wendell and Merrill Carlsmith

Carl Wendell Carlsmith

The most influential figure in the history of Carlsmith and in my own career was Carl Wendell Carlsmith. (Indeed, I would go so far as to say that he was one of the most influential figures of mid-20th century Hawaii although few know him, but that is generally as it is and should be for the best lawyers.)

Wendell was born in Hilo in 1904, the third of Carl and Nelle Carlsmith's four children. He attended the Hilo public schools, graduating from Hilo High School, and, like his parents before him and all of his siblings, went to Stanford University. (In fact, this Stanford family in its first three generations had sent over a dozen Carlsmiths to Stanford where they acquired at least four Stanford spouses.) He graduated from Stanford Law School in 1928 and returned home to become his father's junior partner in the same office on Waianuenue Avenue where the firm had been located already for a half century-plus. He took over the reins of firm management from his father in 1932, a position he would hold until I took over from him in 1965.

This book is in large part about Wendell and so those stories are to be told. Suffice it to say for now that in his time Wendell was not only one of if not the best corporate, labor, public utilities and all-around business lawyers in Hawaii, but was at or above par with the best nationally and internationally.

But Wendell's secret was that he was far more than just a lawyer; he was a true counselor. Clients valued (and paid for) not only his legal knowledge (they could get that elsewhere); they valued his judgment and ultimately his wisdom. "You've told me the relevant facts and the law and my options, now what should I do?" That's what they wanted and that's what he provided.

He also was a master at achieving their goals. Partly this was just solid organization and implementation. But mostly this was his uncanny ability to see way down a road through multiple forks and just know how best to get from point A to point B. Many a time did an opposing client and lawyer (or a Carlsmith lawyer) arrive at a destination point with no other practical option than what Wendell had foreseen several steps back; he was always a few steps ahead.

Restless, driven, always moving and talking, relentlessly goal-focused, not especially tactful (except when it served a purpose), not especially respectful of personal and family time (except when it served a purpose), not one to suffer others' shortcomings quietly, sometimes controversial, he was a challenge to work for and with. But the mark he made on Hawaii, Carlsmith, clients, community and me is inescapable. He practiced law fulltime with Carlsmith for a half century before semi-retirement and died in 1982.

Two lessons. First, a strong central figure can make an incredible difference to any organization. Second, seek out mentors early in a career and try to find the best at what they do.

Merrill Lawrence Carlsmith

If Wendell was the driving force behind Carlsmith from 1928 through the 1960s, his brother Merrill was its stable home base.

Merrill was born in Hilo in 1905 and, like Wendell, attended Hilo public schools and Stanford University before graduating from Stanford Law School in 1930. He returned home and went into partnership with his father and brother in the firm renamed "Carlsmith & Carlsmith", by which it would be known for a quarter century (with the short interlude of Carlsmith, Carlsmith & Cox from 1949 to 1951) until 1959.

Like father Carl Carlsmith and David H. Hitchcock before him, Merrill was a quintessential trial lawyer. He was soon the best trial lawyer on the Big Island and in time among the best statewide. His specialty was land disputes, which led him to become a recognized expert on Hawaii land law generally.

Wendell and Merrill were great complements to each other. They practiced in different areas of the law and so were able to assist each other and cross-sell and expand clients. While Wendell was managing the firm and driving toward expansion, eventually moving to Honolulu,

Merrill took care of the basics of the business throughout his Hilo career.

In fact, Merrill was far better known and involved in the community than Wendell, in part because of his outgoing personality and in part because of talents and interests outside the practice of law. One was that he was a top-ranked golfer.

Parents Carl and Nelle both played golf and Merrill learned the game at an early age, becoming captain of the Stanford University golf team. He was the foremost golfer on the Big Island for twenty to thirty years and captured several state titles. In his mid-50s Merrill competed in the United States Senior Men's Amateur Golf Championship, winning two titles.

One of my favorite stories about Merrill, golf, and coincidences goes this way. Stanford played the University of California in golf in Merrill's senior year. Cal had an extremely good golfer. Merrill beat him to clinch the match for Stanford. Some 33 years later Merrill reached the finals of the U.S. Senior Men's championship. His opponent was the former captain of the Cal golf team. Merrill beat him again.

Merrill was also one of the original watermen. In the 1930s he had acquired a beachfront parcel at Honomalino Bay in South Kona where he and his family and friends would spend weekends and vacations fishing by days and playing cribbage and partying by night. His skill as a spearfisherman and lobsterman was legendary; it was nothing for him to go off on a fishing expedition with his original Hawaiian sling and spear crafted at Hilo Iron Works and his secret underwater flashlight and return with ulua and lobster. My own family owes him a debt of gratitude, for he would invite us as well and in time allow us to stay on our own, from which our children also grew up in the ways of the ocean.

Merrill's career with Carlsmith would last almost fifty years until he retired in the mid-1970s; he died in 1983. I don't mention him often in these stories because I mostly was not a trial lawyer and I mostly worked with Wendell. But he played a critical role in creating a strong law firm, delivered on the essential elements of a sound practice, and gave Wendell the base and support needed to take Carlsmith to the next levels.

6. The Sugar Act of 1934

That opportunity for Wendell and Carlsmith to practice law on a broader scale and with the full attention of the entire sugar industry came with two back-to-back events in the mid -1930s. The first was the Sugar Act of 1934.

The U.S. Congress was then considering legislation to regulate both the import of foreign sugar and the adherent planter contracts. The domestic sugar industry wanted quotas placed on the importation of foreign sugar.

Why was this quota system important? The problem simply was that the international sugar industry was not a truly competitive industry.

The biggest problem was Europe. Beet sugar growers in France and Germany were very influential in their (pre-European Union) governments. The result was that the European countries paid sugar beet growers 28 cents per pound for the sugar and then resold it to consumers in Europe at something like 20 cents per pound. It was so lucrative that beet sugar growers multiplied, so much so that a lot more sugar was grown than Europe needed. The excess was dumped on the world market at cut-rate prices.

Many nations in the Middle East, the Caribbean, and Central America also grew sugar cane. In fact, before the Castro revolution Cuba was a huge producer – something like 8,000,000 tons of sugar per year. Many of these governments went into sugar directly as a government operation. The purpose was not to grow sugar profitably but to create jobs. They were low cost producers and like Europe grew much more sugar than they consumed. The excess sugar was dumped on the world market at cut-rate prices.

Hawaii, Florida, Louisiana, and Texas also grew cane sugar. California, Minnesota, North Dakota, and South Dakota grew beet sugar. They were highly productive and highly efficient, with Hawaii sugar in particular ranking at the top worldwide in tons per acre. They could compete very well in a truly competitive international market, but that was not the case. A system of quotas on foreign imports would control domestic supply and demand and protect domestic producers from unfair below-production low prices on the world market.

Arrayed against the domestic sugar producers were powerful interests. One was the foreign governments themselves, who saw this as an important aspect of overall foreign policy with the United States. Another was United States sugar refineries, who liked the status quo which allowed them to buy sugar at international dumping prices, process it, and sell it to grocery stores for home consumption. Their partners were bulk industrial users of sugar like Coca-Cola, Pepsi Cola and large bakery chains.

It was a complicated issue and negotiation and the outcome was critical to the future of Hawaiian sugar and through it the Hawaiian economy. The Hawaii sugar industry hired Herman Phleger, a prominent senior partner at Brobeck Phleger and Harrison, at that time San Francisco's second largest law firm, to represent them in the negotiations. At the same time the industry was aware that Wendell Carlsmith knew more about sugar generally and adherent planters specifically than any lawyer in the state. So the industry retained Wendell to be Phleger's co-counsel.

At the age of 30 Wendell was sent to Washington, D.C. with Phleger for six months where, in close consultation with industry leaders back home, they successfully negotiated out the details of the new Sugar Act with the administration and Congress. After its enactment, the Sugar Act would underpin sugar's preeminent role in Hawaii's economy and social fabric for several decades.

For Wendell and Carlsmith, the executives of Hawaii's foremost industry became very well acquainted with Wendell and his capabilities during his six month representation. For his part, his work was a major factor in giving Wendell access on a first-name basis to all of the highest Big Five executives and other Hawaii business leaders.

7. The National Labor Relations Act

The second event of critical importance to Carlsmith's development was the National Labor Relations Act, passed in 1935, which gave workers the right to organize and bargain collectively. Soon thereafter the International Longshore and Warehouse Union (ILWU) under legendary leaders Harry Bridges and Jack Hall decided to attempt to organize all dock workers in Hawaii.

The ILWU struck the Hilo docks as its first target. Violence broke out, with the police brought in with guns and other force to defend the wharves against the striking workers. Luckily nobody was killed, but some of the strikers were injured.

(Strangely enough, one of the injured men and a leader of the ILWU in Hilo, Bert Nakano, became a long-time friend of mine. I negotiated with him many times during my years as a Big Island labor lawyer representing employers. We often differed on our positions, but we always tried to find a way to reach a contract that would work for both the employer and the union and their workers.)

Wendell was at the forefront in representing the entire dock industry. Moreover, the entire state took interest in the strike because it was the first test of wills between the ILWU and the Hawaii business establishment and because the Hilo docks were essential to bringing goods to Hawaii and taking sugar and pineapple back to the mainland. Wendell became, instantaneously, the state's foremost labor law lawyer.

Next, the ILWU struck the Maui docks. Wendell was hired by the sugar industry to represent it and basically all business on Maui involving labor relations. Shortly after, he was hired by the industry to represent the entire industry in all labor relations involving the ILWU and the sugar industry, including Oahu and Kauai.

In this situation Wendell represented and worked with something like thirty different sugar plantations statewide owned or controlled by the Big Five. He had to work directly across the industry to get industry consensus on what to do, and to negotiate directly with Jack Hall who was running the show for the ILWU in Hawaii.

That gave Wendell access again to the leaders of business in Hawaii. He had proven to be a good litigator, negotiator and business lawyer and gained their respect and trust.

As the 1930s and Wendell's first decade as a lawyer ended and Merrill's career was established, Carlsmith's position on the Island of Hawaii was stable and secure. But Wendell now also directly represented the entire sugar industry and had secured a statewide reputation with the overall Hawaii business community.

8. The 1940s

Carlsmith and Wendell and Merrill hit a pause of sorts in the 1940s as the War and its aftermath dominated. Sugar, ranching, agriculture and small business went on and people still needed agreements and got in disputes, so good lawyers kept practicing. The only major new work that came Carlsmith's way and may have laid some of the further foundation for Carlsmith's next chapters was representing various businesses before the Alien Custodial Property Board. The owners of such businesses were nationals of countries with which the United States was at war and federal law provided for the potential seizure of their property and payment of compensation.

Throughout the 30s and this period and as their father had phased out his practice Wendell and Merrill has basically run Carlsmith as a two-lawyer shop. But as the post-war period kicked in and opportunities for growth became apparent they looked to staff up for the next steps.

In 1947 they hired Gilbert E. Cox as an associate. Cox had graduated from law school in Texas just before Pearl Harbor. He joined the legal department of the U. S. Army, which sent him to Hawaii. At the end of the war he decided that he would like to remain in Hawaii and found his way to Carlsmith in Hilo. He was very talented and in short order was made a partner in what became known as Carlsmith, Carlsmith & Cox.

Wendell assigned Gil to assist him in his corporate and labor law practice. It was just a short time later that he was doing all of the labor law work, Hilo Electric Light Company work, and other Hawaii Island corporate work. However, as happened with many others, Hilo life was not quite right for him and his family. He moved to Honolulu in 1952 to join Smith Wild Beebe & Cades (now Cades Schutte) as a partner. He subsequently became President of American Factors and, later, President of Alexander & Baldwin.

This, then, was the situation with Carlsmith as I returned home to begin my legal career in Honolulu in 1949 and to join Carlsmith in Hilo on November 1, 1951. It was a top Hawaii Island firm with top Hawaii

Island lawyers. But moreover, it was known through the state as the largest (at three lawyers!) and best firm outside Honolulu (so said the Honolulu lawyers with more than a little condescension), and Wendell had a statewide reputation and statewide representation of the Big Five and other prominent businesses. Though seemingly a small platform for growth, it was well positioned to take advantage of the changes and opportunities of post-War Hawaii, though the explosive growth that in fact followed was difficult to foresee then.

Part Three: *Setting the Stage* (1920s-1940s)   43

C. Wendell Carlsmith

Merrill and Wendell Carlsmith, ca. 1930

Hilo, 1929 (HAWAII STATE ARCHIVES)

Part Three: *Setting the Stage* (1920s-1940s) 45

C. Brewer & Co., Fort Street, Honolulu, ca. 1890 (HAWAII STATE ARCHIVES)

Pepeekeo Plantation, Hamakua Coast, 1935 (Pan Pacific Press Bureau, Hawaii State Archives)

PART FOUR

Career Foundations in Post-War Hawaii
(1951-1965)

9. The Dillingham Contingent Fees

My baptism of fire with Carlsmith and Wendell came immediately with the Dillingham contingent fee cases.

The Dillinghams were a prominent Hawaii family tracing to Benjamin Franklin Dillingham (1844-1918). Dillingham had arrived in Honolulu in 1865 as first mate on a packet. While riding horseback he fell and broke his leg and his ship sailed without him. After his recovery he decided there may be a future for him in Hawaii and stayed on.

He turned into a very successful businessman, among other things founding Oahu Railway and Land Company which ran railroads between all of the sugar plantations and the wharves, and owning and operating Oahu and Hawaii Island sugar plantations. His son, Walter F. Dillingham (1875-1963), was equally if not more successful, among other things founding Hawaiian Dredging & Construction Company (one of whose early projects was to dredge out Pearl Harbor).

In 1950 Walter Dillingham and his siblings owned the family businesses but Walter and his two sons, Lowell S. Dillingham and Benjamin F. Dillingham II, ran them. Walter and his sons had also formed their own family partnership called Dillingham Brothers. If the Dillinghams were not technically Big Five, they were akin to it; Wendell was known to them and they were known to Wendell.

The various Dillingham organizations decided on two courses of action. For reasons that are lost to time, but may have included secrecy concerns or potential legal conflicts, they decided not to retain or even tell their usual law firm, Anderson Wrenn & Jenks (today Goodsill).

Instead, they secretly hired Carlsmith through Wendell. Exactly how and why they came to hire Wendell is unknown, but it could well have been a strong recommendation from Ernest Cameron, of whom more later. Whatever the reason, it was highly fortuitous for Wendell and Carlsmith and, as time went on, me.

The Dillinghams and Wendell negotiated a contingent fee engagement. For each engagement, if and only if it was completed successfully, the firm would be paid a flat fee of $100,000 (about $1,000,000 in 2017 dollars).

Kahaluu and Ahuimanu

As background for the first engagement, at the end of World War II the Dillinghams had come up with an idea which was unique at that time in Honolulu. The grocery store practice then went like this: a housewife would telephone the store and place orders, the store would then deliver the goods to the house, and the grocery store would send a bill to the house at the end of each month.

Here was the innovative idea: the shopper would go into the store and purchase goods for cash. This new "Cash & Carry" system would allow the store to lower the price of groceries tremendously. How revolutionary!

They opened their new store in Iwilei just after the War. Nobody came. Everybody liked the credit and everybody liked the home delivery. Dillingham Brothers lost about $700,000 over just a few years.

Before I joined Carlsmith the Dillinghams had decided to close the grocery business. The tax law then, and it's not too different today, was that you could carry forward your operating losses to reduce future taxes for five years, after which if not used they're gone. Dillingham Brothers needed a profitable project on which their grocery business operating losses could be applied to reduce future taxes. Everything had to be in place by December 31, 1951. If it was, Dillingham Brothers would get their operating loss carryover and Carlsmith would get its $100,000 fee.

Wendell Carlsmith had found out that the Catholic Church owned both Kahaluu Valley and Ahuimanu Valley in Windward Oahu. If Dillingham Brothers with Carlsmith could acquire and resell the land by the tax deadline it would fit the bill.

Ahuimanu had been leased to a dairy, but the lessee had not used good husbandry in caring for the land as required by the lease and guava trees and other noxious weeds grew everywhere. The Church wanted to get the lessee off the land without getting embroiled in litigation. It wanted to sell the land as it felt it was of little worth.

Kahaluu was a tract of land next door to Ahuimanu. It had never been developed and there was no lessee. However, the Church did not want to get into the development business, and wanted to sell it as well.

Somehow Dillingham Brothers, with help from Wendell, was able to negotiate and finance the purchase of both properties from the Catholic Church on favorable terms. When I started work on November 1, 1951, both needed to be sold in just two months.

For Kahaluu Valley, there were then no subdivision or zoning requirements which would entail long drawn-out permitting timeframes and expenses. Dillingham Brothers subdivided the property into larger farm lots, put in basic roads and set a dirt-cheap price of about $5,000 for a five acre lot. Buyers didn't get any amenities but they were able to acquire a large piece of land in fee simple for a very favorable price. The development sold out in short order though the documentation logistics for all of the transactions occurring at once were a nightmare.

The goal with Ahuimanu Valley was to resell it to a single investor. That was achieved by forming a separate Dillingham entity, Dillingham Partners Company, to purchase the land. I was assigned the primary responsibility of doing so. It was fascinating work for a corporate and tax lawyer and included drafting and negotiating a complex partnership agreement among Walter, Lowell and Ben Dillingham, and Wendell Carlsmith who took a partnership interest as an investor to help raise the purchase money.

Between that and the Ahuimanu loan and completing the land transactions for both Kahaluu and Ahuimanu, the ensuing weeks were what my wife has sometimes referred to as "My Working Christmas Day." Everybody in the firm worked 8, 10, 12 hours and more a day, Saturdays and Sundays, even Christmas Day, to get that land sold by December 31st. And we did; we received the $100,000 contingent fee.

The Honolulu Waterfront

On the second engagement, Dillingham subsidiary Oahu Railway & Land Company owned the whole waterfront of Honolulu Harbor. In the early '50s the Dillinghams determined to sell it. Interisland service for passenger vessels was dead. Interisland service by freight on ordinary vessels was also dead; it was all moved now by barge companies. The waterfront was land Oahu Railway didn't need for railway operations. Dillingham engaged Carlsmith to assist with the sale on a contingent fee basis; if and when the waterfront was sold Carlsmith would be paid $100,000.

This job, which ended up stretching into the mid-1960s, was one of many in which Wendell demonstrated his skill and value as more than just a lawyer. He knew his client, he could think and act like his client, and his client completely trusted him. Wendell was in effect his client. His job was to get the docks sold. He conceived of how to do so and then implemented his plan through negotiation, contacts and the wide array of other talents and tools available to him.

First, though, while Wendell was masterminding the sale, the legal status of title (ownership) of the waterfront lands needed to be addressed. Complicated to begin with, title was a mess and had to be cleaned up. Merrill Carlsmith stepped in to clear title with his own version of "My Working Christmas Day" only at high intensity over many years.

Unbeknownst to anybody at the time, and maybe still not well known today, Wendell tried several buyers for the docks. He became convinced that the best buyer was the State of Hawaii. In today's world where the waterfront is public land it seems unfathomable that the State would not be interested, but it wasn't then. How was he going to persuade the State to spend a great deal of money to buy the docks?

The angle came from an unusual direction and relationship. Year after year dating back to the dock strikes of the 1940s, Wendell had been negotiating the longshoremen contracts but remaining on friendly terms with Jack Hall, the head of the ILWU in Hawaii. Jack Hall was an honest and highly competent negotiator. He and Wendell formed a lasting friendship although they were on opposite sides of the table.

They could get behind the scenes where Wendell would say "Now look, Jack, why are you really doing this?" and Jack would tell him, or vice versa. And then Wendell would tell him why the industry didn't want to do something that Jack wanted but would it work this way, or vice versa. These conversations were outside the theater of the negotiating room where negotiators couldn't be frank and actually discuss various solutions when the room was packed with people. That's how Wendell handled labor relationships on a high level with Jack Hall.

By the 1960s the 1954 Democratic Revolution was well established, Democrat John A. Burns was Governor and the unions were very powerful politically. A direct overture from the Dillinghams, on the wrong side of the revolution, to Governor Burns and the Legislature to sell the docks to the State, at least at a reasonable price, was not going to work.

Wendell went to Jack Hall to convince him that the State was the best owner of the docks for his longshoremen and for the general public. Jack Hall agreed: after all it was better for his ILWU members if they worked and negotiated with the known quantity of the State rather than some private owner/successor to Oahu Railway they didn't know. So Jack Hall (not Wendell or Dillingham) went to Governor Burns with the idea, which Burns embraced. He and the Legislature, with Jack Hall's ILWU in strong support, passed the law authorizing the State's acquisition of the Honolulu waterfront and appropriating the funds for the purchase.

It had taken Wendell a decade and a half to achieve his client's goal, but he and Carlsmith had persevered and eventually found a way to make it happen. Carlsmith was paid its second $100,000 contingency fee.

10. The Fair Price Hearings

The Sugar Act of 1934 had also established a system of regulation of the relationship between sugar plantations and their adherent planters (sometimes called "independent growers") that had been the subject of Carl S. Carlsmith's successful representation of the plantations and Wendell Carlsmith's early training back in the 1920s.

The Act required that the U. S. Department of Agriculture dictate annually the price which Hawaii plantations had to pay adherent planters for their sugar cane. It also set minimum wages which the plantations had to pay their employees and imposed other requirements on sugar operations.

USDA set these "fair prices" following annual hearings with representatives of the plantations and the adherent planters. The hearings were held once a year in Hilo by the chief officer of the USDA. They usually lasted a week though preparation for the hearings took a good two months.

There were then thirteen sugar plantations on the island of Hawaii, all controlled by four of the Big Five. There was quite a wide spread between them of what might be called a fair price because while the general analysis was the same the facts differed from plantation to plantation.

The adherent planters received a plot of land free of rent from the plantation on which they could grow sugar cane. For one reason or another, the land was not suitable for the plantations, usually because it was too steep for the mechanical equipment, such as tractors, mechanical harvesting machines and trucks, for the plantation to cultivate. The adherent planter had a full-time job at the plantation but became an adherent planter after hours. The entire family cultivated, fertilized and did other tasks which they could do but the plantations could not do. Their costs were very low; almost any payment they got from the plantation was higher than their own cost of growing sugar cane on that land, if they could do it at all. The extra cane helped spread overhead costs for the plantation. The purchase was worthwhile for the plantation as long as the overall profit of the plantation was increased because of the purchases.

Despite individual differences, the plantations decided, as did the adherent planters, to negotiate and advocate collectively. Wendell had brought the work in after enactment of the Sugar Act. By the time I joined Carlsmith Gil Cox was in charge of the fair price hearings; I was assigned to assist him.

We would ask each plantation to give us their financial statements: costs of cultivation, costs of harvesting, and, most of all, cost of processing. We also asked for revenues from the sales of sugar and molasses. We then tried to assemble these statistics into an overall scenario which showed the point at which it would be profitable for the plantations to buy the sugar cane. We estimated the costs of cultivation of the adherent planters.

I did most of the assembling of the data, and suggested an overall fair price to Gil. Gil would look it over, ask questions and make decisions, and I would prepare a draft brief for review by the thirteen plantations and the four representatives from the Honolulu owners.

If you assumed that the decision-making meeting of representatives from thirteen plantations, four of the Big Five owners, Gil Cox and me was a circus, you would be right. Somehow, decisions were made and I would draft our brief for presentation to the USDA at the fair price hearings. This draft obviously drew multiple "suggestions". Gil and I discussed these suggestions, Gil made further decisions, and I re-drew the draft. The final brief, about one inch thick, suggested a fair price for the year. We submitted it to the USDA hearing officer on the designated date, with copies to the attorney for the adherent planters, and, of course, to the thirteen plantations and the four members of the Big Five.

The attorney for the adherent planters throughout my fourteen or so years of fair price hearings was Nelson Doi. Born and raised on the Big Island, Doi led a long and distinguished career as a State Senator (elected in the Democratic Revolution of 1954), Lieutenant Governor and Circuit Court Judge, among others. But I knew him not as the politician but as an excellent attorney and, though we were often legal adversaries, a person I could resolve matters amicably with and a friend.

Nelson would similarly meet with representatives for the adherent planters on each of the thirteen plantations and prepare and submit a similar brief suggesting a proper fair price for the year. A full hearing before the USDA officer followed at the Hilo federal building/courthouse across Waianuenue Avenue from the Carlsmith office.

It was a strange procedure. We submitted our brief with a short explanation. Nelson Doi asked questions of Gil Cox. Gil answered or huddled with our group. Then Nelson submitted his brief with explanation, Gil asked questions of Nelson, and Nelson either answered or huddled. Then the hearing officer asked questions of either Gil or Nelson and they either answered or huddled. The hearing finally concluded.

Some weeks later the hearing officer announced his decision. We always felt that the hearing officer favored the adherent planters. But the system, at the required price, was still better for both the plantations and the adherent planters than no adherent planters at all. There never was an appeal of a decision.

In 1952, shortly after my first fair price hearings, Gil Cox announced his move to Honolulu to accept a partnership at what is now Cades Schutte. Our clients told Wendell Carlsmith that they were comfortable with my taking the lead role on this work, but that Wendell should make sure that I didn't get off track. Thereafter I did all the work but conferred with Wendell on tough "political situations", such as what to do when two of my clients disagreed on some issue. This supervision diminished as time went on.

This work proved immensely valuable to my later career. I now knew the managers and chief financial officers of every plantation on the Big Island on a first name basis. The same was true of the executives of the four of the Big Five who had executive authority over the plantations. The four members of the Big Five continued to use their Honolulu attorneys for their own primary corporate work. However, if a matter involved all or most all of the Big Five, they used me because they were all familiar with me and none wanted to use a law firm which "belonged" to someone else. Just one example was my later retention by California & Hawaiian Sugar Company ("C&H"), the sugar refiner jointly developed and owned by the Big Five and operating mainly out of Crockett, California to avoid dependence by Hawaii sugar on the larger mainland sugar refineries.

Lesson learned: It is extremely difficult to work with multiple clients. Try to do something to avoid this. For example, try to persuade clients that meetings of large groups are nearly impossible. Ask the clients to form a representative steering committee. Think of some way of representing a large group that simplifies the task.

11. Bank of Hawaii: On Relationships

Bank of Hawaii had commenced business in the late 1890s. In the first quarter of the twentieth century the bank embarked upon an expansion campaign by opening or acquiring branches in many localities on all the islands.

One of Bankoh's targets was the Bank of Maui, Maui's first bank founded in 1901 as First National Bank of Wailuku by some Maui investors represented by my grandfather, Daniel H. Case. In order to avoid paying legal expenses in cash, they granted my grandfather stock in the Bank of Maui. When Bank of Maui merged into Bank of Hawaii in about 1930 that stock was converted to Bankoh stock. I and my grandfather's other descendants still own that stock, at an original cost of less than One Cent per share.

Bankoh acquired the First Bank of Hilo and its four branches in 1922. I don't know when or how the First Bank of Hilo or Bankoh began using Carlsmith, but I started representing the bank when I joined Carlsmith in Hilo in 1951 and continued with all of its Big Island work, including work that came in from its Kohala and Kona branches, for many years.

In part this was sheer proximity, for Bankoh's main Big Island branch was directly across the street from the Carlsmith office, not even thirty seconds away and that without jaywalking. I could walk over to meet with bank officers and they could walk over to see me to discuss some current issue or new legal work.

In part this was about connections, a key theme running through my story. Essentially, a connection, wherever and however it has arisen (whether through happenstance or conscious effort), gives a lawyer an initial chance to meet with a potential client. At that meeting you must persuade the client that you can do the job he/she wants. Thereafter, the continued connection depends on the quality of your work.

My connections with Bankoh across the island arose largely from my days as a boarder at Punahou School. As one example, Walter Ackerman had been manager of the Kona branch when I boarded with his three children; I had met and knew him from then. Similarly, Charles Vannatta was manager of the Kohala branch; his sons had also boarded at Punahou and one son, Bill, became manager of the Hilo branch during my time in Hilo. These relationships got me in the door, but after that it was up to me to keep and expand the work.

Today's Goodsill firm had represented Bankoh on its general matters from its founding; we did not represent the bank on non-Hawaii island branch matters through the 1950s. However, as we expanded our Honolulu presence in the late '50s and '60s we worked our way into increasingly representing Bankoh if Goodsill could not because of a conflict of interest with another client. Then, largely through the efforts of later partner Tom Van Winkle (of which more later), we directly took on more of the bank's work until by the '80s it was (and still remains) one of Carlsmith's largest clients.

As I moved my practice increasingly to Honolulu in the early '60s and other attorneys in our Hilo office took over Bankoh's Big Island representation, I developed a different relationship with the bank. I often represented clients who required financing, one of my specialties being to help them to determine the best type of financing for their needs and then to persuade the best lender to grant the loan. Because I knew Bankoh and its guidelines very well, unless the client had a specific reason to approach another lender I routinely recommended starting with that bank. I never asked for a loan which I thought Bankoh wouldn't approve, and helped clients secure dozens of major loans.

Lesson learned when dealing with financial institutions and lending: Never ask for the moon; ask for something the bank will find acceptable. Banks must make loans; that is their business. Go in with all the information that they need. Make sure it is a good loan for the bank. Don't ask for a loan if you are worried that your client might default on the loan.

12. Ernest Cameron: On Referrals

One of the critical lessons of my career is the importance of referral sources, for they can feed a lawyer and firm they trust in many and varied ways both expected and unexpected. In this sense Ernest R. Cameron (1890-1953) was almost as important as Wendell Carlsmith to the growth of Carlsmith in these years, and his influence on Carlsmith and my career lasted long after both were gone.

As Wendell Carlsmith started representing major Honolulu clients in the 1930s, he decided to retain a major Honolulu accounting firm to advise on Carlsmith's accounting and tax work for both its clients and itself. Partly this was because the practice was becoming more sophisticated every year. But partly this was a shrewd calculation by Wendell that through that firm he would have access to the firm's other statewide clients (provided he and Carlsmith earned its trust).

Ernest Cameron, Certified Public Accountant, then headed one of Hawaii's two major accounting firms. Another Stanford graduate (a persistent theme throughout), he had moved to Hawaii in 1915 and had commenced his practice in 1918. By the 1930s he and his firm did most of the tax and much of the auditing work for most of Hawaii's mid-to-large businesses and many of its families.

Cameron was a very competent tax man to start with. But, like the difference between a good and a very good to great lawyer, he had the unusual ability to go beyond straight CPA work and think like a businessman. His clients sought not only his accounting advice, but his business judgment. He and Wendell were a very good match and Wendell did earn his full trust and referrals.

By the time I joined Carlsmith in 1951 the firm was known as Cameron Tennent & Dunn. While Cameron focused on tax work, Hugh Tennent headed up the auditing and accounting side of the practice. His wife was the famous artist Madge Tennent; his son, Val Tennent, was in my Punahou class and headed the firm's Hilo office in the 1950s. Herb Dunn and another four or five very good accountants rounded out the firm; I worked with all of them throughout much of my career as my clients would be their clients as well (or we would cross-refer).

I had been trained in corporate and tax law and practiced in that area in my first job in Honolulu, and on joining Carlsmith I was designated the firm's corporate and tax attorney. However, Wendell thought I was too inexperienced in 1951 to be fully entrusted with the major tax issues the firm and its clients were facing.

I thought, of course, that he underestimated me. But he nonetheless assigned Cameron Tennent & Dunn to watch over me, which in turn led to my own long relationship with the firm and its professionals.

(The anecdote also points to a mostly friendly and sometimes not-so-friendly rivalry between lawyers and accountants that's as old as the professions themselves. Attorneys think we know much more about taxes than CPAs because major tax work involves reading and interpreting tax law, regulations and cases and advising our clients of options and solutions, while CPAs think lawyers just serve to confuse the law and clients where things are perfectly clear. At least in Hawaii, businesses tend to think CPAs are best for taxes … until they get audited.)

In 1960 Cameron Tennent & Dunn was merged into Peat, Marwick, Mitchell, one of the country's five largest accounting firms. I represented Cameron Tennent & Dunn in that merger, and thereafter was Peat, Marwick's attorney in Hawaii. This was important not only for Peat, Marwick's Hawaii firm, but because Peat, Marwick had offices worldwide, a fact that would influence my later career. (Peat, Marwick was since subsumed into today's KPMG.)

13. Robert Hind Estate and Aina Haina

Robert Robson Hind (1832-1901) emigrated to Hawaii from England via British Columbia in the 1860s. After stints in Honolulu and on Maui, he settled in North Kohala where he was a pioneer in the sugar, cattle and coffee industries. His many descendants flow through the history of Hawaii, especially West Hawaii, to this day.

By the 1940s Robert Hind Estate, Limited was a large landholding company with operations in three areas. First, it owned Puuwaawaa Ranch on the Big Island. Founded by Robert Hind's son, also Robert, in 1895, it was really three different ranches: Puuwaawaa Ranch on the slopes of Hualalai in North Kona above Puuanahulu; Holualoa Ranch above Kailua-Kona; and Honomalino Ranch in South Kona.

(Puuwaawaa Ranch proper played a role in my early career which was not then but became later a humorous family anecdote. It was acquired in 1958 by Dillingham Investment Partners which included Wendell Carlsmith, and the Dillinghams and Wendell would often decamp there to plan their next moves. On more than one occasion this resulted in a call to me from Wendell at all hours weekends included. "Jim: Lowell and I have an idea and would like you to come over right away to discuss." And I would leave Hilo to drive the then-three hours of bad roads to Puuwaawaa to discuss some idea. Wendell felt that the ability to order up his lawyers on a moment's notice demonstrated commitment to the client's needs whether or not necessary.)

Hind Estate also owned Captain Cook Coffee Company, founded by the Hinds in the late 1800s. It was then by far the largest coffee grower and processor in the state, processing and selling real Kona coffee through Hawaii, the rest of the United States and Europe.

Finally, Hind Estate owned Hind-Clarke Dairy, founded in 1924 in the ahupuaa of Wailupe in East Honolulu. Shortly after the War and as Honolulu began to outgrow itself, Hind Estate decided to develop these dairy lands into a complete residential and commercial neighborhood it called Aina Haina (Hind's Land).

The estate put Robson Hind, grandson of the original Hind, in charge of the project. He and his planners did a marvelous job of creating a plan for one of the first large scale master planned developments in Hawaii. Aina Haina was to include large residential areas in the middle and upper parts of the valley, a shopping center on Kalanianaole Highway, and school, church, office and recreational spaces. In short, they planned what was then somewhat revolutionary though today common: a town and community in itself.

Though the concept was masterful, what Robson Hind and the Hind Estate hadn't fully foreseen was the large injection of capital required to pull it off. Soon after the initiation of the project it became clear that the estate was headed for a financial nightmare and needed rescue.

Ernest Cameron represented Hind Estate. In 1950 he came to the difficult conclusion that the current management and attorneys for the Hind Estate did not have the expertise to get them out of the big trouble they were in. He recommended to the Hind Estate that Wendell Carlsmith could do the job and the estate agreed.

This directly affected me since the estate's attorneys then were Pratt, Tavares and Cassidy, which I had joined a year earlier. One day the news swept through the office that we had lost the Hind Estate account, and to make matters worse not to another prominent Honolulu firm but to some three-lawyer Hilo firm. Perhaps it was then that I started thinking I should cast my lot with Wendell Carlsmith after all.

Wendell immediately hired Willis C. Jennings, then manager of Hakalau Sugar Company, to take over management of the Aina Haina development. Wendell knew Willis Jennings because Wendell represented Hakalau. He knew that Willis was an extremely talented executive, one with great imagination. Jennings immediately reorganized projects in order to keep the development alive, but doing so within the confines of the cash which was available.

Wendell then looked for financing. He obtained for the estate a loan from the Employees Retirement System of the State of Hawaii of $10,000,000 secured by the Aina Haina development. The project now had the necessary cash to keep the development going.

When I started working for Carlsmith in November 1951, Wendell assigned me as point man working with Willis Jennings, though Wendell supervised me to make sure that I wasn't getting in over my head. I did all the Aina Haina work from 1951 until the reorganization of the Hind Estate in 1958. This included the legal work for the residential sales, the leases for the shopping center and office spaces, and handling the few litigation matters which came up.

One very difficult problem involved the hillside homes on the Diamond Head side of the valley. The engineers wanted to protect the homes from rainfall moving down the wall of the valley into homes. They devised a brilliant solution: a large ditch just above the highest home running along the walls of the valley to a catch point where it was diverted into another ditch taking it down to the sewer system on the bottom of the valley.

The problem arose after the homes had been built. There was a huge rainstorm, the ditches overflowed, and the water did just what it wasn't supposed to do: it ran through the homes destroying furnishings.

Why? The engineering solution was proper, but the Hind Estate had not established a routine to make the ditches do their job. They had not inspected the ditches from time to time and removed branches, leaves, and dirt, and so small and then larger dams developed which obstructed waterflow.

I researched the law and with heavy foreboding advised Willis Jennings that the estate was liable for all of the damages. Would he change lawyers and get a better opinion? He thought for just a brief time and said: "OK, Jim, I want you to contact every homeowner and arrange settlements for each one of them. Just don't let them take advantage of us."

I contacted every homeowner and arranged settlements with each one of them. I spent many unexpected nights in Honolulu hotels. My wife wasn't happy though my client was.

14. Hawaii Energy Part One: Hilo Electric

Like agriculture, tourism and other underpinnings of the Hawaii economy, Hawaii's energy industry wove in and out of my career throughout. The first chapter in that was Hilo Electric Light Co., Ltd.

By the 1950s Honolulu was a small city of about 300,000 and Hawaiian Electric was well on its way to consolidating virtually all power generation and supply on Oahu under its roof. But the energy industry on the Neighbor Islands had developed differently and was then still not centralized.

In the early years of electricity the sugar plantations were the source of power. Every plantation was a village of its own. It grew the sugar cane, had a little sugar mill, had to run the mill on its own, and was otherwise very, very independent.

Bagasse is the part of the sugar cane which is fiber as opposed to juice; it remains after the juice is extracted and converted into raw sugar for refining. The plantations stored their bagasse and powered their mills with boilers that used bagasse for fuel. Some plantations also had small hydroelectric plants. Grove Farm on Kauai, for example, generated electricity from bagasse, but it also had a little hydroelectric plant on Huleia River.

These plantations distributed their excess electricity to employees using distribution lines. Grove Farm, like many others, either distributed the electricity free to its employees as a benefit or, in some cases, sold it to people who did not work for the plantation. In effect, every plantation was also a small electric company.

After fuel oil was discovered in Pennsylvania, electric companies were started across the country using fuel oil for fuel. Hawaiian Electric, started in Honolulu in 1891, was different from the small plantation electric companies in that it had a comparatively huge customer base and relied almost entirely on fuel oil.

Hilo was the second largest "city" in Hawaii. A group of Hilo investors started Hilo Electric Light Co., Ltd. (often called "HELCO") in about 1891. Notice "Hilo" and not later "Hawaii Island" or today "Hawaii"; it was an electric company formed to serve the town of Hilo.

As Hilo got larger, HELCO started sending transmission lines up the Hamakua Coast. The plantations often had excess electricity, and the plantations like Hilo Sugar and Onomea would sell their excess electricity to Hilo Electric. Otherwise, that excess electricity would have disappeared. HELCO didn't pay much for it, about 2 cents a kilowatt hour in the early days. It was HELCO's cheapest source of electricity, but as it depended on whether the plantations were burning bagasse or otherwise producing power it was an interruptible and not steady ("firm" in utility jargon) supply source.

Prior to the Second World War one of Hilo's primary businessmen, James ("Jim" or "Kimo") Henderson, became President of HELCO. He was an entrepreneur. All of his children had boarded at Punahou with me, including Helen Henderson, and Jack Henderson who lived in the boys dorm with me.

Henderson ran the company as though he owned it completely. As one example he would routinely send HELCO employees to take care of the grounds up at his house. But he wasn't the only stockholder; there were other prominent owners.

William "Doc" Hill was another early Hilo businessman. His real name was William H. Hill, but people called him Doc Hill because he got his business start by peddling eyeglasses. He eventually became one of the wealthiest men in Hilo, not to mention a legendary Hawaii territorial and state legislator for almost four decades.

In the late 1940s the HELCO Board of Directors, led by Doc Hill, decided to remove Henderson as President and retained Wendell Carlsmith for the job. The takeover was successful. Doc Hill became Chairman of the Board, a young businessman named William ("Bill") Mackenzie was made President, and Carlsmith suddenly became HELCO's attorneys though it had never done work for an electric company before.

Here then was the energy situation on Hawaii Island when I started work at Carlsmith in 1951. The electricity in the Kau area was generated by a separate electric company run by the two sugar plantations there. Kohala had a separate company run by five plantations owned by Castle

& Cooke. Kona had its own company with a little diesel which sold electricity down in the central parts of Kona. HELCO had run electric lines up to Honokaa, south into Puna, and then up as far as Volcano. Electricity on the island was thus run by a disjointed number of unconnected small companies.

The HELCO board of directors decided to continue expansion, beginning with upgrading its system with a larger power plant of its own right on the shores of Hilo Bay. The board concluded that the company did not have enough of its own money to do so and decided to put out a public stock offering, meaning it would sell ownership shares and use the sales proceeds for the expansion.

In those days as now the public offering of stock is closely regulated by the federal government mainly through the Securities & Exchange Commission ("SEC"). The requirements include preparation of a prospectus fully disclosing to potential buyers and others all relevant information about the company and sale. Failure to follow these detailed requirements or misrepresentation in the prospectus not only exposes the company and its board and management to legal liability but also the lawyer and firm. Wendell assigned the job to me.

I hesitate to relay this part of my story as it goes against every instinct or advice to any lawyer and firm today, but it is part of my story for better or worse. I knew nothing about the SEC and the other Carlsmith lawyers were not much better, but we and I were not going to turn down the engagement and so plowed forward.

Public offering statements were matters of public record, so I reviewed prior statements on file with the SEC. I then went to what is known today as the Hawaii State Department of Commerce and Consumer Affairs where public business records are filed and reviewed public stock offerings prepared by the big Honolulu firms like today's Goodsill and Cades and their SEC lawyers. I borrowed from these various public offerings and drafted the SEC materials for what was required. We used Dean Witter (now Morgan Stanley) as our banker to manage the offering, and I worked closely with the head of Dean Witter in Honolulu who in turn worked with the main office in San Francisco. This is how I became a securities lawyer and began to develop a reputation and referral sources for this work.

The HELCO public offering was very successful and nobody got sued. The company raised enough money to build a state-of-the-art power plant in Hilo located where the Wailoa River enters Hilo Bay. The plant was destroyed by the 1960 tsunami; you can still see its foundations behind the green clock frozen at 1:04AM, when my family and I were at Merrill Carlsmith's house to which we had evacuated from Keaukaha.

It soon became clear that the plantations just couldn't do the job of a modern utility. One of the major reasons was that they produced power intermittently while modern appliances, instruments, highrise buildings, and other power users required the reliable, constant voltage of firm power. Hotels couldn't run elevators subject to power interruption, and appliances would burn out if the voltage dropped too far or spiked. This remains a problem for much of the world in the computer age.

The sugar plantations did not want to make investments in a modern electric system. So HELCO embarked on an acquisition campaign. I helped HELCO buy Kau Electric, then Kohala Electric.

We next tried to buy Kona Light and Power. Manager Lloyd Osborne was very happy with where he was. Osborne had lived in Kona a long time and knew a lot of people in Kona that were loyal to him.

So we went to the Hawaii Public Utilities Commission (the "PUC", which regulates Hawaii public utilities, meaning mainly power, water and transportation companies) with an application for authority to offer all Kona Electric shareholders cash to buy them out. Osborne opposed it and we had public hearings and contested case hearings. The PUC approved our application and HELCO made an offer to all stockholders. Almost all shareholders accepted the offer. With this acquisition HELCO became the sole electric company for the entire island of Hawaii by the late 1950s and I gained valuable expertise in PUC work.

Throughout this period I represented HELCO on most of its general work as well. This included negotiating power purchase agreements with all the sugar plantations through which the plantations sold their excess power to Hilo. This work proved invaluable in my later career when I represented wind and other alternative energy companies negotiating power purchase agreements with the electric utilities.

This also included rate cases, an important part of PUC work. The PUC regulates what utilities can charge their customers and these rates are set on application from the utilities in cases akin to court proceedings. Not only are the rates to cover day-to-day operations, but longterm capital improvements as well.

This was especially important to the utilities as coverage expansion and evolving technology required larger injections of capital. The depreciation for these new improvements was often large, and inflation frequently increased the other various costs of doing business. Customers were demanding expanded coverage and reliable electricity to power communities and growth. HELCO often had to file applications with the PUC for approval to raise the rates. Everybody on the island usually opposed it; they wanted good, reliable electricity but they didn't want to pay for it.

Bill Mackenzie, who had been hired by Doc Hill in the early 50s, continued as President for a number of decades. I worked with Bill throughout most of those decades, even after my move to Honolulu in 1965 as we still had our Hilo office and it was simple enough to fly to Hilo.

I did virtually all of my HELCO work with Bill Mackenzie except for unusual work such as public offerings. In these larger cases Bill and I would consult with Hill or the HELCO board. I would explain what we wanted to do, what it would cost, and how it was going to work. Bill consulted me on all important issues and often on issues that though not especially material to HELCO were just troubling him. Doc Hill did also on a higher level.

As a result I got to know HELCO and Bill and, to a lesser extent Doc Hill, very well. And they got to know me very well also and came to use me as not just a lawyer but a counselor, which they valued even more.

Lesson: if you want to be very valuable to a client, learn all about the client and its business, goals and concerns.

My representation of HELCO beginning in the 1950s not only made me competitive statewide in securities law, but took me into expertise on PUC rate cases, condemnation cases, power purchase agreements, and company acquisitions and financings. It would prove invaluable in representing other public utilities in the next chapters in Hawaii energy.

To complete the HELCO story and impart another lesson, with rapid expansion on the Big Island in the 1960s HELCO needed ever more capital to keep up which became more and more of a problem for the company. Sometime in the late 1960s the HELCO board decided to pursue a transaction under which HELCO would merge into Hawaiian Electric.

Peter Lewis, general counsel and corporate secretary of Hawaiian Electric and a fellow Williams College alumnus, came to see me in my Honolulu office. He said that he understood Carlsmith and I would represent HELCO in the details of the merger and he would be the point man for Hawaiian Electric. He wanted to set up how we were going to handle it.

I was very busy on other matters at the time and asked Tom Ingledue, one of our junior partners, to handle it. Tom did a good job and the merger was completed in 1970. (Similar acquisitions and mergers were completed in the same time frame such that today Hawaiian Electric is the virtually exclusive provider of electricity to some 95% of Hawaii's population; only Kauai operates an independent utility, of which more later.)

With the merger, Carlsmith's and my representation of HELCO ceased. Goodsill had been Hawaiian Electric's statewide attorneys for a long time and Hawaiian Electric moved the HELCO work there. It was a rather abrupt end to a long and good relationship.

Lesson learned: Lawyers lose clients for many different reasons. A lawyer may do fine legal work for a client, but he may still lose a client for reasons not associated with the caliber of his legal work.

In this case, the lawyer for the purchasing company became the lawyer for the acquired company. Or a company may decide to dissolve for many different reasons; the lawyer loses the client when the dissolution is concluded. Or a company may be forced into bankruptcy; the trustee in bankruptcy (who takes over management rights) will almost always retain its own lawyer. Or, as will been seen in the next chapter, the shareholders of a company may change and the new shareholders may want a new attorney. All of these scenarios occurred to me in my career, on both sides of the fence.

Regardless, the best way to keep and get a client is to do the best possible legal work, help the client solve its problems, and develop a reputation for doing so. You will certainly gain clients along the way, and, although you may lose clients for reasons unrelated to your work, sometimes the unexpected happens.

15. Hawaii Tourism and InterIsland Resorts Part One: Beginnings

Early Years

Hawaii tourism developed almost independently on Oahu and the Neighbor Islands. Many great companies and personalities contributed to its rise, among them Outrigger Hotels and the Kelley family in Waikiki. The foremost on the Neighbor Islands was InterIsland Resorts, which I represented for thirty-five years.

In early Honolulu, there was a hotel downtown whose name will sound familiar: the Royal Hawaiian Hotel. It was across the street from Iolani Palace in the late 1800s and was the major hotel in Honolulu. Waikiki at that time was the second home area of the king and major chiefs; there were no hotels.

The next real tourist hotel in Hawaii was the Volcano House on Hawaii Island, which was very important and known all over the world during the late 1800s. The Volcano House is probably the oldest hotel in Hawaii. It's still there, although under subsequent transformations.

As Honolulu grew, more and more visitors wanted to go to Waikiki because of its beach and surfing. One of the earliest hotels, a major hotel on the beach at Waikiki which is still there, was the Moana Hotel. It was built in 1906 and was the major start of Hawaii's tourism industry on Oahu.

The Matson Lines, then owned by four of the Big Five before federal antitrust regulators broke up ownership, was already running passenger and freight ships back and forth between Hawaii and the West Coast. It decided that it should go into the tourism industry and built Hawaii's most glamorous hotel of its day, the Royal Hawaiian Hotel, in 1926. Thereafter, the Matson ships would run on a weekly basis between California and Honolulu. They would bring people to Honolulu, land them early on a Saturday morning, pick up the people who'd been here and take them back, leaving for the mainland on Saturday afternoon. So Waikiki when I was old enough to understand it, which was around 1927 or 1928, was starting up as a major tourist resort.

The hotels on the other islands were really business hotels. On Kauai the Lihue Hotel was one such hotel, not a resort. On Maui there were two business hotels, quite good ones, right in the town of Wailuku. Hilo had a downtown hotel called the Hilo Hotel. There were small inns in Kailua-Kona. One of them, the Ocean View Inn, is still there, although now just a restaurant. These hotels were not set up to be tourist hotels on the beach where you could swim, sun, and surf because that entire concept was still being invented.

Thus, Hawaii's tourism industry in the first half of the twentieth century was almost completely centered in Waikiki.

Inter-Island Steam Navigation Company

Inter-Island Steam Navigation Company was a shipping company founded in 1883 that moved freight and passengers among all the major islands. Originally it had smaller ships, such as the Humuula, which serviced the major and smaller ports throughout Hawaii, Those ports are a roll call of that era in old Hawaii: Nawiliwili on Kauai; Honolulu; Lahaina and Makena on Maui; and Kailua, Napoopoo, Hookena, Hoopuloa, Honuapo, Punaluu, Kukuihaele, Honokaa, Kukaiau and Hilo on Hawaii Island, to name some.

In the 1920s Inter-Island Steam Navigation Company upgraded its fleet with modern ships like the SS Waialeale and the SS Hualalai. Those ships were quite a bit larger and more luxurious than previous ones. They were designed to carry passengers and freight between the islands much faster and more comfortably. Those were the ships that I learned to travel on. You would leave Kauai at ten at night, you had a stateroom or else went steerage, and you arrived in Honolulu in the morning. The trip to Hilo took longer; on return you left Hilo at four in the afternoon and landed in Honolulu in the morning.

Then Inter-Island, thinking along the same lines as Matson, started two major new ventures. In 1929 it formed subsidiary Hawaiian Airlines, which commenced flying aircraft between the islands. The planes were originally amphibious as there weren't any airstrips really good enough to take large passenger planes. So they took off from Pearl Harbor and landed at Nawiliwili Bay on Kauai, Hilo Bay, and the Keehi wetlands on Maui.

I was one of the early passengers. In around 1932 my grade school partner and I had entered an annual competition put on by the 4-H Farmers of America, a national organization teaching young people how to be farmers. We won the Kauai competition and then the statewide competition in Honolulu. The winners were awarded a trip to Washington, D.C. for the national competition. But it was the middle of the Great Depression and the 4-H Society had to cancel the trip. My grandparents on Maui felt sorry for me and gave me a trip on the airplane to visit them, a truly memorable experience.

A few years earlier Inter-Island formed a hotel subsidiary which it named InterIsland Resorts. This new subsidiary then built the Kona Inn in Kailua-Kona, which opened in 1928. It was the first major oceanfront resort hotel on the Neighbor Islands and was the beginning of the resort hotel industry there.

Then InterIsland Resorts acquired the Lihue Hotel and tried to turn it into a resort hotel as the Kauai Inn. This was a mistake because it was in the middle of town and not on the ocean. All of my years of working in the hotel industry taught me the obvious: tourists coming to Hawaii for a resort experience want to be on or close to the ocean. There have been no successful major hotels ever built in Hawaii that have not been built on or close to the ocean. The only luxury hotels not on the ocean are the Volcano House, which has not been successful for the most part and is a small hotel, and the Koele Lodge on the island of Lanai, which is a gorgeous hotel but consistently loses money and at this writing has been closed for years. InterIsland Resorts would not make that mistake again.

Walter D. Child

Walter D. Child grew up in Utah and came to Hawaii in the early twentieth century as a chemist on a sugar plantation. He somehow decided to get into the hotel business.

So he and his friend bought a hotel on Fort Street in downtown Honolulu called the Blaisdell Hotel. The Blaisdell was not a glamorous hotel but it was quite successful. It was located where operated the majority of the city's saloons, nightclubs, and other entertainment spots of various degrees of repute. It was especially popular in the 1940s when military members patronized downtown; rumors are that the Blaisdell's occupancy rate consistently exceeded 100% during that time.

Then Child and his partner acquired a Hilo hotel built in 1939 situated right on Hilo Bay with an incredible view across the bay to Mauna Kea. It was then serving as a combination businessman's and resort hotel for tourists travelling to the Big Island mainly for the Volcano but also the rest of the island, this being when the only real airport was at Hilo. It was called the Naniloa Hotel.

Walter Child was a successful businessman though a tyrant in a way: if you made a mistake you were fired. He followed a cost-cutting approach to hotel ownership and management: never put in an amenity unless you were sure that it would add to your bottom line, and give minimal service. Essentially, he never made the transition from the Blaisdell or businessmen's hotel model to a quality resort.

After the War more and more hotels were being built in Waikiki. The first high-rise ever built in Hawaii was the Biltmore Hotel in 1954 where the Grand Hyatt Hotel now stands. It was the former beach home of a Honolulu businessman called James Steiner. But though resort tourism was taking off in Honolulu, there were still no major resorts on the Neighbor Islands, with the Kona Inn remaining the only oceanfront resort hotel.

Walter Child owned the Naniloa on Hilo Bay, but Inter-Island Steam Navigation Company through Inter-Island Travel Service, its travel agency affiliate that handled arrangements for Hawaiian Airlines, always sent people to the Volcano House or Kona Inn. Childs' hotel was being bypassed.

Enter again the accounting firm of Cameron, Tennant and Dunn, senior partner Ernest Cameron, who were Walter Child's accountants. Ernest Cameron suggested to Child that he engage Wendell Carlsmith to solve his problem, which Child did. The trio of Walter Child, Ernest Cameron, and Wendell Carlsmith developed the idea of trying to buy InterIsland Resorts from Inter-Island Steamship Navigation Company.

Divestiture and Takeover

They were aided in the late 1940s when the federal government through the Department of Justice brought an antitrust action against Inter-Island

Steam Navigation Company for being a monopoly. It surely was, as Hawaiian Airlines by then was the only real way to travel between the islands and its sister company, Inter-Island Travel Service, directed all tourists to other sister company hotels. Any presumed competitor faced a complex airline/resort hotel monopolistic arrangement, as Walter Child had already experienced.

The Department of Justice forced Inter-Island Steam Navigation Company to divest itself of subsidiaries Hawaiian Airlines and InterIsland Resorts. The spin-off occurred in or about 1950 when the shares in those two companies were sold publicly.

InterIsland Resorts was now an independent public company with many shareholders. In those days as today every Hawaii company was required to file certain information with the Department of Commerce and Consumer Affairs annually as of December 31st. This report then had to include a list of each shareholder and the shares owned, all a matter of public record. But if ownership had changed during the year one wouldn't know that until the final report was filed (unlike today where material ownership changes for public companies must be disclosed right away under federal law).

The largest owner of InterIsland Resorts shares after the spin-off was a trust formed by George Norton Wilcox. This was the same G.N. Wilcox who had started Grove Farm Plantation where my father, Hib Case, had gone to work in 1919. He and partners had also founded Inter-Island Steam Navigation Company. He had died in 1933 but his trust had retained his holdings in Inter-Island Steam Navigation Company; the trust had essentially traded in those shares for shares in InterIsland Resorts. The manager of the trust was G.N.'s nephew and Grove Farm manager Gaylord Wilcox, while the treasurer and day-to-day operator of the trust was Hib Case.

Pursuing their plan to acquire InterIsland Resorts, Walter Child and Wendell Carlsmith went to see Wilcox and Case somewhere in 1951 and persuaded them that they could offer the Wilcox trust a very good price for its shares which would enable the trust to reinvest the proceeds at a much better return than InterIsland Resorts was making or expected to make, but under a pledge of secrecy. The Wilcox trust agreed, and Child secured the right to purchase that block of stock for an agreed price.

Child kept buying stock options that way, week after week after week for a year, until one day in early 1952, shortly after I joined

Carlsmith, he had acquired and exercised options on enough shares to obtain majority control of the company. The Board of Directors of Inter-Island Resorts didn't know this had happened as, due to the interaction of the annual filing requirements with the means of acquisition, it wasn't a matter of public record.

I was now assigned to the InterIsland Resorts matters and directed to prepare documents demanding a shareholders meeting. This was a great surprise to management and the board who tried unsuccessfully to object. We went to the shareholders meeting with a majority of the shares and a slate of new directors: Walter Child, Wendell Carlsmith, and about three other business friends of Child. They were elected directors, Walter Child was elected President, Ernest Cameron and his accounting firm was selected the company auditors, and Carlsmith was selected new lawyers for the company.

Now Walter Child and Wendell Carlsmith directed me to undertake a very difficult task. Dudley Lewis of Honolulu had been the lawyer for the company for a long time. He was a solid lawyer, born and raised in Honolulu and eleven years my senior, whose father ironically had been in the same first graduating class as Carl Carlsmith at Stanford. (And, as a further irony, he was the father of Peter Lewis, who eighteen years later as attorney for Hawaiian Electric would switch the HELCO work over to Goodsill.)

Walter and Wendell told me: "Jim, we want you to go and see Dudley Lewis. Let him know he is no longer the lawyer for the company and ask him to turn over all legal matters to you immediately." I called up Dudley Lewis and went to see him. It was not a pleasant meeting; in fact, it was a very brittle meeting. But after he looked at everything he decided he couldn't do anything about it. So I acquired all the legal records for InterIsland Resorts. The takeover was completed.

I was suddenly directly involved in InterIsland Resorts. Wendell became the outside general counsel and I became his assistant. This meant the whole range of the company's interests, including the Kona Inn, Kauai Inn, InterIsland Travel Service (by then the largest travel service in the state), and the Gray Line transportation franchise on Hawaii Island. I was in the hotel industry, and started a crash course on hotels, travel services, Gray Lines, and other components of Hawaii's exploding tourist resort industry.

As one of my first jobs, Walter Child decided to merge the Naniloa

Hotel into InterIsland Resorts. It was a natural fit to put Naniloa into the same company with the Kona Inn and Kauai Inn, and also gave him a larger share in InterIsland Resorts.

Wendell asked me to draw up all these complicated merger papers. That required a special meeting of shareholders, a notice of the meeting, a merger agreement, resolutions of the Board of Directors and shareholders (a large portion of the shares still being held by people and entities not controlled by Walter), and much more.

I had never worked on a big corporate merger before, and I didn't know how to go about it. As with HELCO I decided to go to the Department of Commerce and Consumer Affairs and review how other law firms like the big Honolulu firms, with more expertise than me at the time, had handled past mergers. I apparently didn't feel any remorse about borrowing their ideas and language; they knew more than I did at the time, and I thought that if their language was good I might as well not try to invent new language. That was really a compliment to them, although I didn't tell them that.

I drew the documents. Wendell and Walter gave me suggestions (that meant "Orders"). We proceeded to send the documents out to the shareholders.

Then Wendell said: "Jim, you now know all of the details. I want you to explain the details to the shareholders: what's going to happen; and how it's going to happen. Then answer the questions. If you aren't sure of the right answer, turn to me. Walter probably won't know anything about the details."

The meetings went very well. The merger was completed.

The Waiaka Lodge: On Client Communication

Around 1957 an opportunity came along for InterIsland Resorts to buy a lodge on the ocean near the Kona Inn named the Waiaka Lodge. It was a small hotel but it gave InterIsland Resorts additional rooms right in the center of Kailua-Kona, where it could be managed by the Kona Inn management and used as an overflow from the Kona Inn.

I learned one of my best lessons when Walter asked me to negotiate the purchase of the Waiaka Lodge. It's a lesson that I often tried to explain to younger lawyers.

The owners of the Waiaka Lodge were tough negotiators. Walter told me that he would not pay more than $500,000 for the hotel. He would accept any price at $500,000 or less. Walter told me: "One thing I want you to do. I don't like to pay legal fees. I want you to make them pay your legal fees."

One thing I have learned over the years: never be the lawyer on a transaction where the other side pays your fees. How can you go back to the opposing party who's paying your fees and explain what a wonderful job you did, much less your own client? The more you explain it, the madder they are at you if you've done a good job. But I was young and didn't have enough experience to argue this matter with Walter Child.

I got into the negotiation with the other side and ended up getting a very good deal for Walter Child. Instead of $500,000, I reached an agreement to buy Waiaka Lodge for $450,000. My legal fees would have been $25,000. The other side told me that they weren't going to pay my fees. My deal was $25,000 better for Walter than the one he had authorized me to make.

I went to Walter with the good news:

"Walter, I've done a wonderful job. Instead of paying $500,000, I've got it for $450,000. In order to settle, I waived the requirement that they would pay my fees."

Walter said: "You didn't get my permission to give up my demand that they pay your fees. Now I want you to tell them that I require that they pay your fees."

I couldn't do that. I was in a sharp pickle and had learned a lesson. It is never enough to do a good job for a client; you must have their permission ahead of time before you can settle a case.

At the end he said. "Jim, I told you that I wouldn't pay your fees, and I won't." You had no right to do that. So we'll settle on the $450,000, but thank you for the free legal work." We closed the deal and absorbed the fees.

Lesson learned: No matter how good a job you do for a client, it's still the client's decision on what to do. That is something so simple. A lawyer sometimes can get caught up in a negotiation, but what you can never do is get out there ahead of your client. Whatever you do in the legal world, you must have your client with you the whole way. After all, the clients are always right - even when they aren't.

16. The Koehnen Flood

Not all of my cases and clients in this period of my career, or for that matter throughout my career, were the sugar plantations and HELCOs and Dillinghams and InterIsland Resorts and the like. In fact, much of it was the work of helping people and their families and businesses get through their usual lives and solve their problems large and small.

A man from Germany, Fritz Koehnen, and his wife moved to Hilo about 1900. They opened a store, Koehnens, at the foot of Waianuenue Avenue, which sloped mauka from Hilo Bay a block from the Wailuku River. It was extremely successful. By World War II it had grown to be the foremost high-class furniture, silver, linens, and jewelry store on Hawaii Island.

They had two children: Helie and Fred. An American soldier named Carl E. Rohner was stationed in Hilo during the war; he and Helie married. At the end of the war Carl, Helie and Fred all joined the store as employees. By the mid-1950s the elder Koehnens had retired and the younger generation had taken over. My wife and I knew Fred and his wife socially. Carlsmith had always represented Koehnens.

One weekend night in August 1957 a huge rainstorm hit Hilo. It was raining one inch per hour. During our family dinner I received a telephone call from Fred Koehnen: "Jim: A large amount of rain is pouring into our basement. We don't know why. We are all working to save our inventory. Could you please come over here and find out what is happening?"

I left dinner right away and went down to Koehnens. I took an umbrella and a flashlight. Rain was pouring in through ground-level windows from the street on the mauka side of the building.

I gathered two or three other people (to act as witnesses) and went out on the street. We could hardly keep from falling; the running water almost swept us off our feet. It was coming from the Wailuku River side of the street. We followed the water.

It wasn't coming from the river; it was pouring down a street next to the river. We followed the torrent of water. We were completely doused with rain. It was hard to see because of the rain in our eyes.

Two blocks up the street there is a bridge crossing the river called Wainaku Bridge. The water was pouring over the bridge from Wainaku, the town right across the river from downtown Hilo. It then made a ninety degree turn to the left and went down the street for two blocks. It then made a ninety degree turn to the right and went along the street mauka of Koehnens. It then made a turn into the Koehnens basement.

We crossed the bridge. There was no traffic. We noted a most important fact: the bridge was paved completely. There was no place for water to go if it got on the bridge but out the other side. We also noted that the bridge was slightly higher on the Wainaku side. Next, we found water pouring along Wainaku Street to the bridge. We walked along Wainaku Street. There are slopes on the mauka side all along. Water was pouring down all the slopes on the mauka side of Wainaku Street.

We decided that we had seen enough and returned to the store. First, we had to tell Fred that there was no way to stop the flooding except to pray for the rain to stop. I tried to call my wife but the phones were down. I pitched in. We moved dry stuff upstairs or to a higher shelf. There was hardly any way to save the stuff on the floor. The Koehnens finally decided that we couldn't save any more.

Next morning I thought it over. I decided that the design of the bridge had allowed the water to cross over the river. If the bridge had been designed with escape holes or grates so that rain would fall into the river, it would have never happened.

I realized that I had been through this problem once before when I had done work for the Hind Estate in Aina Haina and re-researched the law. It was still clear. If people left the natural terrain alone, then an upper slope landowner could not be held responsible for adverse consequences to a lower slope landowner. However, if the upper landowner made changes to the terrain, then the upper landowner was responsible if the changes caused damage to a downhill landowner.

I was confident that in this case the County of Hawaii was responsible for all damages to Koehnens because it caused water on one side of Wailuku River to flow across the river, and that the erroneous bridge design had caused the damage. I wrote up a full and exact account of what we had seen, and got the legal authorities together in case the County resisted paying Koehnens its damages.

I then went down to see Helie, Carl, and Fred. I told them our view of the law and the facts. I emphasized that they should make an immediate inventory of what had been lost and its original cost and retail value.

After receiving Koehnens' detailed items of inventory lost and their original cost, I demanded that the County of Hawaii reimburse Koehnens. The County Attorney refused to discuss any settlement, other than saying that the County hoped to change current law. We filed suit.

James W. Boyle had recently graduated from Stanford Law School and joined our firm. I decided that Jim Boyle should be the lead attorney. This was primarily a test of the law and Jim was expert at that. Taking the lead would give him the opportunity to go to court under favorable circumstances and gain experience and confidence. Boyle did a good job in the Circuit Court. We won a decision for the full amount of our claims.

The County appealed. After exchanges of briefs the Supreme Court of Hawaii set the matter for oral argument. I was in a dilemma: should we take it all the way or try to settle? What would the Koehnens say about Carlsmith and me if we didn't settle and lost? I took the choice to them. They said: "Go for it. We've read the briefs. We think we're right."

The Supreme Court rendered its unanimous opinion upholding the lower court in the case entitled *F. Koehnen, Ltd. v. County of Hawaii*, 328 P 2d 214 (1963). It has been cited ever since as the basic Hawaii law on the subject.

Many years later I was approached by the Association of Owners of Makaha Towers, a condominium located at the bottom of a steep valley wall in Makaha, Oahu. A huge landslide had come down the slope and smashed into the lobby and much of the rest of the lowest floor.

Willard C. Hatch was my fraternity brother at Williams College. He went on to be senior partner of a Seattle law firm and was generally regarded as the best bankruptcy lawyer in the Northwest. Willard and his wife had been coming to Hawaii for twenty or more years for vacations and eventually bought a condo at Makaha Towers. He recommended that the Association board of directors get my advice on whether they had a case against the City and County of Honolulu for failure to prevent the landslide.

I met with the board, which asked me to take the case on a contingent fee basis and file suit against the City. I investigated the facts and could find no evidence that either the City or anyone else had ever made any changes to the hill above the building. I told them that we would not recommend a lawsuit and would not take the case.

The board hired another lawyer who told them he could get a settlement with the City. Bill Hatch advised the board not to do it. He said that he had read Hawaii law, particularly the Koehnen case, that I was right, and that they would spend money with very little chance of success. They spent a substantial amount of money, eventually decided that they couldn't win, and dropped the case.

I had inadvertently become an expert on this rather small segment of the law. It didn't produce much legal work because the law was clear and the facts usually were also. But I always felt good about helping Koehnens.

17. Ala Moana Shopping Center

I had a small but unusual, ticklish, and funny hand in the development of the Ala Moana Shopping Center, the premier and ahead-of-its-time mall in central Honolulu.

In 1957 I made a business trip to Los Angeles and stayed with my aunt and uncle, Sally and Leonard Shea. Sally was my mother's sister and Len was then Senior Vice President of the Western Division of The Melville Corporation, which owned Thom McCann. Thom McCann was the primary manufacturer and marketer in the U.S. of good but relatively inexpensive shoes. Len's job was to build up the Thom McCann shoe business in the western United States including Hawaii.

I was very close to Aunt Sally and Uncle Len. During my Williams College-Navy-Harvard Law years from 1937 to 1949 and except for my Waikiki year 1941-42, I returned home very rarely; in fact, only once in college, a few times transiting through in the Navy, and never in law school. Sally and Len then lived in a beautiful apartment in New York City with an extra bedroom and had no kids. Their apartment was essentially my home and they were my second parents during those years.

Over dinner in Los Angeles Len said that it was a coincidence, but he had met that day with two people from the Dillingham Corporation in Honolulu. The company was building a new shopping center to be called The Ala Moana Shopping Center. The two men with whom he had met that day were the executive in charge of the development, Don Graham, and the company's attorney, Jack Russell of Goodsill. They wanted Thom McCann to lease space for one of their shoe stores in the new Ala Moana Shopping Center.

Len asked me: "Do you know anything about Dillingham Corporation, the proposed Ala Moana Shopping Center, or Graham or Russell that might be of help to me?"

Of course I knew Dillingham Corporation, as I had then been representing it for some six years, and I knew both Graham and Russell. I was also a lawyer for the Ala Moana development, with one of my assignments being to make sure that charging tenants like Thom McCann their electricity and other utility costs did not make them a public utility subject to PUC regulation. In a difficult situation, I gave Len some innocuous answer like: "Yes, I know them and it sounds like it will be a successful development."

Somehow Graham and Russell were staying at a hotel about two blocks away. With the greatest dash of humor I have ever seen, Len called them up, told them that his nephew was staying with him, and could his nephew catch a ride with them to the airport in the morning? They said: "Of course". The next morning Len went to the curb with me and introduced me to them. I have never seen such surprised and shocked expressions on anyone's face.

I got into the front seat, and one of them asked me what my relationship was with Len Shea. I told them the whole story, modified and embellished within reason.

Silence!!!

Then: "Did you discuss the Ala Moana Shopping Center with Len?"

I said: "Yes, I told him that I had done some of the legal work for the development of the center and that I was currently working on many legal jobs for Dillingham Corporation."

Silence!!!

Then: "What did you tell him?"

I couldn't keep this going. I said: "I told him that I just couldn't talk with him about his negotiations with you." I couldn't see their faces because I was in the front seat, but I think that there was considerable relief in the back seat.

Now, you would think this would have been the end. But Don Graham, who became the acknowledged dean of Hawaii commercial developers and lived to the ripe old age of 96, was not shy. He said: "Jim, we're having a problem with Len. We have signed up a shoe store already and we want Len to take the space next door. Len doesn't want to do that. Can you help us?"

Now I thought: "I just can't keep this going any longer". So I said: "Don: Let's talk about the weather". We all dropped the subject and talked about everything else under the sun.

Len eventually decided to take the space next door after obtaining considerable concessions from Graham. The Thom McCann store was very successful in its day as of course has been Ala Moana Center.

Len and Sally often came to Hawaii and stayed with us. Len always laughed with glee about the time he had obtained that taxi ride for his nephew. Sometimes a little joke can break the ice.

18. Hawaiian Dredging & Construction in Kuwait

By the late 1950s the main components of the Dillingham companies like Hawaiian Dredging & Construction Co., who had traditionally used Goodsill for most of their work, started using Goodsill for their routine work and Carlsmith for their more complicated issues.

One of the most interesting and complicated issues came up around 1958. The Suez Canal had somehow or other silted up. Shipping in the entire world was disrupted. Hawaiian Dredging and Construction Co. bid and received the contract to dredge the canal. Hawaiian Dredging moved all of its dredges and a huge number of people to Egypt to dredge the Suez Canal. The job was completed very successfully.

Kuwait, a small and then-lesser known country, was situated on the Persian Gulf between Iraq and Saudi Arabia. It was one of the largest oil-producing countries in the world, even though it was not much bigger than Hawaii. It was a very, very rich country. However, it had no deepwater harbor.

The Sheikh of Kuwait decided to build a complete deepwater harbor. This required dredging out and expanding the small natural harbor, creating passages through the reefs and sandbars outside the harbor, and building docks; in short, the whole works for a complete harbor.

The Sheikh put it out to worldwide bid. An Italian firm was the low bidder; Hawaiian Dredging was second. The Sheikh soon decided that the Italian firm didn't have the expertise to tackle this project, but that Hawaiian Dredging, which already had dredges and expertise in the Middle East, did. So Hawaiian Dredging was given the opportunity to negotiate a construction contract with the Sheikh of Kuwait.

Hawaiian Dredging formed a joint venture with an Oakland construction company called J.H. Pomeroy to add capital strength to the venture. Hawaiian Dredging hired Wendell Carlsmith to represent it, and I was assigned by Wendell to the job as his chief assistant. Pomeroy assigned its General Counsel, Bill Maxeiner, to represent it. Wendell and Maxeiner went to Lebanon to set up the venture's Middle East headquarters. They spent almost six months negotiating with the representatives of the Sheikh of Kuwait.

They would negotiate with the Sheikh of Kuwait and his representatives, then send me a radiofax of what they wanted in the final contract. I would draw drafts of the documents in Hilo and return the drafts to them by radiofax. The final draft was a fifty-some-odd page agreement outlining some complicated international arrangements.

For example, how were we going to move money, the dredges, the equipment, and people around? We were afraid of the tensions in the Middle East, afraid of revolutions. We were afraid that if there was turmoil in the Middle East, we'd never get our dredges out. (Has anything changed since 1958?)

We decided to go through a Canadian bank to move money around. Kuwait had to start the process by depositing about $6,000,000 in a bank in Canada which we both trusted. We would then move our dredges from the Suez Canal to Kuwait. Then, if Kuwait put another $3,000,000 into the Canada bank, Hawaiian Dredging would move its people there.

I drafted revision after revision of this agreement; I think I went through forty drafts. Then, when we thought that we had reached an agreement, the Sheikh of Kuwait said:

"Now, Mr. Carlsmith, we don't consider ourselves great lawyers here; we always use Freshfields in London. Freshfields is the leading international law firm in London. They also represent the Bank of England, and have been in business since the 1700s. They are our lawyers on important matters. Now we'd like them to take a look at this."

So, Wendell and Maxeiner had to go to London to work with Freshfields. Freshfields, one of the most storied firms in the history of law, was very competent on international matters. Its team was headed by (later Senior Partner and, knighted in 1968, Sir) Charles Percival Law Whishaw, Oxford University, 1931, who would surprisingly reenter my career a decade later.

We worked very well with Freshfields as we each understood the other's concerns and tried to solve them as best we could. We did not want to use Kuwaiti law to settle disputes; they understood and we agreed to use English law. They understood why we didn't want Bank of England as the banker for the transaction and we stayed with the Canadian bank.

Freshfields would draw up proposed changes to the basic agreement, Wendell would radiofax them to me in the Carlsmith office on Waianuenue Avenue in the small town of Hilo, Territory of Hawaii, and I would review and comment or redraft when I thought it was necessary and radiofax any changes back to London. They asked for very few further changes.

The parties eventually signed the contract. Everything went forward as provided in the contract. The actual construction took about five years. Kuwait ended with a modern deepwater harbor courtesy of a Hawaiian company and its Hilo lawyers. There were no disputes!

19. Sam Chang: On the Unexpected

One day around 1960 I got a call in Hilo from a man from Honolulu named Sam Chang. I had never met or heard of him, but he explained that he was an architect whose firm had been retained by a mainland developer to draft preliminary plans for a major golf resort in Hilo and could he come see me the next day.

As I got to know Sam over the coming years I learned of his fascinating history. When the Communist revolution in China deposed Chiang Kai-shek, Chiang and his entire government moved to Taiwan. Most educated people in China (businessmen, engineers, architects, educators, etc.) moved to Taiwan with him. Sam Chang was part of an educated, influential family in Shanghai who fled China. He had been sent to Belgium to study architecture and had chosen to settle in Japan. From there he had moved to Hawaii where he obtained a position with a large Honolulu architectural firm. He was fortunate in that he had been assigned to work on large projects like highrise buildings, hotels, and condominiums. He was an erudite and personable man.

The next day we met in my Hilo office and Sam Chang explained that his client had developed major golf course resorts all over the United States. He wanted Sam to pursue acquisition of about 150 acres of property along the ocean immediately Hilo town side of the Hilo Yacht Club that had come to his attention. He needed local counsel who would help to assemble the property, get necessary permits, secure other partners or equity, and otherwise put the project together. I don't remember how Sam found his way to me, but he did and I was retained.

Sam and I assembled the overall property by securing options to acquire individual parcels. Sam developed broad plans for the golf course, hotel, and other structures. The mainland partner decided that he would look for equity by filing a prospectus with the SEC for a public offering of stock. I knew how to do that from my work with HELCO.

We were successful in assembling the entire package, including

SEC approval of our prospectus. Now came the moment of truth to find investors to buy the stock. Very few people bought the stock. I believe in retrospect that investors had correctly foreseen that future resort development would occur on the sunny, warm Kona Coast - not the rainy, cool Hilo side.

After many years working on the project, my client folded its tent. The dismantling was not too complicated as we had been careful to secure only preliminary, non-binding arrangements such as options and not commit too much front money until it looked like the project would work.

I tell this story at this point for two lessons that come up repeatedly. The first is the importance of relationships and referrals, for Sam Chang would appear in several more chapters of my career. The second is this: even a failed project can sometimes set the stage for much larger and more successful engagements in the future.

20. Martin Pence: On Confidences and Information

The confidentiality of lawyer-client communications is central to the ethical responsibilities of the legal profession. In addition, lawyers representing their clients to the best of their ability trade on available information: who is doing what and why and how do I use that to my client's advantage, and conversely how can I control the information coming from my client's side to my client's advantage.

I was told at my 1949 orientation meeting at Pratt Tavares & Cassidy that I could not talk with anyone outside the firm – including my wife – about cases I was working on. Suzi is not only naturally curious but was new to Hawaii and wanted to know what I was doing every day. I said: "I can't tell you." She understandably said: "Why can't you tell me what you're doing every day." Things were tense for a while until we developed a policy. If the news was public, I could talk to her. But if it was still within the firm I couldn't. This she understood and it also allowed her to answer questions from others about what I was doing with more than just: "I have no idea." We followed this arrangement during my entire career.

During most of my years working out of Carlsmith's Hilo office, there were no lawyers practicing law on Hawaii Island outside the town of Hilo. There were no comparable population centers and the judges would largely travel from Hilo along with lawyers to hear cases at the smaller district courts around the island. The other lawyers outside Carlsmith were almost always sole practitioners, although there were two-lawyer partnerships from time to time.

Martin Pence was Hilo's leading sole practitioner. Originally from Kansas, Martin had found his way to Hilo where he had commenced practice in 1936 and served as Circuit Court judge from 1945 to 1950.

Martin almost invariably represented plaintiffs, while Carlsmith by this time almost always represented defendants such as insurance companies, sugar cane plantations, ranches and other businesses. In perhaps one-third to one-half of all litigation cases before the Circuit Court, Martin Pence would be representing the plaintiff and Carlsmith would be representing the defendant. He was a formidable foe.

We represented the Hilo Gas Company, a subsidiary of the Honolulu Gas Company. Around 1960 a gas pipe had exploded outside a building and had severely burned a person standing on the sidewalk. The plaintiff retained Martin Pence to sue the Gas Company and the Gas Company retained me to defend it.

It was quite a complicated case. There was no question that the bystander had been harmed. But had she done something to cause the explosion? Why did the pipe explode? Had the Gas Company been delinquent in not keeping its pipes in good shape? Real evidence was hard to come by and liability was not clear.

The Gas Company felt that it had done nothing wrong while the plaintiff felt that she had been harmed and the Gas Company should pay. The legal action proceeded until it was ready for trial.

Pence and I got down to hard negotiating because neither of us wanted to take our chances in court if we could get a fair settlement for our client. Pence would give me his client's position, I would then call the Honolulu executive responsible for the Gas Company operations to get my marching orders, and I'd go back to Pence with our response and position. We finally got fairly close to a settlement. The trial had been set for the next Monday. On the Wednesday before I gave Pence what I called our last and final offer of a firm settlement that was well beyond what the Gas Company thought it should pay.

On Thursday my wife attended a meeting of the Hilo Womens Club which included Lucy, Pence's wife. Now, Pence was an avid bird hunter. He tramped the mountains of Mauna Kea and Mauna Loa to shoot chukar and other game birds. He would also go on vacations to places like Montana for bird hunting.

One of the women asked Lucy if she and Martin were planning any mainland vacations any time soon. Lucy answered: "Yes, we're leaving Saturday morning for Montana."

That night Suzi told me about her meeting and said: "The Pences are leaving on Saturday to go hunting in Montana." I nearly fell over. "Say that again!" She did. I decided to shut up and said only: "I'm sure they will enjoy the trip."

The next morning, Friday, Pence called me up and made me a counter-offer. With as straight a voice as I could muster, I said I would call my client and call him back that afternoon. I didn't call my client. I merely called Pence a few hours later and told him that we would not change our offer. "If you don't accept our previous offer, I'll see in court Monday morning." He called back in a few hours and accepted our offer.

With one exception, I never told Pence or anyone else (not even my client) what had happened. I accepted everyone's congratulations on securing a fair settlement. This kept my knowledge private and protected. Good thing too, because a year later Martin Pence was appointed as one of Hawaii's federal judges, where he served with great distinction over almost forty years. Carlsmith and I appeared before him many times, and we remained good friends for the remainders of our careers.

I, in turn, always made an extra effort to explain to beginning (and on too many occasions not-so-beginning) lawyers that they had to keep everything secret. As just one prime example, watch those elevators: if you have been talking with your partner while you wait, you have to absolutely shut up when you enter the elevator. But it could be anywhere, any situation.

Oh, the exception? I confess that I did tell Suzi why the news from Lucy Pence ended up being so important. She kept that secret.

21. InterIsland Resorts Part Two: Growth

W. Dudley Child, Jr.

As Walter D. Child was taking control of InterIsland Resorts, his son, Walter D. Child, Jr. (Dudley Child; 1931-2004), was finishing his studies at Cornell University School of Hotel Administration, generally acknowledged then and now as the top hospitality and hotel administration school in the world. He joined InterIsland Resorts in his early 20s and was assigned by his father as manager of the Naniloa Hotel.

Robert Herkes, Dudley's classmate at Punahou, would become his lifelong friend and business associate. Bob Herkes had grown up in the Philippines in a sugar family and attended intermediate school in Hilo; he would later also graduate from Cornell's hotel school. In addition to a quarter century with InterIsland Resorts, Bob would enjoy careers in the restaurant business and in politics.

Bob joined Dudley at the Naniloa as assistant manager in 1953. As I took on more of InterIsland Resorts' work, Dudley and Bob became not only clients but friends. Dudley's children were about the same ages as ours and it was routine for me to pick up Dudley's oldest, Debbie, in the mornings as I was driving Ed from Keaukaha to preschool in Hilo. It turned out to be a lifetime relationship.

After a few years Dudley was promoted to manager of the Kona Inn, which was a much bigger and better known hotel; Bob Herkes went along as his assistant manager. The Kona Inn years were a wonderful time for Suzi and me. Dudley had bought a boat. Suzi and I would go over to Kona (after farming the kids out to family and friends in Hilo) for a business meeting (on Fridays, if possible) and stay in the hotel. Then on the weekend we'd go on his boat up and down the Kona Coast. We worked well together and had a good time on the boat.

InterIsland Resorts was doing well and was poised for statewide growth. Walter Child gradually gave Dudley more and more overall responsibility as did Wendell Carlsmith with my own representation, though Walter with Wendell's close counsel continued to make the major decisions. But in 1957 Walter suffered a debilitating stroke and Dudley at age 26 took the reins as President. By the late 1950s he would move to Honolulu to run the next chapters; Bob Herkes again joined him as Vice President.

Tradewind Tours

Walter Child had acquired Inter-Island Travel Service with InterIsland Resorts back in 1952. He ran the Travel Service like other things - on the cheap. He tried to sell tickets to people, but he wasn't a very good salesman. The business withered.

An entrepreneur named Bob MacGregor started a company called Tradewind Tours. And he was a salesman! He put together tour packages where you paid a total amount and Tradewind would put you in this hotel in Honolulu for a while, then off to Coco Palms on Kauai, and then off to some other hotel, few or none of which were InterIsland hotels. However, he had lost money in his expansions and was in dangerous waters financially.

Dudley invited Bob MacGregor and me over to the Kona Inn for a weekend of discussions about these two companies. We had the whole weekend available: breakfast, all morning, lunch, all afternoon, dinner. It was obvious that each party had something that the other critically lacked: InterIsland Resorts had money and properties and Tradewind had package market expertise and reach.

InterIsland and Tradewind Tours decided to form a joint venture, pouring all of their Travel Service assets and liabilities into a new entity. They agreed to a seven member Board of Directors; InterIsland would name three directors; Tradewind Tours would name three; and the parties would both name a seventh neutral director (beginning with Rudy Peterson, President of Bank of Hawaii).

The venture commenced in 1959. Bob MacGregor ran the sales side of the business; he loved it and was good at it. Inter-Island stayed out of his way except to be sure the finances remained sound. Bob got guaranteed rooms and rates for his packages, while Inter-Island got included in Bob's packages on favorable terms, not to mention a new and expanded guest base. It was a very successful marriage.

Lesson learned: Most of practicing law is about finding a way to make things happen, not cleaning up if they don't.

Gray Line

On a less successful note, InterIsland had acquired the Gray Line transportation franchise for Hawaii Island in the 1952 acquisition. Gray Line itself is not mainly an actual operating company but a franchising company (similar to, for example, McDonalds). It grants franchises to other companies to operate tour buses within the brand and rules of the parent Gray Line. The parent Gray Line polices each franchisee to make sure it is operating under the franchise standards, the intent being that everyone makes more money if operating under a common recognized brand.

There were three other Gray Line franchises in Hawaii: Kauai, Oahu, and Maui. Each was owned by a different family. InterIsland decided to buy these Gray Line franchises one by one by one. This took many years, but InterIsland eventually owned all Gray Line franchises in Hawaii.

This sounded good. The problem once again came down to forecasting the future. Nobody in InterIsland Resorts foresaw the impact that U-drive car rentals would have. The tour companies, which provided tours to an area or city, dwindled as tourists took to the idea of renting cars and seeing the islands on their own. Gray Line didn't do well and InterIsland eventually sold all the franchises.

Kauai Surf

By the mid-1950s Dudley Child, harboring the ambition of taking InterIsland Resorts statewide like Wendell Carlsmith with his law firm a generation earlier, said to his father something like: "You know, all these tourists are coming to Honolulu. Only one hotel on the outside islands is up to date - Coco Palms on Kauai. All others are old-fashioned hotels. The best one we have was built way back in 1928. I think we should build a major modern up-to-date hotel on the outside islands."

Dudley continued: "Moreover, Coco Palms on Kauai is taking all of the business from our Kauai Inn. They are on the beach; we are not. They are modern; we are not. We just have to be competitive with Coco Palms. Otherwise, we will have to close Kauai Inn. We should build this new hotel on Kauai."

Walter and Wendell agreed. But where exactly on Kauai should they build this hotel? Dudley was charged with conducting a search.

From my long observation of him, I believe that one of Dudley's best talents was his sense of location. Where exactly should a hotel be located and why? The world's best hotels all have location while the world is also littered with beautiful hotels that do not.

Dudley concluded that Kalapaki Beach was ideal. On Nawiliwili Bay, just minutes from the airport and Lihue, it was undeveloped with a beautiful and sheltered beach and ocean and a waterfall and flowing water. Guests could relax and stay or easily visit Hanalei and Kauai's north shore going one way or the west side and Waimea Canyon going the other.

Dudley recommended that InterIsland try to buy 29 oceanfront acres at Kalapaki from its current owner, build a state-of-the-art resort hotel there, and close the Kauai Inn. Everyone agreed.

Ownership of Kalapaki Beach, a portion of the ahupuaa of Kalapaki, had devolved after the Great Mahele to Princess Ruth Keelikolani, one of the ruling chiefesses in Hawaii. It was Princess Ruth's second home, her main home being in Honolulu. Princess Ruth had sold it in 1879 to William Hyde Rice, who started Lihue Plantation.

Rice's son, Charles Rice, had inherited it and made it his home in 1899. I grew up one mile from Kalapaki and it was nothing for my friends and me to ride our bikes down to the beach to swim and body-surf. Even closer in, Charles Rice Wichman, who by then had joined Carlsmith and would be my law partner for over a half century, was the grandson of Charles Rice and had spent much of his childhood living there. (Charlie would be studiously walled off from the negotiation and engagement.)

By the time of InterIsland's initiative Charlie Rice wasn't living at Kalapaki anymore because the 1946 tsunami had demolished his home. He had moved into another home that he liked perfectly well and didn't wish at his age to rebuild at Kalapaki, so he was receptive to an offer to buy.

Walter Child and Wendell Carlsmith went to Charlie Rice and said: "We would like to buy Kalapaki, so we'd like to put in an offer". Rice said: "I have a surprise for you. I have decided to sell the property. You should know, however, that my relatives, the Kimball family, who own the Halekulani Hotel in Honolulu, have the same thought you do. And so I don't know what to do."

Charlie Rice knew his way around. He spoke fluent Hawaiian, was a former senator from Kauai, knew and could deal with all kinds of people. He knew what he was doing.

Either his lawyer or we suggested that he put the property up for sale under a silent sealed bid auction, highest bidder takes it, no further negotiations. That appealed to him: the bidders would all have to offer their highest price out of the gate.

Now we had to decide how much to offer. Wendell used his best psychology, and I'm talking here about client psychology, how to get his client to do what Wendell knew he'd have to do to get the result.

Wendell said: "Now look, Walter. You know the Kimballs and the Kimballs know you. They know that you usually only pay bottom prices. They will offer a fair price. And they'll expect to win because you'll never offer a fair price. But Walter, you've got to offer more than a fair price."

So we calculated it all out. I can't remember the exact numbers, but let's say we figured the Kimballs would think Walter would never bid more than $775,000 or so, so they would bid $800,000, so we bid $825,000. The Kimballs did bid $800,000, and InterIsland got the property and ideal location.

For the hotel, Dudley wanted to hire an imaginative young architect named Frank S. Roberts. Walter Child wasn't sure that he could trust a young architect, so he hired Ted Vierra, who was a well-known architect, to review the plans to make sure that they made sense. His name on the plans would carry a lot of weight. Roberts designed a beautiful ten-story high-rise hotel on Kalapaki Beach. Vierra approved the plans.

Bank of Hawaii offered to make a construction loan provided that InterIsland put other financing in place before the start of construction. This take-out financing would pay off Bank of Hawaii. The only way we could do that, we felt, was to make a public offering of stock in InterIsland Resorts.

However, Walter Child didn't want to lose control of InterIsland Resorts and so that precluded an offering to new shareholders. This is where I came in given my prior experience with clients like InterIsland Resort on the initial acquisition and HELCO.

Hence, we made what's called a rights offering. An offer would be made to all current shareholders, as follows: You have a right to buy one new share in the company for every share you now own for a price which is slightly less than current market price. This offering required the approval of the U.S. Securities & Exchange Commission. I had done it before and didn't even have to consult the forms at the Department of Commerce and Consumer Affairs again.

We registered the stock and made the rights offering. Walter Child bought enough of the stock so that he still had control of the company. InterIsland raised enough money to pay off the Bank of Hawaii construction loan. The hotel was built and opened in 1959, and is still one of the nicest conceived in one of the nicest locations in all the islands. InterIsland had made a big stride forward.

Dudley Child was the pusher and I was the lawyer. Walter and Wendell came in for the big decisions and implementations but mostly stood back to make sure Dudley and I didn't make any serious mistakes. The generational clock was turning over.

Kaanapali

Pioneer Mill was a sugar plantation encompassing most of West Maui and owned by Big Five member Amfac. Pioneer Mill's plantation lands included a one mile stretch along one of the most beautiful beaches in Hawaii a few miles north of Lahaina called Kaanapali. Sensing that tourism had a better future than sugar, Amfac in the late 1950s withdrew its lands there from sugar and embarked on development of a complete resort.

Amfac owned lands throughout Hawaii and ran them from a large land department in Honolulu. They hired Robert R. (Bob) Midkiff to focus on development of the Kaanapali Beach Resort. Midkiff's family was already five generations deep in Hawaii. We had known each other for a long time dating back to our years at Punahou together.

In the middle of Kaanapali Beach is an elevated rock promontory jutting out into the ocean called Black Rock. It has spectacular views not only to the ocean but up and down the beach both ways and back to the West Maui Mountains. The property includes beachfront land on both sides. In short, it was and remains a spectacular location for a hotel.

For Dudley Child and InterIsland Resorts it was a perfect opportunity. Their natural next move was to Maui and Waikiki and this was just right for Maui. They felt that as first-in they could get a good deal on a site there and that Kaanapali would prove successful.

Walter Child and Wendell Carlsmith gave Dudley and me the green

Part Four: *Career Foundations in Post-War Hawaii* (1951-1965) 99

light to pursue a development lease (all that was being offered) on Black Rock from Amfac. I contacted Bob Midkiff and told him InterIsland Resorts wanted to acquire the lease and could we discuss it.

Amfac and Midkiff wanted to lease the site out to a credible hotel company as much as InterIsland Resorts wanted to acquire the lease. It is hard to imagine today but there was nothing at Kaanapali then and Amfac needed someone to say yes to get the ball rolling. This meant both parties wanted the same goal, which is always promising.

Midkiff lived on the beach at Kahala (thus one of my most complex later engagements, but that for later). By this point I was going from Hilo down to Honolulu more and more, maybe one or two days a week. Midkiff and I found it was mutually convenient for us to meet at his Kahala home. I would go over for dinner and Bob's wife, Evanita, was kind enough to let us discuss business before cocktails and after dinner.

Bob and I worked through how we were going to make this arrangement work. Eventually we agreed on a lease. The lease gave us suitable time for us to arrange development financing before the lease became firm.

Dudley and I then rounded out the plan by arranging the financing. Walter and Wendell approved the plan (they had, of course, been involved along the way).

Dudley and I then put the entire proposition before the InterIsland Resorts Board of Directors. Rudy Peterson, the president of Bank of Hawaii, was on the board. He decided that it was too risky to be the first hotel into Kaanapali and declined to recommend our plan. His voice was almost tantamount to running the company because he was the usual financier for InterIsland. The other directors did not wish to approve something against the opinion of Rudy Peterson. After Dudley and I had done all that work, the Board voted us down.

Amfac turned elsewhere and one month later leased Black Rock to Sheraton on the exact same terms we had negotiated. Sheraton built in 1963 and operates to this day the highly successful Sheraton Maui Beach Resort and Spa. Rudy Peterson went on to be President and CEO of Bank of America in San Francisco and was very successful at that job.

Lessons learned: Bob Midkiff, Dudley Child and I had negotiated a very good transaction for both sides. I am sure that our plan would have resulted in a world-class hotel, which would have been a great boon to both InterIsland and Amfac. Rudy Peterson was a competent banker, but in this instance I think his banker's desire to avoid risk caused him to make an unfortunate decision. A good banker may not be successful as an entrepreneur, which by its very nature requires risk-taking. A good CPA may not be successful as an entrepreneur; he or she may worry too much about costs as opposed to market share and growth. A good lawyer may not be successful as an entrepreneur; he or she may be unwilling or unable to become the decisionmaker. A person eminently qualified and successful in one position will not automatically succeed when placed in a different environment.

22. Kahekili Highway: On Extortion

As a mainly land and business lawyer throughout my career, I interacted frequently for my clients with all levels of government. On many occasions these officials, whether elected, appointed or civil servants, had decisionmaking discretion that could make or break a client or at least make or cost it a lot of time and money. For the most part I encountered honest, reasonable and committed officials; I didn't always agree with them but I thought they treated my clients and me fairly and within the boundaries of the law.

On occasion, though, we'd run into officials whose actions were unethical at best and skirted if not broke the law at worst. It was never so obvious as pay-me-money-for-a-favorable-decision, but usually quite subtle so as to be unprovable. These occasions presented difficult enough choices for my clients, but also had the potential for very difficult decisions for me as a lawyer governed by our profession's code of ethics. I recount two of those situations, which we handled differently but which added up to the same lesson.

The first arose as Dillingham Partners, which we had assisted to acquire Ahuimanu Valley in Windward Oahu at the end of 1951, pursued its longterm goal of increasing the value of its landholdings and reselling them. Ahuimanu was then virtually landlocked because the only road from Honolulu to Kaneohe to Kahaluu and then on up the North Shore was the Pali Highway to Kamehameha Highway along the coast, there were no roads of note leading inland to Ahuimanu. Wilson Tunnel, which would offer an alternative route from Honolulu to Kaneohe over Likelike Highway, began construction in the mid-'50s and was completed in 1960, but it didn't solve the Ahuimanu problem since it also hooked into the coast road.

It was obvious that the key to Ahuimanu lay in construction of a new inland road for the five mile stretch from Likelike to Kahaluu, what was referred to then as the Kahaluu cut-off road and today as Kahekili

Highway. We set our minds to the task.

First, we looked for partners. The obvious ones were all of our fellow landowners between Likelike and Kahaluu who were all in the same boat. The largest of them was the Bishop Estate, which owned most of the ahupuaa of Heeia. Another major landowner was Los Angeles developer Paul Trousdale, who had built the original International Market Place in Waikiki in 1957. He had bought a portion of Ahuimanu from Dillingham Partners and was developing it as Valley of the Temples Memorial Park; his local representative was Hod White. There were several other smaller landowners who came on board.

Second, we hired George Houghtailing to come up with a plan. Houghtailing, from a kamaaina family, was Hawaii's premier traffic engineer. He had worked for the City and County of Honolulu for almost three decades, including over a decade as director of public works, before starting his own private consulting business. Houghtailing engineered an efficient road utilizing the lands of private owners who were willing to dedicate them, meaning condemnation would not be an issue.

Third, at Houghtailing's suggestion we focused on a city ordinance that authorized creation of an improvement district. This law, a very common one throughout the country and elsewhere, said that if a supermajority of the landowners adjoining the proposed road approved creation of an improvement district to pay for the road, the road would be built and dedicated to the city and all of the adjoining landowners would bear the cost. That was no problem here since virtually all of the adjoining landowners supported creating the improvement district and paying for the road to be built.

We packaged up our proposal in strict conformance with the improvement district law and in 1962 submitted it to the Honolulu City Council for approval. We were expecting prompt and smooth approval as we had complied with the law and our read of the law was that if we were in compliance the proposal had to be approved.

But then an entirely unexpected figure entered the picture. Richard Kageyama was a longtime Councilmember with a colorful past, including an earlier impeachment attempt on him mounted by the city clerk for allegedly lying on his candidate application. Kageyama contacted Ben Dillingham and told him something like this:

"Ben, as you have submitted your proposal I oppose it. I don't think

Houghtailing has prepared a good plan. If you hire so-and-so for $50,000 to review the plan and he approves it, I'll support you. But if you don't do that, I will do everything I can to kill your plan."

Was it extortion? Of course. But it was generally plausible that a City official could question a plan for a road the City would have to accept and ask for a second opinion. Kageyama had a minimally credible denial if he was ever called on it, though it was laughable that he could credibly question Houghtailing.

Baird Kidwell, a partner at Goodsill and later an Associate Justice of the Hawaii Supreme Court, represented Trousdale and Valley of the Temples. We convened a meeting in his office: in attendance were Kidwell, Hod White, Ben and Lowell Dillingham, Wendell Carlsmith and me.

What should we do? There was no question this was wrong, but calling Kageyama on it publicly was problematic on a number of fronts. In the big picture and given what was at stake, $50,000 was not a lot of money and we would get the road built on schedule.

We didn't think that a threat to Kageyama to expose him publicly would back him off, so the practical choices looked to be yes or no. One of them asked me what our plan would be if we went with no. I said that I thought Kageyama would in fact try to persuade his colleagues to vote no, that we should argue in the Council and if necessary in court that we had met all legal requirements for approval, that it could cost a lot of time and money to do so, and that we had a solid chance of winning.

Ben Dillingham led off and recommended doing it: "It is a cheap price to pay." What would Lowell Dillingham and Hod White say? If they said yes, I felt I would be participating in extortion. I thought that Carlsmith, Wendell and I just could not do this and that we would have to withdraw as counsel. And what would Wendell do? He was in the predicament of being both a partner in Dillingham Partners and the lead attorney for Dillingham Partners (a perfect example of why such dual arrangements are today generally disfavored by firms and their malpractice insurers).

Kidwell turned to Lowell: "Lowell, what do you want to do?" I trembled.

Lowell said: "We don't pay bribes. Jim: Do what you need to do."

Kidwell turned to Hod White: "Hod, what do you want to do."

Hod said: "We don't pay bribes either. Ben: tell Kageyama no. Jim: Do what you need to do."

True to his word, Kageyama tried everything he could to defeat our proposal, but the Council ended up voting 8-1 for the district. Then, in 1964 as the district was about to be implemented, Kageyama sued the City, Mayor and City Council in Honolulu Circuit Court to stop the plan. That was pretty brash considering that he had started off by trying to shake us down and we hadn't called him on it.

The landowners intervened (got admitted as parties) in the lawsuit and agreed that I would represent them all. As in the Council, never once did we ever reference Kageyama's extortion attempt. Instead, we stated the facts, that we had satisfied all legal requirements to form the improvement district, and our view of the law, that the City was therefore required to approve it. The judge ruled in our favor and Kageyama dropped it.

Kageyama was defeated for reelection later in 1964, likely because he had tried to charge off an extended trip to Europe as a City expense. Kahekili Highway was built and opened in 1966. Dillingham Partners sold Ahuimanu to Trousdale and reinvested its proceeds in the purchase of much of the Robert Hind Estate lands on Hawaii Island. Trousdale, in partnership with Texas-based Centex Construction, developed most of the beautiful communities now lying along the highway along with the Koolau Center shopping mall. Walter F. Dillingham is buried at Valley of the Temples.

Lessons learned: First, extortion is rarely black-and-white but if the thought occurred to you it probably is extortion. Second, acceding to extortion is the wrong choice, not only on moral grounds, not only especially for lawyers on code of ethics grounds, but because as a practical matter clients and lawyers who make known that they will fight it get a better result both then and down the road. Third, as to how to fight it, the options include public disclosure, the threat of public disclosure, and argument on the merits; each situation has its own context and best approach.

23. Macadamia Nuts Part One: Honomalino Agricultural Company

As has already been seen, my career included many fascinating single engagements but also some engagements for clients and industries that took their twists and turn through the decades. One of the latter was my involvement in Hawaii's macadamia nut industry beginning in the mid-1950s.

Macadamia is indigenous to Australia. It was introduced to Hawaii in the late 1800s as a windbreak for sugar cane. In the early 1900s it had been recommended as a nut crop in ideal locations such as Kona. In the post-War period there were some larger plantations and the macadamia nut became popularized as a national gourmet item. But in the 1950s the large-scale production and distribution of macadamia nuts that made the U.S. (largely though Hawaii) the world's top producer (before Australia reclaimed its birthright in the 1990s) was still a decade or so away.

As recounted earlier, Wendell had assigned me to the Robert Hind Estate matters from my first days in 1951. My direct client relationship was overall manager Willis C. Jennings, and virtually all of my early work was the development of Aina Haina.

The Hind Estate's assets included Honomalino Ranch in South Kona. This was a 14,000 acre parcel on the slopes of Mauna Loa in the ahupuaa of Kapua. It was owned by the Bishop Estate (now known as Kamehameha Schools) and leased to the Hind Estate, which used it for marginal ranching.

Willis Jennings was always a thinker and a planner. Around 1956 his (and thus my) thinking turned to Honomalino Ranch. He thought: is there something we can do at this ranch which will be better than ranching? It wasn't necessarily good ranch land. Were there other uses that could yield higher productivity and income for the parts of the ranch that were not well suited to ranching?

Kapua can be roughly divided into three sections from the ocean to the mountain. The ocean (makai) section up to about 800 feet of altitude is very dry with mostly lava and minimal vegetation and has very marginal use. The middle section from 800 feet up to about 2,500 feet has moderate rainfall and vegetation and is good for various crops. Mamalahoa Highway runs through this section at about 1,600 feet. The upper (mauka) section from 2,500 to about 6,000 feet is cold and rainy with heavy native forest cover.

Willis Jennings tested various crops, focusing on the middle section. One was coffee, which was already well established in Kona including Hind Estate's own Captain Cook Coffee Company. He thought that coffee might grow well particularly between 1,000 ft. and 2,500 feet just like it did in central Kona. He also planted macadamia nut trees, avocados trees, lilikoi vines (like they were grapes, the vines on top of little chicken wire fences), and a few other crops. (His test groves from the late 1950s are still there. If you are driving Mamalahoa Highway, just a half miles or so north of MacFarms of Hawaii, you will see on the mauka side some very beautiful old macadamia orchards, and strangely right in the middle of them some avocado orchards and coffee trees.)

Jennings found that coffee grew well there. But coffee prices all over the world were way down (this decades before Kona coffee would command the premium prices it does today) and Willis didn't have confidence that there was a future in coffee. Avocados and lilikoi also grew well, but he didn't know how to market them and also didn't think there was a big enough market for all the avocados and lilikoi he could grow.

He had found that below about 1,000 feet and above about 2,500 feet he couldn't make a real go of any crop. But about 4,000 acres in the middle section on both sides of the highway were prime for various crops. He needed to pick one crop for economies of scale in both production and distribution.

In about 1958 Willis decided that macadamia had the best future. In the late 1940s Castle & Cooke had started a macadamia nut plantation at Keaau outside of Hilo under the Mauna Loa Macadamia Nuts brand; C. Brewer had bought it and it looked like the trees (which took from planting at least seven years to first harvest and ten-plus to full production) were doing well. Further, the University of Hawaii Extension Service had become world experts in macadamias and Brewer was still experimenting so there was plenty of good information being developed on best practices.

It looked like macadamias might have a real future in Hawaii, and the Hind Estate decided to go into the macadamia nut business bigtime, setting aside the Honomalino Ranch middle section for largescale farming. But it also decided it couldn't finance the venture itself. While ranching and coffee were breaking even, Aina Haina was sucking up all of its available cash and financing ability. It needed capital partners.

Finally I became useful. I recommended that the Hind Estate raise the money it needed through the formation of a series of limited partnerships. There would be more than one of these limited partnerships because it was much easier to raise money and run the operation than if everything was in one limited partnership.

First the estate would form a wholly-owned subsidiary which would be the general partner of each of these partnerships; the subsidiary would not contribute money but would run the partnership and the farm. Then the partnership would look for limited partners, anywhere from one to about ten; they would invest their money but not have any direct role in running the partnership and the farm. These investors would put up all the capital we thought we would need for the particular limited partnership. The investors would have a total 75% partner interest while the general partner would have a 25% interest and they would share profits and losses on that basis.

Our target limited partners were wealthy individuals and entities, mostly on the mainland, who had extra money to invest but who didn't want or need a hand in the actual partnership operation (passive investors). It was a very attractive investment for such investors because the tax laws then allowed you to deduct all of your share of the expenses from planting to harvest (five to ten years), longer than the time required to qualify for a lower longterm capital gains tax rate. So you would have the benefit of deductions for the initial period, following which you could either hold your interest for income or sell at the lower rate. (While this was criticized as a loophole and later revised, it financed the growth of Hawaii's macadamia nut industry.)

I developed and implemented these limited partnerships in consultation with Cameron Tennent & Dunn. Meanwhile Willis Jennings was getting the operation ready through nursery cultivation of optimum plantings and otherwise. By 1961 we were ready. We formed Honomalino Agricultural Company as the Hind Estate general partner subsidiary and set up the first limited partner ("Mac One"). We went looking for our first limited partner investors.

Before and during the War and before he went on to Hakalau Sugar and the Hind Estate, Willis Jennings was manager at Hana Sugar on Maui. I knew his daughters, Patricia and Monica, who had boarded at Punahou with me. During the War Patricia met Alexander "Bill" Morriss, a Navy Hellcat pilot from St. Louis stationed on Maui; they were married and moved back to St. Louis where he embarked on a promising business career.

Bill Morriss had lots of friends in St. Louis who were good potential investors. Many of them had inherited wealth or had successful business careers. For example, two brothers and their family owned a very large nut company. Honomalino was a wonderful investment because they were already in nuts -- not macadamias but other kinds.

Willis interested Bill and his circles in investing. Further, Willis needed someone he could trust to run Honomalino, Bill was very capable and Patricia wanted to come home. They returned in 1961 as Honomalino Agriculture Company was being formed to run the operation.

Mac One was formed with about seven St. Louis investors. Jennings and Morriss smartly assembled Mac One's orchards part lower down, part in the middle, and part higher up so that the partnership had an array of land, staggered production and diversified risk. With the investments from the limited partners Honomalino then cleared the land, planted the macadamia nuts and cultivated them toward production and nuts sales seven-plus years later.

George Shattauer, the original manager of the orchards, was a key contributor. George's father had been the manager of Puu o Hoku Ranch on Molokai and George and his two brothers had been Punahou boarders with me. George Shattauer managed those orchards for many, many years and became a true expert on macadamia nuts.

While getting Mac One up and running we were also forming and repeating the process with further partnerships; we called them Mac Two, Mac Three, etc. We'd do about one a year based on our own capacity and investor interest until we got up over Mac Ten.

I went all over the United States for actual and potential investor meetings. Many of those were back to St. Louis, but some were to more exotic locales like Hollywood where I encountered some famous and interesting people.

One was Jimmy Stewart. His business manager was Guy Gadbois, who represented not only Stewart but many other movie actors and actresses. Gadbois knew that a limited partnership like this was an attractive investment for such people who, like sports figures, had a potentially short period to earn the great majority of what they would earn over their lifetimes. They could put their money away then and it would be worth a lot more when their careers ended. Stewart invested into Honomalino, as later did others like Julie Andrews and Ann-Margret.

Of course Suzi was starstruck when she heard I would be meeting with Jimmy Stewart and made me ask for his autograph. And I admit I was as well. What was Jimmy Stewart like? He was never really an actor; in person as in the movies he was just himself, the same Jimmy Stewart whose personality came through regardless of role, the same drawl. He had graduated from Princeton where he majored in drama and was interested in a lot of things to include Hawaii. Besides his Honomalino investment, he and Gadbois bought and developed Hoomau Ranch which he owned until he died and the family disposed of it. The ranch is still there on the mauka side of Mamalahoa Highway just north of the Honomalino orchards.

Some other very interesting investors to whom we were introduced were the Brown Family Investment Group out of Providence, Rhode Island. Their lineage traced to the founders of Providence. In the 1700s they made their fortune as merchant traders, built a home at the Providence waterfront and founded Brown University. By the 1960s they were investing all over the country and the world out of the Brown Family Investment Group's offices in the old Brown family home right on the Providence waterfront. Their investments included large Midwest farms and they had accumulated a wealth of knowledge on farming.

I went to see the Brown Family Investment Group. But I first stopped off to see one of my best friends from Williams College, the Navy and Harvard Law School, Charles E. Clapp. Charlie was the tax partner for the largest law firm in Providence. I explained to him how the Honomalino limited partnership worked and he agreed it would work like that for investors such as the Brown Family Investment Group. Armed with that information, the group sent one of the family out to Hawaii to check it out and then invested a large amount in Mac Eleven.

Somewhere along the line, Honomalino decided that it wanted to do more than just farm macadamia nuts; it wanted to process and sell them as well. Honokaa Sugar Company on the other side of the island was a Theo. H. Davies plantation. Honokaa had actually gone into some of the earliest cultivation of macadamias in Hawaii when a manager thought: "Why don't we plant macadamia nuts on the hillsides where sugar cane won't grow -- they don't need irrigation in that particular climate, and we can have a sideline of macadamia nuts."

Honokaa formed a subsidiary called Hawaiian Holiday and later built its own processing plant. We went to Davies and proposed that we would co-invest with them in Hawaiian Holiday and Hawaiian Holiday would process and sell our macadamia nuts. They agreed and I helped Honomalino form a 50-50 joint venture with Hawaiian Holiday. Now Honomalino had a processing plant which also marketed the nuts.

The person at Davies I negotiated the deal with was Francis Swanzy Morgan, vice president in charge of all sugar and agricultural operations. Frannie Morgan was from an old kamaaina family which had owned Kualoa Ranch for generations. He had been my Punahou classmate and friend from ninth grade on. He had also been my client for several years as I represented the Davies and other Hawaii Island plantations in the annual adherent planter fair price hearings.

In the Hawaiian Holiday negotiation, though, Francis Morgan was on the other side of the table and Davies was represented by its usual Honolulu lawyers, Cades. But after the deal closed Hawaiian Holiday retained me going forward as by that time I knew more about macadamia nuts than Cades or possibly any other lawyer in Hawaii. I worked thereafter for many years on all facets of the macadamia nut industry, from development to growing and through to processing and sale. This led to further chapters in the industry after Honomalino, in addition to a very difficult chapter involving Frannie Morgan and the Davies Hamakua sugar plantations.

Later Davies decided to get out of the macadamia nut industry and concentrate on sugar. It sold its Hawaiian Holiday partnership interest to Paul and Anita De Domenico, whose family owned Ghirardelli Square in San Francisco. Honomalino Agricultural Company sold its interest at the same time. Paul and Anita came to Hawai'i to run the company, which I continued to represent for a time. They were good salespersons: Hawaiian Holiday published recipes to encourage chefs to use macadamias in their cuisine; and the De Domenicos were early on into what is sometimes now referred to as agricultural tourism, bringing tour groups to their processing plant at Honokaa and appearing all over trade publications touting macadamia nuts. But Paul De Domenico wasn't up to the job of managing a profitable business and eventually the company dissolved.

In that first decade of Honomalino as the various partnership were being formed and the orchards were not yet to full production, the general partner, Honomalino Agricultural Company, was short of capital. It wasn't getting income from its partnership interests, it had the expenses of planting, cultivation, management and labor, and it was dependent exclusively on its limited partners for their investments. Each partnership agreement and financing plan thus required the limited partners to make not only an up-front investment but also contribute annually until there was enough production to switch from a negative to positive cash flow.

Some of the partnerships ran into financial trouble when their limited partners, such as members of the movie industry with variable annual incomes, were either unwilling or unable to make their annual contributions. They wanted Honomalino Agricultural Company to put in the money, which it didn't have. This led Honomalino to sell a 50% share of its interests in the partnerships to two other investors who lived in Kona and had some money to invest.

By 1978, with the partnerships all formed and the orchards in various stages of production, we determined to sell our remaining 50% in Honomalino Agricultural Company. We had a big closing at the Carlsmith office and sold the interests to the same two Kona investors. Suddenly the job I had started with the Hind Estate and Willis Jennings in 1956 ended. But especially tragically, Bill Morriss, who had been with us for the most of the way, returned to his home in Kamuela and died that night of a heart attack.

24. Carlsmith Goes Statewide

In the fourteen years from when I joined Carlsmith in 1951 to when the firm officially shifted its center of gravity to Honolulu in 1965, Carlsmith grew from a Hilo-based practice of three lawyers to a statewide practice of fifteen. These were years of what then seemed explosive growth, not only by Carlsmith's standards but by the state's, for the large established Honolulu firms only grew by a few from their base of ten at the most in the same period. Amidst such growth it is sometimes hard to tell what's causing what, more lawyers or more clients, but the fact was that Carlsmith's reputation was growing far and wide and its lawyers and clients were also.

Donn Wendell Carlsmith
Wendell had started planning for this transition and growth in the late 1940s. He then "found" that his eldest son, Donn Carlsmith, wanted to practice law. That was an uncharacteristically quaint way to put it, as I'm sure there was never much doubt in either Wendell's or Donn's mind that Donn would go into law as the first of the third generation of Carlsmiths at the firm.

Like Wendell and Merrill, Donn was born and raised in Hilo and graduated from Hilo High, where he was student body president. He graduated from Stanford and then, likely much to the family's surprise and shock, went to law school at Harvard. He returned home in 1953 and joined Carlsmith, where he practiced law throughout a fifty year career until his death in 2003.

Donn had much of Wendell in him. He combined all of an imaginative mind, restless energy, encyclopedic and broadranging knowledge, the ability to mastermind a large and complex task, the powers of charm and persuasion, a keen business mind and more into a package that many and varied clients trusted to solve their problems and achieve their goals.

He demonstrated that in his first year, when he helped the Fujimoto brothers, his schoolmates at Hilo High, regain the control of Hilo-based

Hawaii Planing Mill (today's HPM) which they had lost during the War. He went on to represent all manner of entities on the Big Island, the rest of the state and beyond, just a representative few of which were Parker Ranch, Dillingham Investment Corporation, the Magoon Brothers and Guenoc Winery in California, and the Waterhouse Estate. To this he added wideranging philanthropic interests and worldclass knowledge and contributions in the areas of Hawaii plants, birds and history.

His full life included being a passenger aboard ill-fated Aloha Airlines Flight 243 from Hilo to Honolulu in 1988. He was sitting in the front section of the aircraft as the fuselage ripped off and spent the rest of the crippled flight staring into space. Cut, bandaged and bruised, he came to work in the Honolulu office the next day explaining that he had had "a difficult flight over".

Donn's interests and abilities translated anywhere in the state and beyond and he spent much of his career in Honolulu. But somewhat like Merrill he preferred the Big Island and anchored the Hilo Carlsmith office as we expanded our statewide presence.

Charles Rice Wichman

Charlie Wichman was the fifth generation of his family on Kauai. He graduated from Iolani School before serving in the Army during the War. After the War he went on to Stanford, where his roommate was Donn Carlsmith.

Wendell liked to claim credit for Charlie becoming a lawyer. As Wendell tells it, sometime late in Charlie's college career Wendell, in San Francisco visiting Donn, asked Charlie what he wanted to do. When Charlie said he didn't know, Wendell, who of course already had Charlie slotted into the next Carlsmith generation, said he should go into law to "protect your family properties". Charlie said, if I do will you give me a job, and Wendell said, yes, but only if you graduate in the top of your law school class. Which Charlie did, graduating from Stanford Law School at the top of his class alongside such classmate luminaries as later U.S. Supreme Court Chief Justice William Rehnquist and Justice Sandra Day O'Connor.

Charlie joined Carlsmith in Hilo in 1952. He started out as a labor lawyer in the union negotiations of that time but that wasn't his thing and he gravitated into the high level land, tax, trusts and estates work in which he would specialize throughout his career, representing many of

Hawaii's large landholding estates and families. After two years in Hilo the lure of Honolulu got Charlie as it had others prior and since, and he took a job with the U.S. Attorney's office with the tacit understanding that if and when Carlsmith opened up in Honolulu we'd come looking. This happened a few years later, and Charlie went on to the rest of a half-century career with Carlsmith.

Donn, Charlie and I formed the nucleus of firm leadership from the mid-50s to the mid-80s and, as we picked up speed, Wendell started to ease off, at least on firm management. We were very different but we liked, respected, trusted and complemented one another and, although we sometimes disagreed and that sometimes strongly, it didn't get personal and we were usually able to find the best overall solution and all get behind it or at least agree outside our leadership group. I was truly fortunate to have found this team.

By 1957 the time had come to open a Honolulu office. Wendell was there most of the time, I was there a lot of the time, our clients were increasingly in Honolulu and wanted us to be there, our consultants and potential clients were there, and the perception of a truly Hawaii-wide firm required us to be there. We had gone deep into the game without doing so, perhaps holding on to our Hilo firm mystique, but could not advance further.

We opened up in the Hawaiian Trust Co., Ltd. building overlooking Iolani Palace, at ten stories high the first high-rise building in downtown Honolulu. There was a reception room, a small room for other staff, and two offices. We persuaded Charlie Wichman to leave the U.S. Attorney's office, take a pay cut, and rejoin the firm as manager and sole fulltime attorney in the office. The second office was for Hilo attorneys in Honolulu on business, though in fact Wendell occupied the office nearly full time. The rest of us Hilo attorneys rented suites at the Alexander Young Hotel a block away where there was space to work. This new office and our new Honolulu presence started to outgrow itself right from the beginning.

Carlsmith Carlsmith Wichman & Case

Through a hundred-plus years the Carlsmith firm had never had more than three partners nor a formal partnership agreement. That changed in early 1959 when Wendell and Merrill "invited" Charlie, Donn and me to join them as full partners and Wendell asked me to draft a partnership agreement.

I had just finished drafting a formal partnership agreement for Cameron, Tennant & Dunn. Wendell gave me broad latitude for the soon-to-be new partnership, even telling me that I should come up with a proposed method of sharing partnership profits.

I grappled with this problem. In most healthy law firms there are three basic tiers of partners: the senior partners, who are primarily responsible for bringing in the business and maintaining the overall quality of the practice; the mid-level partners, who maintain a lower level of overall client responsibility; and the junior partners, who, following a period (traditionally around five to eight years) in which they are associates, primarily help the senior partners and work on their own business development. I thought that the agreement should give the more senior partners larger shares in good years and smaller shares in bad years but provide a more stable and predictable share base for junior partners from year to year.

I came up with the idea of giving every partner a guaranteed amount of money every fiscal year. We called it a "salary", but legally it was just a first draw on the profits. A larger share of the remainder of the profits went to the senior partners. The junior partner got a lower share of the remainder of the profits. The middle partners had pretty much the same share of the salaries and the net profits after salaries. What this meant was that more of the expected total compensation of the senior partners for any year rode on the ultimate success of the partnership for the year.

I then came up with proposed salaries and shares of the profits after salaries based upon what I thought might be a normal year. We all agreed that Wendell should have the largest share, Merrill should have a share about in the middle, and the three junior partners should have equal shares of the remainder.

One of my major ideas was the creation of a fiscal year starting July 1st and ending June 30th. This differed from the more normal practice where the calendar year was the fiscal year. Our partnership always ran on a cash basis method of accounting. The result of this provision was that cash income in the latter six months of a year was not taxable in that year, but was taxable in the following year. All of the new partners got a tremendous boost in their disposable income that first year because they only paid taxes on the first six months of income.

(The Internal Revenue Service subsequently decided that it didn't like our way of adopting a fiscal year. It issued regulations requiring that partnerships using a cash basis method of accounting must use the calendar year as their fiscal year. However, we were grandfathered.)

Carlsmith Carlsmith Wichman & Case was officially formed on July 1, 1959. We all signed my partnership agreement, which remains Carlsmith's partnership agreement up to the present although it has been amended to change with the times.

As with a partnership agreement, Carlsmith during its first century had had no need for a formal management structure. All partners effectively constituted the executive committee and there was no need to delegate authority to a smaller group.

With the official formation of Carlsmith Carlsmith Wichman & Case and under our partnership agreement, an Executive Committee structure was formally set up. At first the Executive Committee consisted of all five of us partners (and I undertook managing partner responsibility for the Hilo office), but within a few years we had more than five partners and there was true delegation to this committee. Within a few more years, as the number of partners grew and Wendell and Merrill stepped off, it became just Donn, Charlie and me and remained as such throughout much of the firm's explosive growth post-Statehood.

As with any other organization in the world with more than a few owners, law firms don't do well as purely democratic, consensus-based operations. Most of the lawyers in the firm should be focused solely on practicing law and developing business, and in truth too many are not especially good at management (though I hardly met a lawyer who didn't think at some point he or she could do a far better job of managing the firm than the Executive Committee). Firms do best when firm management is delegated to a central committee, and the organization, selection and operation of the committee is thus of paramount importance to the firm. Firms across the world have different philosophies and methods of doing so. Whatever the standard, the goal must always be to choose a small group trusted with the power to make decisions in the best interest of the entire firm.

Just because the goal is achieved doesn't make the decisions to be made inside the Executive Committee or the explanation and acceptance of partners and others outside the Executive Committee any easier. Here are two examples.

One of the most important decisions of a partnership is the admission of new partners. The responsibility of recommending (or not recommending) associates for admission usually falls (and with Carlsmith fell) to the Executive Committee.

On occasion doubts arose about whether an associate had the competence and judgment to become a partner. I believed in the "up or out" theory and was inclined to make the decision to let the associate go and open up the lines of opportunity for someone better. The issue was not usually that they were bad lawyers, as in the ability to understand the facts and apply the law to identify options. The question was: did they have the competence and judgment to advise our clients on complicated matters on their own without being supervised by other lawyers.

Your partners must trust you to manage complicated matters and earn the client's trust. If you are going to run a good organization, whatever it is, you must spend the money to get good talent and train them well toward that goal. If it doesn't look like they'll reach the point when they can handle complicated matters on their own, you should let them go. I did not ever look at it as bad; I looked at it as the way an organization ought to work. And very often the people I had to let go ended up very well for themselves in another environment.

But both inside and outside the Executive Committee, there was sometimes a reluctance to make the tough decision and let someone go because short term concerns obstructed the long term goal. For example, if that person was working for Donn, then Donn did not want to let that person go because it would make it more difficult for Donn in the immediate future. He would have to train another person and bring that person up to speed on his particular projects. However, if the firm always followed that philosophy, it could never improve its workforce. Is the firm willing to take a short term hit in order to have a brighter future?

Another critical decision for a partnership is whether partners will take profits today or reinvest them in the future. For Carlsmith in the 1950s and 1960s the question became whether we were willing to distribute less profits today in order to give higher beginning salaries than other firms in Hawaii in order to attract the best talent with which to grow tomorrow. This meant that the partners had to transfer much of their current distributions over to associate salaries and/or inject more capital into the firm when needed in the hope that a larger and better firm would be more rewarding in the future. After a not insignificant and ongoing discussion in both the Executive Committee and the full partnership about the whethers and how muchs, we decided to follow the investment course.

As a result, throughout much of the 1960s the incomes of the junior partners were no different than those of the senior associates and additionally at greater risk since the associates got salaries while the partners' incomes depended on profits. We desperately tried to keep this information from the associates because we were afraid that the associates would draw the wrong conclusion that we were in financial trouble instead of the fact that we were funding the expansion to their ultimate benefit. And it made for a sometimes awkward discussion with an incoming partner: congratulations on being invited to join the partnership but you might not be making as much. But we did in fact achieve a larger, better and more rewarding firm as a result.

25. Fork in the Road: The Dillingham Offer

The Carlsmith partners had an annual partnership meeting in June of each year to close out the current fiscal year on June 30th and prepare for the new fiscal year. These were always important meetings with key recurring decisions such as new partner admissions, Executive Committee membership and partnership share distributions along with other major decisions on the specific issues of the day.

The June 1964 partner meeting was especially important. The partners were still Wendell, Merrill and Donn Carlsmith, Charlie Wichman and me, and the biggest decision we made was to move Carlsmith's central office and presence to Honolulu. It was the natural next step in the modern-day evolution of Carlsmith.

We then came to the question: who should be Chair of the Executive Committee? It had been effectively Wendell since 1932 – a period of 32 years. Out of the blue (or was it?) Charlie Wichman proposed that I move to Honolulu and become Chair of the Executive Committee effective July 1, 1965.

I was stunned. It was a huge responsibility and opportunity. What would my wife think? I did the proper thing: I said that I would think it over and talk with her and get back to my partners.

One afternoon a few months later, while my partners were giving me the time to mull over my decision, Wendell called me from Puuwaawaa Ranch and said: "Something very touchy and important has come up. Could you come over to Puuwaawaa immediately and spend the night here." Such an invitation was akin to a command. I didn't exactly say "yes, Sir" as if I had been in the Navy, but I said I'd be right over. The car trip was little better than it had been when I was first summoned to Puuwaawaa in 1951. What was so important?

When I arrived Wendell got right to the point: "I have a terrible problem here. The firm has asked you to move to Honolulu and become Chair of the Executive Committee. The Dillingham family is our most important client. Lowell has decided that he should hire an in-house General Counsel to run all of Dillingham's legal affairs and also serve on its five person Executive Committee. He has asked me to discuss this with you. He would like to offer you the job. I believe that your compensation would be considerably higher than it will be in the foreseeable future here at the law firm. You would be a top executive at one of Hawaii's largest companies.

"I personally do not want you to leave the firm which I have managed for over thirty years. However, Lowell is one of my best friends and Dillingham Corporation is our best client. I owe it to Lowell not to influence you. You must consider your own best interests. You must call Lowell and make a date to see him. Hear all about it from him. Then, make up your own mind."

We then had a wonderful steak dinner and didn't talk about it again. Early next morning I went back to Hilo. I called up Anita Rodiek, Lowell's administrative assistant and the most competent at her job of any in the state. I told her that I had a matter that I wanted to talk to Lowell about. She said: "Yes, of course. Lowell told me that you would be calling." We set up a date for the following week and Lowell made me the offer.

I could hardly wait to discuss this surprising turn of events with my wife. We put aside for a moment the issue of whether we even wanted to move to Honolulu and focused on the coming offer. The Dillingham position would pay considerably more than I would be earning as a partner. I would be an important executive of one of Hawaii's most important companies.

Suzi said: "It seems to me that you are in the same position now as when Hawaiian Pineapple offered you a job as General Counsel in Honolulu way back in 1951. Has anything changed?" The more I thought about it, I decided that indeed nothing had changed.

There was an opportunity at Carlsmith that would be more fulfilling. It looked to me like we could grow as a firm and achieve what Wendell had started – to become one of Hawaii's major firms. It would be a challenge for me, but I would have a major influence on the outcome. The more I thought about it, the more it seemed that I would enjoy continuing the practice of law in a major law firm than working in a corporate setting. And I felt I could do well financially over time. Our consideration actually did not take long.

I met with Lowell and told him that he had made me a wonderful offer, but I thought I would enjoy taking over the reins which Wendell was giving me and having the challenge of making it work. Lowell said: "Look, Jim, we would have loved having you here. However, in all honesty I can't tell you that you are making the wrong decision. In fact, if you think that you would enjoy the law firm more, there shouldn't be any further discussion.

"Now, however, I would like some advice. Do you have any recommendations for a general counsel?" I thought for a moment: "I can't think of one right now but will try to think of someone with a broad vision and the competence to do the job you want. You should think over all of the lawyers who have worked for you and with you, even those who have been your opponents in the past. For example, you remember Bill Maxeiner; he was counsel for the construction firm in San Francisco who was your partner when you did the Kuwait project."

I thanked him for his offer and said that I would continue to make sure that our firm would represent him well. I think we did, and Lowell hired Bill Maxeiner for the job.

26. A New Chapter

That left Suzi and me with the last decision on whether to accept Carlsmith's offer and move to Honolulu. We enjoyed our life in Hilo. We had a beautiful house right across the street from the ocean in Keaukaha, we had good friends, and we had meaningful community interests. Six of our seven children had been born there and were at various stages of a great childhood amidst all that was and largely still is the Big Island. Suzi had actually finally graduated from University of Hawaii-Hilo after our fifth child (and I was able to finally tell her dad that we had lived up to our promise). And I had enjoyed a fulfilling and challenging legal career to date.

But, I pointed out, I was already spending up to three days a week in Honolulu. Chairing the Executive Committee would be not only a real challenge but a real opportunity to steer the firm's next chapters. Living in Hilo would be easier, but I worried about topping off my career too early and I was not ready to go into semi-retirement at 50.

Suzi understood but wondered whether we would we be able to buy a home in Honolulu like the one we would be leaving and otherwise afford to live as well there as Hilo. I said: "I'm going to Honolulu next week. Why don't you come with me? You can look at houses and see what is available."

We studied the Honolulu newspapers the week before we went to Honolulu, and did so with greater concentration while we were having breakfast in Honolulu. We decided that Suzi would look at four houses. She went off house-looking and I went to work.

We finally met for dinner. "Tell me about them", I said. She summarized them and one in particular looked good to both of us. But somewhere in the course of the discussion what stood out in particular to me was that she had decided we were going to move to Honolulu. (She thinks I had already decided; I have always steadfastly denied that.)

We managed to both sell our Keaukaha home and buy our Honolulu home, where we still live, by the summer of 1965. We and our children were and still are deeply grateful for our years in Hilo, but it was time to go. I started my fulltime job in Honolulu as Chair of the Executive Committee as planned on July 1, 1965. With that my own career accelerated and, with the formal and informal transfer of the center of gravity of Carlsmith from Hilo to Honolulu, so did the future trajectory of Carlsmith.

Donn, Wendell, Merrill and Carl Carlsmith at Carlsmith & Carlsmith, Waianuenue Avenue, Hilo, 1953 (Sonny McNichol, Hilo Photo Supply)

Part Four: *Career Foundations in Post-War Hawaii* (1951-1965) 125

Walter F. Dillingham (Men of Hawaii 1921)

Lowell S. Dillingham (Men and Women of Hawaii 1972)

Hilo Canec labor contract negotiations, Hilo, 1954 (Wendell Carlsmith second from left, Jack Hall third from right) (R. T. KANEMORI, MODERN CAMERA CENTER)

Part Four: *Career Foundations in Post-War Hawaii* (1951-1965)   127

Ernest R. Cameron (MEN OF HAWAII 1935)

Sam Chang

Walter D. Child, Sr. (MEN AND WOMEN OF HAWAII 1972)

Kona Inn, Kailua-Kona, ca. 1930 (HAWAII STATE ARCHIVES)

Part Four: *Career Foundations in Post-War Hawaii* (1951-1965)   129

Walter D. (Dudley) Child, Jr. (MEN AND WOMEN OF HAWAII 1972)

Kaanapali Landing (Black Rock), 1935 (HAWAII STATE ARCHIVES)

Kauai Surf at Kalapaki Bay

Part Four: *Career Foundations in Post-War Hawaii* (1951-1965)   131

Weekend tennis, Hilo ca. 1954 (back from left: Jim Case, Wendell Carlsmith, Charlie Wichman, Donn Carlsmith)

PART FIVE

Full Speed Ahead
(1965-1985)

27. The Guiding Principles: Taking Stock

As I assumed responsibility from Wendell Carlsmith just half a decade into Statehood, I reviewed the principles by which Wendell had run the firm and which I believed would best guide me and us in our next chapters:

#1: Dare to be first.

#2: Do the highest quality work.

#3: Dare to invest in the future.

#4: Hire and grow the best lawyers and staff.

#5: Invest in the best offices.

#6: Be willing to expand.

#7: Aim to diversify, develop new niches, and provide full service.

#8: Dare to be the best.

Taking stock as Carlsmith's second century was underway, these principles had served us well. Dating back to Almeda Hitchcock, we had already been the first among Hawaii lawyers and law firms on a range of items now taken for granted: regular mainland recruiting trips; a professional office manager; branch offices (in an ironic twist, Honolulu as Hilo's branch); and a summer associate program (hiring of law students in summers to consider permanent fit). We were doing some of the highest quality law work in the state and in some specialties nationally if not beyond.

We were actively deferring partner profit distributions to invest in associate and staff hiring and training, new offices, client development and other future-oriented initiatives. We were in expansion mode, having not only made the move to Honolulu but having by then taken the penthouse space in the Hawaiian Trust building with room for not just two but a whole ten attorneys (though we would outgrow that as well in just a few years).

We had developed a cadre of promising associates and (in 1963) new partners coming up behind Charlie, Donn and me. The best of them was Jim Boyle, who would grow into one of the best corporate and business attorneys in Hawaii.

Jim had come out of Vermont and served as a paratrooper in the storied 82nd Airborne in Korea before graduating from Stanford University and Stanford Law. He had seen five times more of life than most others his age by the time he started practicing law, and I think, like others who had prior real life experiences especially in the military, that made him a superior lawyer and counselor. With a long nose, penetrating gaze and deceptive smile, he scared the daylights out of generations of associates, but each and all of them would credit him for molding them into better lawyers. He was a trusted partner and friend who worked literally next to me for decades.

(Jim and every other one of our lawyers to that point had started off in Hilo. Some stayed there and some moved to Honolulu, but I believe all of them benefited from the same basic experiences that all of the Carlsmiths, Gil Cox, Charlie, Donn and I had absorbed in that incredible diversity of smalltown practice early in our careers. It was not until Tom Van Winkle joined us in 1966 that the you-must-start-in-Hilo tradition ended.)

We had certainly diversified, developed new practices such as in tax, trusts and estates, diversified agriculture and energy, and refined our expertise in our bread-and-butter practices like sugar, land and labor relations, though we were still far from being able to fairly call ourselves a full service firm. And the culture of the firm was deeply rooted in daring to be the best.

In short, Wendell had handed off a firm poised for its next chapter. It was now up to us to make or break it on our own and we were confident that we could and would. But I don't think any of us really reasonably expected where things would go in the next two decades.

28. Haleakala: How Much is Too Much

In 1965 Suzi and I and four of our children (Ed, John, Suzanne and Russell) embarked on a four-day, three night hike though Haleakala Crater on Maui. The first day is a downhill hike from the 10,000 ft. crater trim to Kapalaoa Cabin at 7,000 ft. The second day is an easy hike to Paliku Cabin over a level trail. The third day is another easy level hike to Holua Cabin at the base of the crater rim and trail out. The fourth day is a hike over a longer, narrow, winding and somewhat scary switchback trail up from 7,000 ft. to about 8,500 ft. and the main road.

There were no telephones at the cabins, except for one emergency handcrank phone which connected only to Park Headquarters. In 1965 there were no cell phones. On the second day we had finished breakfast at Kapalaoa and were about to set out for Paliku. Then the phone rang. A person from Park Headquarters said that a Wendell Carlsmith had called them. He told them that there was an emergency in Honolulu and that I should return to Honolulu immediately. No explanation was given. Had my father died? Had my mother died? Had one of my brothers died? Had one of my major law partners died?

I couldn't even reach Wendell without hiking from Kapalaoa back up and out and then to Park Headquarters, about three hours. By that time my family would be at Paliku. I couldn't even reach them at Paliku without hiking back down and then hiking at night over the crater floor to Paliku.

What was I to do? I looked at my wife; she was ashen faced. She would have to spend at least two days and nights handling everything herself. I was actually quite sure that she and they could do it. Ed was 12, John 10, Suzanne 9 and Russell 7. In spite of their young ages, they had hiked all over Hawaii Island and were in their element. My wife had done the same. So I said: "I just have to do it. I can't even find out the seriousness of the problem without hiking out." I waited for my wife's reply. She turned to the three kids and said: "Ok, let's go". They hadn't thought it was a problem at all.

I turned around and hiked back out to Park Headquarters; it was about three in the afternoon when I got there. I telephoned Wendell. Wendell said: "I need you back here right now. Dillingham Corporation has always used Marshall Goodsill for its Securities and Exchange Commission work. Dillingham wants to make a public offering and needs SEC approval. Marshall is in Europe and refuses to return. This is our chance to get major corporate work."

I was furious inside, but what could I do? It actually was easier to go to Honolulu than to hike at night all the way over to Paliku. I could meet with the Dillinghams and Wendell and then come back to Maui and meet the family at Holua. So I went to Honolulu.

The next day I met with Wendell and the Dillinghams. I told them that I could do the work. I mentioned the numerous SEC filings I had done for Hilo Electric Light Company and InterIsland Resorts. They hired us. I told them what they needed to put together for me: financial statements, purpose of the offering, etc. Then I said I would be back two or three days later.

I flew back to Maui in late afternoon. I thought: "I can't hike down that trail at night without a flashlight." So I got one, drove up to Park Headquarters and started down the switchback trail about 8:00 P.M. It was totally dark. About thirty minutes later I saw two flashlights heading my way. Who in the world would hike up that narrow, steep, winding trail at night? It was Ed and John and they had a story to tell!!!

The group had reached Paliku without trouble, spent the night, and reached Holua near sunset the next day. John and Suzanne went up the hillside back of the cabin for a little adventure. Somehow a big rock had been dislodged. Suzanne thought that John had done it; John thought Pele was at work. The rock hit Suzanne on the head and she fell dizzy and spinning. Everyone came to help and got Suzanne down to a bunk at the cabin.

What should Suzi do now? She had no idea where I was and for some reason she couldn't reach Park Headquarters on the emergency phone. So she dispatched Ed and John to climb up the trail to Park Headquarters to get help. They had gotten about halfway out when we met.

We decided that I should turn around and go back out and they would return. There was someone on duty at Park Headquarters and I called Dr. Haywood down in Wailuku. After much conversation he decided that we should not move Suzanne, but keep her in bed, poke her from time to time to wake her up, and keep an eye out. If we couldn't wake her up, someone would have to climb the trail again to call in a helicopter. I turned around and hiked back in arriving at Holua around midnight.

Suzanne slept, but she woke up every time we poked her although still dizzy and vomiting. Finally she asked for some water. Everyone took turns staying awake, but she got better during the night although she woke up with a black eye which we covered with a scarf.

In the morning we all decided that Suzanne could make it if we took it easy. We would hike a bit, stop, hike, stop. We got to the top. We called Doc Haywood and said we were on our way to see him. He decided that she had indeed had a concussion, and that it would be best if we spent a quiet night at a hotel before returning to Hilo. The children all thought that was a good idea. Our trip ended in Hilo the next day and the episode entered into family legend as "The One-Eyed Akua of Holua".

The following day I returned to Honolulu. The SEC work went well, and from that moment on we started doing all major corporate work for the various Dillingham enterprises we had not already been doing.

Was Wendell right or wrong in what he did? Hard to say. It wasn't really necessary for me to come out, he probably knew that, and his telephone call was the start of an impossible and difficult story for my family and me which luckily turned out well. But we solidified Dillingham as a client.

In fact, Dillingham now represented 25% of our total gross revenue and as much as any client had fueled our expansion. We began worrying about that: what would happen to us if one day Dillingham suddenly stopped using us, whether by choice or acquisition or other circumstance. We consciously decided to diversify and broaden the work we had been doing so that we could both keep the Dillingham work but not be at such risk to one client. That we did.

29. InterIsland Resorts Part Three: Glory Years

By the mid-1960s Walter Child was no longer involved in running InterIsland Resorts and Wendell Carlsmith had also withdrawn. Dudley Child was firmly in charge, I continued with sole responsibility as InterIsland Resorts' lawyer and there was a ton of work to do.

In 1964 a new wing had been constructed at the Kona Inn. The shift in tourism on the Big Island from East to West Hawaii had not yet caught the Naniloa in Hilo. The Kauai Surf remained the best hotel on the Neighbor Islands. But the goal of a truly statewide company had not been achieved.

The Kelleys of Outrigger

A natural next step was Oahu and Waikiki, then absolutely taking off with the advent of jet travel and mass tourism. And natural partners were the Kelleys who were pioneering budget travel to Waikiki.

Roy and Estelle Kelley had moved to Honolulu in 1929 and Roy, an architect, had gone to work for noted architect C. W. Dickey. They had developed a side business in building and operating Waikiki apartment buildings which took them in 1947 into the hotel business with construction of the Edgewater Hotel on Seaside Avenue, the first new hotel in Waikiki in over twenty years and the first to cater to mid-income family travelers. That was followed by further hotels capped in the mid-'50s by the prime beachfront property known today as the Outrigger Reef Waikiki Beach Resort.

In 1963 the Kelleys had entered into a longterm lease of the Waikiki Beach oceanfront property owned by the Queen Emma Estate where had long stood the Outrigger Canoe Club and before that the Queen's beachfront estate. Roy Kelley thought it was just possibly the best tourism location in the world, and he set his sights on his first Outrigger hotel (known today as the Outrigger Waikiki Beach Resort).

InterIsland Resorts and Dudley Child, with their recent successful grounds-up development of the Kauai Surf, were natural partners. The two were not unknown to each other. Both were already well established as the leading local hotel companies, and InterIsland Resorts had its headquarters in Waikiki (and at some points in its history its offices in Outrigger properties). Dudley and Roy and Roy's son, Dr. Richard Kelley, Dudley's contemporary who would succeed to the reins of Outrigger in 1971, were all friends, and the two were already doing business together (Bob MacGregor at Tradewind Tours put all his guests in Kelley hotels on Oahu because they were cheap). For the Kelleys it was the opportunity to partner with a proven and trusted friend on a major development, and for InterIsland it was a chance to break into Oahu and Waikiki.

The parties entered into negotiations for a partnership agreement to develop and operate the Outrigger Waikiki. But it was soon obvious that their approaches were fundamentally different. Dudley Child wanted to build luxury hotels in the best locations. Roy Kelley, although he equally valued location, had succeeded with cheap budget hotels and could not break that mindset. At the end of the day InterIsland did not want to operate the kind of hotel Kelley wanted to build, and the parties parted ways; it was not a successful venture.

Lesson learned: The parties to any type of joint venture must share the same vision of what they want to achieve and how they want to achieve it. They may each have an excellent answer, but it must be the same answer.

The parties nonetheless remained friends and did continue to do business together. And it is interesting to reflect on who had the better answer. Outrigger grew into a major chain and brand which, after almost seven decades of stewardship by three generations of the Kelley family, was sold in 2016 to a mainland company. Yet despite its success it is still living down its Roy Kelley image as a budget hotel chain, and I'll bet that if others had the Outrigger Waikiki to do over again they'd choose Dudley's way. InterIsland Resorts of course no longer exists and perhaps much of that is having never fully broken into Waikiki, so should it have gone in with the Kelleys notwithstanding the disagreement over hotel operation?

Whatever the answer, this collection of fascinating people were giants individually and together in the development of Hawaii's tourism industry. In 2007, the 26 inaugural inductees into the Hawaii Hospitality

Hall of Fame, alongside other giants as Duke Kahanamoku, Don Ho, Henry Kaiser (today's Hilton Hawaiian Village) and Bill Mullahey (Pan American World Airways), included Walter and Dudley Child, Roy and Estelle Kelley, and Bob MacGregor.

For me and my career the InterIsland connection to the Kelleys paid many dividends. First of course was the significant legal work generated including Outrigger's which not only continued to fund Carlsmith's expansion but assisted in diversifying its client base.

It was also the Kelleys' custom to have a family lunch every Thursday noon at their Waikiki offices. Roy would invite his family and often guests to join and he would sometimes include me. The discussion ranged throughout the issues facing the industry and company. What was going on in the tourist industry? How could a particular hotel do a better job? Not only did I get to know the Kelley family members, but I also got quite an education in the nuts and bolts of running a hotel business.

My relationship with the Kelleys and their enterprises continued in various ways for many years. As a major example, Carlsmith represented the Kelleys in the effort to build a world-class convention center in Waikiki. As it turned out, this was not a successful undertaking for Outrigger and the tourism industry as, although a fine facility was built, it was not built in any of the preferred and optimum locations any of them had advocated.

Maui Surf

Dudley Child had not forgotten Maui after the InterIsland board's rejection of our Kaanapali project in the early '60s. He turned back to it in the late '60s and found the going a little easier, as conditions had changed: the Sheraton Maui at Black Rock was successful and Kaanapali had shown that it would work as a destination resort. But again he didn't have enough capital available, at least without selling stock and risking control, and so would have to borrow to finance construction and initial operation of what was already envisioned as the Maui Surf.

InterIsland launched into the initial legwork of retaining an architect to design and a contractor to build the hotel. My old friend Sam Chang signed on as architect and came up with a great design. And Hawaiian Dredging & Construction signed on as contractor.

We also of course had to negotiate another ground lease with Amfac, which continued as fee owner of this and other Kaanapali properties. This ended up being pretty straightforward as we had already negotiated with Amfac previously and just used the same basic lease we had preliminarily agreed on with Amfac for Black Rock. We reached agreement with Amfac in short order and Amfac gave us time to try to line up financing.

Construction costs were projected at $10 million. I came up with a basic financial plan: (1) InterIsland would form a joint venture with a partner to construct and own the hotel; (2) each of Interisland and its joint venturer would put $1 million into the venture; and (3) the venture would borrow $8 million and mortgage the hotel to the lender as security.

I was then engaged in representing some Honolulu developers in developing a luxury condominium project in Honolulu overlooking the Ala Wai Harbor known then and now as Yacht Harbor Towers. We had secured project financing from the Connecticut General Life Insurance Company headquartered in Hartford, Connecticut. (Then as now life insurance companies are major lenders as they have excess cash from premiums to deploy for higher returns.) I had visited Connecticut General's Hartford headquarters (and in fact, in answer to a favorite where-were-you-when question, that's where I was in the summer of 1969 as the first man walked on the moon.) By that time I knew the people at Connecticut General very well: what they were looking for; how they thought; what their risk profile was; and on.

Harkening back to my early days of both representing and proposing loans to lenders like Bank of Hawaii, I thought Connecticut General would be interested in the Maui Surf financing. I called up my friend in Hartford and made this proposal: "I think that this is a deal that will work for you and InterIsland Resorts. The hotel is going to cost $10 million; it is going to be on the beach at Kaanapali; we think that's a great location and that we can make a big success out of it."

I continued: "Look, we'll put up $1 million in equity, you put up $1 million in equity, and you make an $8 million loan to the venture on reasonable terms." I didn't try to negotiate the loan terms; I just said I was sure they'd come up with terms that would be reasonable in the marketplace. He asked a few questions and then said: "It looks good. What if I come down next week?"

He came down the following week and into my office. I showed him all of our plans and forecasts: we're going to do this, this, and this; we'll be in the black in the fourth year. However, for a couple of years we will need a working capital loan from you. He said: "It sounds good. I want to look at the property."

Dudley hired a private plane to take the Connecticut General representative, Dudley and Dudley's whole staff over to Kaanapali to look at the property. They came back to Honolulu and the representative came in to see me. He said: "Okay Jim, we're going to do it. Why don't you write up the letter of intent." We wrote up and signed the letter of intent.

The project was financed. The entire construction cost was $10,200,000, just $200,000 over and well within contingency limits, which made Connecticut General very happy. The beautiful Maui Surf opened in August 1971.

What made Connecticut General and Interisland even happier were the results. In its first year alone the hotel earned back the $1 million equity investment by each of its joint venturers. From then on everything the joint venture earned was gravy other than paying down the $8 million debt. Partly it was that Sam Chang had designed not just a beautiful but functional and efficient hotel which saved operational costs, partly it was that Interisland knew how to run hotels, and partly it was just catching Kaanapali at the right time. The Maui Surf was the highest earner in the InterIsland portfolio throughout InterIsland's ownership, and it continues as one of Maui's premier hotels under its current branding as the Westin Maui Resort and Spa Kaanapali.

Lesson learned: If a lawyer, architect, contractor, and client work together to prepare a plan that is as accurate and credible as possible, potential partners or lenders will form an immediate initial opinion that the project is worth looking at and that they merely need to substantiate their first impressions. In this case Connecticut General trusted me from our prior dealings; we had a good team and credible presentation; he told me over the telephone that it sounded like it would work; after an actual inspection he confirmed that they would agree to the plan as described; and everyone delivered. Finally, it did work, even better than described. Connecticut General would be willing to make further investments with us and tell other people that we would be a good bet if we proposed a plan to them.

Kona Surf

At the same time as InterIsland was completing the Maui Surf, it was also pursuing and would complete a new property in Kona which became known as the Kona Surf, though with a more mixed process and result.

The Kona Inn was still a good hotel but was showing its age. It certainly wasn't and would never be a modern luxury resort hotel along the lines of the Kauai Surf and Maui Surf.

Moreover, the State of Hawaii under Governor Burns in the 1960s had committed to development of the "Gold Coast" in West Hawaii between Kawaihae to the north and Kailua-Kona to the south as the future of tourism on the Big Island. The revolutionary Mauna Kea Beach Hotel, opened in 1965, had paved the way but was still the only true resort hotel on the island. Burns pushed through the opening of a new airport at Keahole in 1970 and the brand new Queen Kaahumanu coastal highway in 1975 which sparked resort and other development up and down that coast.

InterIsland wanted to play a part for both its Hawaii Island and statewide positioning by opening a new luxury hotel in Kona. It initially eyed a property of about five acres in size in Kailua town right across the street from the bay between the Kona Inn and the newly-opened Kona Hilton on the point (today the Royal Kona Resort).

The land was owned by the kamaaina Kona Greenwell family. Dudley Child and I commenced negotiating a land lease with the Greenwells through their attorney, Robert Bunn of Cades Schutte. We completed and signed a quite normal lease for 65 years requiring that InterIsland build a luxury resort hotel on the property within a set period (I believe five years). Rent would be low during the construction period, but would increase to normal market once the hotel opened for business.

Then Bishop Estate, the state's largest private landowner with major landholdings throughout Kona and perhaps eyeing Amfac's success at Kaanapali, decided to build a large, complete destination resort named Keauhou south of Kailua-Kona between Kahaluu Bay and Keauhou Bay. Its master plan provided sites for about five hotels, a golf course, condominiums and a commercial center.

InterIsland Resorts decided that in the long run Keauhou had better longrange prospects for its Kona Surf for various reasons. InterIsland felt having other hotels in the area was a plus - not a negative. Dudley and I negotiated a pretty standard ground lease from Bishop Estate for what we thought was a spectacular location right on the point on the southern end of Keauhou Bay.

But InterIsland still had the lease on the Greenwell property which it now didn't need or want. I contacted Bob Bunn and said that InterIsland would like to surrender the lease and land back to the Greenwells. I said to him: "InterIsland is giving your client back the lease so it can lease it to someone else." Bob Bunn proceeded to teach me several lifetime lessons, starting with the law: "Jim, we have a 65 year lease, and we don't care what you do with the property, but we want the rent for the next 65 years."

I couldn't believe that the lessor could force InterIsland to stick to a lease which it was willing to surrender. I got one of my associates to check out the law. He researched and researched and researched and researched. Finally he told his senior partner and Carlsmith managing partner (that is, me) that Bob Bunn was right and I had been wrong. I now congratulate that associate for telling it straight to his senior partner.

When you enter into a lease with a landowner, you don't have the right to surrender it, period, unless the lease says you can (or in some situations a law has been passed to that effect). That is so elemental that I'm surprised, embarrassed and puzzled to this day that I missed it in my three years of law school and by then two decades of practice. But regardless of how I felt, the Greenwells could charge the minimum rent (about $200,000 a year) for the duration of the lease and InterIsland also still had a duty to build a hotel and pay increased rent when it was completed. Unless we could negotiate out of the lease, our only option was to purposely default on the lease and get sued for damages and that wasn't InterIsland's style. We were really stuck.

After giving Dudley Child the bad news (and I don't remember how he reacted; maybe I blacked it out), I commenced further negotiations with Bob. We settled on what was actually a pretty good deal for both sides. We paid the Greenwells two years rent in advance to cancel the lease now. They could keep that payment even if they found another lessee immediately. Which they did; they turned around and leased it back out immediately and kept our payment. But InterIsland was now free of the Greenwell lease.

Lessons learned (several of them): One of the best learning experiences is when you have made a mistake and get beaten as a result. There are many things I should have done. First of all, I should have known the law and should further not have assumed I knew the law; I should have researched the issue before signing the Greenwell lease, not after. If I had known the law (or even if I didn't), I should have added conditions to the lease that would spell out whether and how InterIsland could surrender it. Now when InterIsland signed the Greenwell lease it didn't know about the Bishop Estate Keauhou opportunity, so I didn't miss that issue. But often you negotiate conditions that address contingencies you don't know will happen as a just-in-case measure. Regardless, I should have completed the lease surrender before signing the Bishop Estate Keauhou lease, as committing to the Keauhou lease first put us in an especially bad situation. I don't think I made any of those mistakes again!

Now InterIsland was ready and able to proceed with construction of the Kona Surf at Keauhou. We got a connection with a Philadelphia insurance company and offered them the same basic deal we had offered to Connecticut General for the Maui Surf. InterIsland and the insurance company would form a joint venture and each put up 50% of the venture's equity; the insurance company would loan the joint venture the construction and initial operating funds; and InterIsland would hire and supervise the architect and contractor and manage the hotel upon completion.

InterIsland retained Architects Hawaii to design the hotel; they came up with a unique design that took advantage of the property's unique setting. Hawaiian Dredging & Construction was retained to both participate in plan completion to correctly estimate construction costs and to build the hotel. The final plans provided for a 350 room hotel with the option to add an additional 200 room wing if and when the project was successful. InterIsland thought that the hotel at the 350 rooms could go into the black in the fourth year.

The Philadelphia insurance company came back to InterIsland and said: "We like the deal so much that we're willing to put up all the money. You won't own the hotel, but you will still manage it for us." InterIsland accepted the deal. It thought that it would enlarge its chain for marketing purposes without putting up any equity or risking any cash. As we will see, it was a major mistake on the part of InterIsland.

Now the Philadelphia insurance company made a series of stupid mistakes. It first cancelled the construction contract with Hawaiian Dredging & Construction and entered into a new construction contract with a much smaller company whose only experience building hotels was a small property on Kauai. Although it didn't know anything about hotel operations, the contractor persuaded the Philadelphia insurance company that if it built the extra 200 rooms now, the insurance company could save a lot of money because building 200 rooms later would be much more expensive. That may have been true as a matter of construction, but did not account for marketing and operating a 550 vs. 350 room hotel from the get-go.

The Philadelphia insurance company told InterIsland: "We're going to build the 550 rooms all at once". InterIsland said: "But we can't fill a 550 room hotel; you will probably blame us for not filling up the hotel; you will lose money; we are telling you as forcefully as we can: "DON'T DO IT". They said: "Well, we're going to listen to our contractor." So they built it and the Kona Surf opened to great promise the same month as the Maui Surf, August 1971.

But InterIsland could never make money on that hotel, although it usually got 80%-plus occupancy on the 350 rooms. Part of it may have been that the Gold Coast up north started to kick in, and part of it may have been that despite its stunning oceanfront setting it had no swimming beach. But its chances of success were crippled early on by the owner's decision to overbuild. The Philadelphia owner got madder and madder at InterIsland, and it finally sold the hotel. It could have been a successful venture.

Many lessons learned: The site was a good one. InterIsland made the first mistake when it turned over the entire ownership to Philadelphia and didn't keep control of the hotel. Philadelphia made much larger mistakes when it listened to its inexperienced contractor and not to the professional hotel operator. Neither Philadelphia nor the contractor understood the hotel business. A businessman must always listen to experts in the field and not amateurs who lack knowledge in the particular industry.

The Naniloa & Sheridan Ing

In the late '60s, while the Gold Coast was developing up and the Kona Surf was coming online, the Naniloa in Hilo, InterIsland's mother property, continued to be very important to the company's present and future. Virtually all Hawaii Island tourism traffic then came through Hilo and the Naniloa was the best hotel there and generated consistent positive cash flow to support InterIsland's overall operations and expansion. But it was showing its age and then was largely destroyed by fire.

InterIsland faced the decision whether to rebuild and how. Perhaps had the full impact of the desertion of tourism from East Hawaii to West Hawaii brought on by Gold Coast development and a changing visitor mix and preferences been then known, InterIsland would have taken its insurance proceeds and rebuilt on a smaller scale. But it either didn't see the full impact coming or concluded that it still needed and could support the Naniloa at the same scale, and so set out on a full rebuild. But, like its other efforts, it didn't have the available capital to do so, at least without issuing new stock and risking family control.

I had earlier been the lawyer for two developers, Bruce Stark and Bob Pulley, who (with Sam Chang as their architect) were attempting to build the Wailana condominium on the edge of Waikiki. Building rules had changed in the middle of the development and Stark and Pulley had run out of money. I went to U. S. Senator Hiram Fong's Finance Factors and asked it to enter into a 50-50 joint venture with Stark and Pulley. Finance Factors did so. A Honolulu-born Harvard MBA graduate named Sheridan Ing served as Finance Factors' point man on the deal. I worked with Ing to put it all together and the Wailana opened in 1970. It was very successful, Finance Factors earned a lot of money for its investment, and Stark and Pulley were saved from bankruptcy.

I now wondered if Finance Factors might be interested in becoming a partner with InterIsland to rebuild the Naniloa Hotel. I went to Sheridan Ing and asked him if Finance Factors would be willing to enter into a partnership under which each partner would put up 50% of the needed equity and share 50% of the debt, with Interisland managing the hotel for the partnership. Finance Factors agreed, everything went well and the Naniloa was rebuilt.

Dudley Child could now claim that InterIsland was truly a statewide hotel and resort enterprise. Its portfolio included four high-end hotels on four islands, a mix of ownership and operation of a number of other hotels, and related interests throughout the travel industry. Despite underperformance in some properties such as the Naniloa and Kona Surf, it remained a very profitable and stable company into the 1980s under Dudley's leadership and based on strong performances especially from the Maui Surf and Kauai Surf.

Of course, for Carlsmith and me this was especially good news as InterIsland continued to need a high quality and quantity of ongoing legal advice and continued to grow as a top client of the firm. And my relationship with Sheridan Ing also paid further dividends down the road as my representation of him and his partners in Honolulu residential condominium developments which had started with Yacht Harbor Towers continued with other iconic condominiums such as the Royal Iolani (opened 1978) and the Admiral Thomas (1980). Sheridan Ing, also a longtime owner of Aloha Airlines, was a pioneer in his own right whose career and life were tragically cut short by a heart attack in 1993 at the age of 70.

30. A Lawyer in London: Dillingham Tries to Buy Davies

Janion, Green & Company was an English company which started a store in Honolulu in 1845. In 1856 it hired a young man of 22 years to move to Honolulu from Liverpool and work for the store. His name was Theophilus H. Davies, known commonly as Theo. H. Davies. Davies worked for the Janion Company for many years in both Honolulu and Liverpool. The Honolulu operation started to get into great financial trouble. Davies acquired the business in 1867 and it was known thereafter as Theo. H. Davies & Company.

A century later the company was still wholly owned by the Davies family. The leader of the family was Theo. H. Davies' grandson, Geoffrey Clive Davies, who lived in England as did most of the company's family shareholders. Geoffrey often came to Hawaii to review the status of the company with management. He owned a beautiful home on Tantalus and was quite involved in local social affairs.

Over the years the company had become a factor (agent), one of the Big Five. Its primary business was the operation of a huge wholesale department. Its headquarters occupied an entire city block in downtown Honolulu. Its sugar plantations on the Big Island were an important component of this empire. Its modus operandi was very similar to that of the remainder of the Big Five: integration of operating a wholesale business, owning and managing sugar plantations, and engaging in other activities that would benefit from the talents and investments of the main office.

By 1968 it became generally apparent that the Hawaiian sugar industry was headed for rocky times what with increased competition both nationally and internationally and higher production and transportation costs. Furthermore, the wholesale business was in trouble. Many companies, particularly grocery stores, started to buy their own merchandise and store it themselves.

In short, the entire business model of the Big Five was crumbling.

Various members of the Big Five took different steps to convert their assets to other uses. They were sometimes successful - sometimes not. Since then Brewer has dissolved, Amfac was sold, and Castle & Cooke morphed into an entirely different structure and operation. Really only Alexander & Baldwin has survived via a fairly smooth transition to a different business model.

Lowell Dillingham knew Geoffrey Davies. He formed the opinion that the Davies family would not want to invest money in transforming the company. He thought that Dillingham had the resources to buy Davies and management expertise to guide its re-direction into a continued successful enterprise. However, he was unsure whether Geoffrey would be willing to sell the company and whether, if a sale was presented to him, he would fight it with his fellow family owners.

Lowell, guided as always by Wendell Carlsmith, decided to form an investigative committee composed of himself, the Executive Vice President of Dillingham, the Carlsmith firm (Wendell, myself, and Charlie Wichman), and a business consultant named Jim Tabor. Tabor, an attorney by profession, had been a Vice President of Hawaiian Pineapple Company (a subsidiary of Castle & Cooke) and President of The Hawaii Corporation and lived on Tantalus about five minutes away from Geoffrey Davies; he knew Geoffrey and other members of the Davies family very well.

I knew Jim Tabor as well. Jim's wife (Troy Elmore) was my Punahou classmate. Jim had served as Hawaiian Pineapple's general counsel before his promotion to the executive ranks; we had worked together during my early years in Honolulu and he had recommended me as his replacement. We had continued to work together when he moved over to The Hawaii Corporation. It was a good team.

The committee commenced frequent meetings at Lowell's office. The primary issue was: How to proceed? The committee (that really means "Lowell") reached a conclusion that if Dillingham paid no more than a specified amount to the Davies family it could work

But should Lowell approach Geoffrey and propose the sale? Or should Dillingham Corporation make a private offer to every member of the family at the proper share of the stated price? The basic argument for selling was that Davies had not earned money in recent years; that it was not earning money currently; that it had no prospects of earning money in the future; that the owners could receive a substantial amount of money from a sale of their position; and that many of them needed the money because they had been accustomed to their style of living from their Davies dividends and were no longer receiving them. How best to propose that sale and what would Geoffrey do?

Lowell and Jim Tabor decided that Geoffrey would not want to sell and would oppose it. The committee then decided that rather than contact Geoffrey first Dillingham would make an offer to purchase directly to every shareholder. English law provided that an offer to a large number of shareholders, even in a private company as was Davies, required a prospectus (a summary of the transaction with pros and cons). Carlsmith was directed to contact a good English law firm and work with it to prepare a prospectus.

Wendell remembered Freshfields and (soon-to-be-Sir) Charles Percival Law Whishaw from the Hawaiian Dredging and Construction Kuwait engagement of a decade earlier. Whishaw, who was Freshfields' senior partner, replied that they'd be happy to take the engagement.

Wendell then told me that he had decided I should travel to London and work with the Freshfields firm. He wanted Freshfields to understand that they were dealing with important people (meaning the firm itself, Wendell and me), so he made reservations for me to stay at The Ritz, one of the most glamorous and well-known hotels in the world, and work from the hotel when I wasn't working at Freshfields. He wanted me to leave in three days for what would amount to a three week trip. I would contact Charlie Wichman when I needed information; Wendell would contact Lowell if strategic decisions were needed.

Jim Tabor would also go to London and stay at a hotel a short walk from mine. He would use the "vacation" to contact members of the Davies family and ascertain their current feelings toward the plight of Davies and their financial situation. He was not to mention the plan or make any offers at all, and we would consult regularly.

My trip to London was certainly one of my most enjoyable business trips, including some very humorous episodes. I had never been to England before; I had never stayed in a hotel like The Ritz before; I had never worked directly with a foreign law firm with the ability, experience, reputation, and just plain class of Freshfields, the most prestigious law firm in the British Empire and well accustomed to working with clients from all over the world.

I landed in London and checked into The Ritz. My quarters included a sitting room about the size of my living room at home. It contained various sofa arrangements, a dining table suitable for private meals for eight or so, a working desk, telephones, a large bathroom, and a walk-in closet large enough for the needs of important visitors. I had travelled all night and went to sleep.

It was time for lunch when I woke up and got dressed. Lunch was being served in the hotel's main dining room overlooking Green Park. The waiter (dressed in evening clothes, of course) gave me the menu. It was entirely in French. I had never studied French. I saw something that looked like veal ("de veau" as I recall). It was not what I expected! Whatever it was named, it consisted of cooked brains from veal. I stumbled through lunch.

I then walked around the City. It was Sunday and warm for London. The citizenry was in all the parks sunning themselves. I chose a more traditional restaurant for dinner.

Next morning I went down to the hotel restaurant for breakfast. It was closed! I couldn't find a place to eat anywhere. I went to the front desk and inquired. "Mr. Case, most of our guests prefer to have breakfast served to them in their rooms. However, there is a little breakfast room over there." Obviously, the front desk clerk was not accustomed to having a mere commoner in the hotel. The little breakfast room was indeed little, but the breakfast was a hearty English meal.

The quintessential English cabs waited outside the side entrance to The Ritz. I said I wanted to go to Freshfields in the old city. Did he know where it was? "Of course, sir." (Freshfields' offices are across the street from the Bank of England, their main client for centuries. There is a tunnel under the street so that the public cannot see major bank executives crossing over to see their solicitors nor Freshfields senior partners crossing in reverse to advise the bank.)

I presented myself at Freshfields and asked for Charles Percival Law Whishaw as Wendell had instructed me to do. The receptionist got up and took me to his office. It was what you would expect: a beautiful old desk, a conference table, leather sofas and chairs.

"It's great to meet you, Jim," Charles said. "I enjoyed working with Wendell and you when he was here on the Kuwait project. I know that you drafted all of the documents. You certainly thought through all the problems and attempted to provide for all eventualities. We just made sure that they conformed to English and Kuwait law and that they were acceptable to our client, the Sheikh of Kuwait. I understand that the entire project was completed without incident. We should both be proud.

"Now we are working for your client. Here is how we would like to work on the project. You will be our contact. We will tell you what information we need, what problems we see and what solutions we suggest. If you can answer us directly, fine. If not, you can contact Wendell, who will, in turn contact Mr. Dillingham if he feels it is necessary. But we will listen only to you; we will not contact your client directly.

"I have assigned one of our junior partners to work with you. He is about your age and has about the same degree of experience. I am sure that he and you will get along very well. He will contact me if he disagrees with something you want to do or if he can't figure out what course should be taken. Don't take this wrong; I hope that I don't see you except on social occasions."

I met the junior partner. He was about my age, we had similar educations, we had similar legal experience; we got along well. In short, we had a perfect working relationship.

I reviewed with him all the material I had brought with me: the history of both Davies and Dillingham in Hawaii; what Dillingham hoped to accomplish; what we knew about the current Davies family; the role of Jim Tabor as a consultant; how I would work with my partners and clients in Hawaii; in short, everything that I thought he needed to know to get started on drafting a prospectus for Dillingham to send to all of the stockholders of Davies.

He was used to working over different time zones. Hawaii was eleven hours away. We worked out a schedule.

I would meet him at his office at 10:00 A.M. every day and I would give him information that he had requested. We would discuss problems and would adjourn when we finished, usually about noon.

During the afternoon he would work on the project. I was free to explore London, and often had lunch with Jim Tabor.

A few days later Charles asked me to have lunch with his partners so that we could all get to know each other. "One rule", he said: "We don't talk business at lunch; we meet so that we can get to know each other personally. This makes for a firm where everyone knows and respects each other." Lunch was served at about 1:00 P.M. every day in their main conference room, which seated about 20 people. It was very enlightening. As a group they knew more about what was going on all over the world than, I believe, any American law firm.

My counterpart at Freshfields would either come to see me at The Ritz or else telephone me at about 5:30 in the afternoon. At 6:00 P.M. London time (7:00 A,M, Hawaii time) I would call Charlie Wichman in Honolulu and explain what problems we had encountered and what questions Freshfields had. This conversation would usually take about thirty minutes.

After this conversation I had the evening free, and again often met Jim Tabor for dinner. However, I had also had work to do during the evenings, like attend the London Symphony, the opera at Covent Garden, current musicals, and London plays, find good restaurants, etc. It was indeed a very difficult regime.

In the morning things returned to reality. I had to wake up early so that Charlie and I could talk about 7:00 A.M. London time and 6:00 P.M. Hawaii time. He would give me the information he had gathered on his own, or from Wendell or our clients at Dillingham.

I now had about three hours before I needed to arrive at Freshfields at 10:00 A.M. I learned how to order breakfast sent up to my room. This was a pleasant learning experience. Sometimes I had breakfast with Jim Tabor in my room so that I could fill him in on what we were doing. He rather liked the breakfast and setting. Sometimes I would have a quick breakfast downstairs and do something interesting on the way to Freshfields.

It was a very productive schedule (I promise). At the end of two weeks we had a prospectus ready to go out to all Davies shareholders. I couldn't find any way to continue my arduous work trip to England and so returned to Hawaii. Tabor stayed in England.

Our final offer was to purchase each shareholder's shares for cash payable in London. We knew that a large number of Davies heirs were high on the social ladder but were short on their daily living expenses. This was, we thought, a very good deal for them. We were still not sure what Geoffrey Davies would do, although we suspected that he would attempt to persuade his family to hold together. We sent out the offer and prospectus to all shareholders.

What happened?

Geoffrey did, indeed, oppose the sale, and worked his tail off to persuade almost 100% of his family to stick with him against the sale. He had an argument for his family that we had not fully considered or at least attributed sufficient importance to. These heirs owned Davies stock which had a very low basis dating back to its value when their ancestors acquired it. They didn't want to sell their stock for cash in England and pay huge English taxes. Their investment was overseas; they didn't want to bring their money back to England. They wanted their investment to stay somewhere outside of England. The Dillingham proposal was soundly rejected.

There was a silver lining for Davies, though, for the Dillingham proposal prompted Geoffrey to recognize the need for transition in their business model albeit in a different way. He merged Davies into Jardine Matheson, an English-owned company headquartered in Hong Kong. Jardine, whose roots dated back centuries to the English trade headquartered in Canton and which was the model for the book and movie *Taipan*, was a huge company throughout the Far East, with businesses in Hong Kong, the Philippines, Singapore, etc. It was just what Geoffrey was looking for.

I'm not sure that the shareholders in England with very little income were better off with a new investment overseas and don't know whether Jardine Matheson paid dividends back to the former Davies owners in England. But it was the end of Dillingham's efforts to buy Davies and Theo. H. Davies faded into Hawaii history after a few last chapters.

First lesson learned: While it is important for lawyers and businesspeople to make sure they know what they want, it is equally important that they know what the other person wants. In this case Dillingham did try to figure this out, but didn't find out. It is obvious in retrospect that we should have talked to Geoffrey first. We might have found a different way to solve the basis issue and complete the acquisition (for example, merge Davies into Dillingham), or else drop the idea earlier (although that would have cost me my excellent adventure in London.).

Second lesson learned: Freshfields illustrated how to keep a large, diverse, important law firm together. Too often today American firms become arenas for internal competition and combat. This is also, of course, true of corporations. You build a true sense of "partnership" when each partner is looking at the overall picture and is attentive to the feelings of others.

Third lesson learned: It is always important that persons involved on any business matter have a firm understanding of the "line of command". Who are your real bosses? The British and American navies are particularly good at this. So it didn't especially surprise me that the senior partner of one of Britain's foremost law firms established lines of command at our first meeting. My junior partner counterpart's superior was (soon-to-be-Sir) Charles who had already assured me that he would take direction only from me.

Thus ended one of my most interesting engagements. Unfortunately, nothing quite like it ever happened to me again.

This is also the final note of substance in my story on the Dillinghams. Carlsmith and I continued representing them on matters large and small until 1983, when they sold their interests to mainland private investors. In their century of operation they had left their mark throughout Hawaii and well beyond, and since 1950 they had driven the growth of Carlsmith and the careers of its lawyers, especially Wendell Carlsmith and me.

31. Hawaii Energy Part Two: Kauai Electric and Citizens Utilities

My early and then-still-ongoing work for Hilo Electric Light Company stood me in good stead when in 1969 I was engaged by a Connecticut company, Citizens Utilities, to represent it in the purchase of Kauai Electric Light Company. It was the beginning of an engagement that would last over three decades.

Electricity on Kauai and Kauai Electric had developed in much the same way as with Hawaii Island and HELCO. Each of the sugar plantations generated its own electricity for its own needs and sold any surplus to nearby communities.

At some point Big Fivers Alexander & Baldwin and Amfac, which owned several of the Kauai plantations, acquired these various electricity operations and merged them into one company, Kauai Electric, which thereafter owned the electric franchise for the whole island and distributed electricity islandwide.

But the electricity was still being produced almost exclusively by plantation operations, mainly bagasse burning and hydroelectric. Kauai Electric built a small diesel generation facility at Port Allen, but it did not produce a lot of power.

Then Kauai began to grow, especially with the acceleration of tourism. Modern hotels like Coco Palms and then InterIsland Resorts' Kauai Surf not only increased overall power demand but required reliable energy at a firm, constant, steady voltage. Kauai Electric could not meet this demand in its then-configuration and engineers estimated it would cost $20 million to modernize the system.

A&B and Amfac decided to sell Kauai Electric. Partly it wasn't their core business and they had other uses for $20 million. Partly, as a utility whose operations, investments and rates are closely regulated by the Hawaii Public Utilities Commission (PUC), it was difficult and time-consuming to manage the regulatory process and make a reasonable profit. And partly public utilities investments only really work for a very specific class of investors and that wasn't them. Somehow they found Citizens Utilities as a potential buyer, but it was an obvious choice.

Power generation and distribution on the mainland, especially with the acceleration of urbanization, had mostly evolved into megacompanies like Pacific Gas & Electric in Northern California and Southern California Edison in Southern California serving the urban and suburban areas. Citizens Utilities, founded in 1935, aimed instead for the marginal, rural markets, places like Redding, California and northern Vermont ignored by the big boys, investing in and operating electricity, gas, telephone and sometimes water utilities. A place like Kauai was a good fit.

Citizens had a tax situation which was most interesting to a tax lawyer. When it was started its original chairman, a brilliant entrepreneur named Richard Rosenthal, had set up two classes of stock in the company. One class (A) paid out dividends in cash while the other (B) paid out dividends in more stock. At that time stock dividends were not taxed when received but only when later sold, unlike cash dividends which were taxed when received. The law was later changed to require stock dividends to be taxed the same as cash dividends, but all of Citizens' B stock issued before that change was grandfathered.

The net effect of this was to provide Citizens with an opportunity very important for public utility companies. The average utility might distribute upwards of 75% of its earnings in dividends because it wanted to provide its stockholders with a good yield to retain and increase investments, leaving only 25% or so of earnings for reinvestment into the company. But Citizens could reinvest 75% of its earnings applicable to B stock and so only had to raise money for the last 25%. Over the years Citizens had reinvested its earnings instead of paying out the cash dividends, which had enabled it to both finance its acquisitions and renovations and increase its earnings and dividends every year. It was in good shape to both buy and, with a reasonable rate increase, upgrade Kauai Electric into a modern utility that could power Kauai's needs for decades while providing Citizens with a fair (and regulated) return.

A&B and Amfac offered to sell their interest to Citizens. Citizens looked at the proposal and replied: "You are almost bankrupt and have to put in a huge investment to make it work. We will buy it and make that investment, but only if you support our application to the PUC for a rate increase and tell the PUC you would have had to do so yourselves if you had retained ownership." Citizens didn't want A&B and Amfac saying: it's not our fault.

Citizens retained me as its Hawaii attorney to work with its New York law firm on the purchase. I think it did so because I had represented HELCO, a small rural electric utility, and not Hawaiian Electric, the Hawaii equivalent of Pacific Gas & Electric. We worked out a complex purchase agreement under which Citizens would buy out A&B and Amfac for just $2 million. Of course, the hitch was that Citizens would have to invest about $20 million more in order to bring Kauai Electric up to modern standards.

Hawaii law provided and still provides that control of a public utility may not be sold without the PUC's approval, so the parties had to go before the PUC to get it to approve the transaction. It seemed that in this situation PUC approval would be straightforward as fully in the public interest, since under its current ownership Kauai Electric could not serve its customers without a large capital injection, the current owners were not going to make that investment, and Citizens was willing and able to do so and had a track record of successfully operating rural utilities.

Then a serious obstacle came out of nowhere that was Ahuimanu revisited. At that time the PUC consisted of five members: one from each of the counties and a chair from Oahu. The Kauai commissioner, John B. Fernandes, came to see me; I knew him because he had been a well-known public figure when I was growing up on Kauai, having served from 1933 to 1958 as a Kauai County Supervisor and State Representative and Senator. He said: "We have an understanding on the PUC that when an issue affects a particular island, the rest of the PUC will vote the way the commissioner from that island asks them to vote. I am not going to approve the sale unless you create a subsidiary on Kauai that is a separate company, not a division of Citizens, and Citizens hires my son to be its senior vice president in charge of public relations."

This was obviously a very hot potato akin to extortion. I immediately telephoned Ishier Jacobson, President of Citizens. We decided that we could not agree to either one of the demands. The first demand was easy to reject, as since the early 1900s electric companies had been prohibited by federal law from owning electric subsidiaries.

The second demand was very tough as we did need PUC approval, Fernandes could easily engineer disapproval, and the temptation of some in that situation might be to consider hiring the son as no big thing considering the stakes. Not knowing Jacobson as well then as I did later (I would not have had any doubt later of his answer), I was worried sick that he would succumb to that temptation. I did not want to participate in extortion. To my relief, Jacobson said without any discussion: "We just will not do this. How shall we go about saying no?"

We agreed that I would contact Fernandes and tell him that (1) we would go public with his demands if he did not withdraw them and (2) we would tell other commissioners and the rest of the state about his attempt at extortion. Which I did. Our joint petition with the sellers was recommended by Fernandes to his colleagues and was approved by the PUC without further incident.

We still had the problem of completing the transaction without violating federal law. As Citizens could not own Kauai Electric as a subsidiary, we could not simply buy the Kauai Electric stock from A&B and Amfac and stop there; we had to bring Kauai Electric all the way into Citizens at the same time. We arranged a complicated closing. First, Citizens transferred the $2,000,000 cash price to Carlsmith's client trust account in Honolulu the day before the closing. Then, at 4:00 A.M. the next morning, I met in Honolulu as Citizens' lawyer with representatives of Amfac and A&B; I gave them the money and they gave me the stock. I then called Ish Jacobson in Connecticut, where it was 10:00 A.M, and told him that Citizens now had the stock. Jacobson had previously called a Citizens board of directors meeting, and the board immediately approved the dissolution of Kauai Electric as a separate company and its absorption into Citizens as a division. That dissolution required a filing with the federal Securities and Exchange Commission. Citizens had its SEC lawyers standing by in Washington D.C. and they made the necessary filing. Within the span of a few hours the transaction was complete and Citizens legally held Kauai Electric.

The first improvement made by Citizens was the construction of a new modern steam power plant at Port Allen. Suzi and I returned to Kauai for its dedication.

Citizens also had a major operational decision to make early on in its ownership as Kauai Electric's general manager was about to retire. Ish Jacobson called me up and said: "Could you look around for about five people you think might be a good manager for Kauai Electric?"

I first went to see a person I thought was very qualified to be the new manager for Kauai Electric. C. Dudley Pratt, Jr., whose father had hired me to my first legal job in 1949 on Wendell Carlsmith's urging, was in mid-career as director of planning at Hawaiian Electric. He knew all about utilities, and I thought he would be a competent president of the company. In addition, he was personally connected to Kauai as his mother had grown up on Grove Farm and would be comfortable living there. Dudley Pratt said: "Let me think about it." He called me up after a short time and said: "Jim, I think I have a good opportunity to be president here, and although I appreciate your offer and everything else, I think I'll stay where I am." He did become President of Hawaiian Electric in 1981.

I then went to talk with my brother Bill, who among us three brothers was the only one to follow our father into the sugar industry, spending his entire almost four-decade career with C. Brewer. Among many other assignments he had previously been assistant manager at Kilauea Sugar on Kauai, and was then Vice President of Brewer in charge of all of sugar plantations. I said to Bill: "I think that somebody who has been or is a factory superintendent in the sugar industry would be good for us. Can you give me the names of a couple of your people you'd recommend?" He said: "Well, I have somebody that's just right for you and I won't have to tell people that you stole him away. We are closing down Kilauea Sugar. Ernie Smith has been our factory superintendent. I think that he would be a very qualified guy for you." I asked Bill to speak with Ernie and ask him to call me if he was interested in the job. Bill called me up a short time later and said: "I have some surprising news about Ernie Smith. He has already accepted a new job. He was told by his new employer to keep it a secret until everything was settled."

I then thought of somebody else I knew, a guy who had grown up with me in Lihue, Kauai named Boyd Townsley. His father had the same job at Lihue Plantation that my father had at Grove Farm: Chief Financial Officer. He worked at Amfac and was in charge of managing their electric installations on the many Amfac plantations. I thought: "Here's a person who has lived on Kauai, probably wouldn't mind moving back there, and certainly has a lot of experience."

I thought of a couple of other names and discussed them all with Ish Jacobson. He said: "Well, you know, I think that this guy Townsley sounds like the best guy. I like the fact that he works in the administrative area rather than just being a mill superintendent. He probably would have a bigger picture than the other people. Why don't you see if he'd be interested in us talking to him?"

Townsley worked in downtown Honolulu, just a couple of blocks away from my office. So I invited him out to lunch and said: "Here's a really good opportunity for you. This company is going to grow and grow, and you can be the president of it. You would be the local guy in charge." He says: "Okay, I'll do that. It sounds like a wonderful opportunity." Ish Jacobson talked to him, he was satisfied, Citizens hired him, and Boyd served as Kauai Electric's president for a quarter century.

From then on I represented Citizens on all of its expansions, rate cases and other matters before the PUC, and all other matters affecting Kauai Electric. Between that and my prior and continuing representation of HELCO and other utility work, Carlsmith developed a solid niche practice in public utility law and several of our attorneys who trained up on the work developed related specialties. Just one example is Alan Oshima, who joined Carlsmith in 1976 and became one of the top PUC lawyers in Hawaii; he is today President of Hawaiian Electric.

I also worked very, very closely with Ish Jacobson throughout his long tenure as president of Citizens. He trusted me not only to handle the day-to-day legal affairs of Kauai Electric, but to provide the more complicated advice that any president of a company appreciates. Basically I handled the rate cases and he called me on everything else.

I also got to know Jacobson personally and to count him as a friend. Though Citizens owned and operated about forty utilities across the country, he came down to Hawaii a lot, to add to my fairly frequent trips back to Connecticut to meet with him and his boss, the chair of the company. I learned that he had served in the Navy during the war, as I did, and had gone to Harvard Law School one year behind me. After graduation from Harvard, he had been hired by Citizens because he was not only a lawyer but had graduated from college with an engineering degree. He was a very competent and educated man who knew exactly how best to use his lawyers. I learned a lot from him and from our representation of Citizens.

But, as already reflected in some of my stories, law firms are often affected by events well beyond the quality of their work and relationships with their clients. In the case of Citizens Utilities, the chairman of the board (Rosenthal) died, Ish Jacobson retired, the shareholders changed and the board of directors changed. In the late '90s the new board and management decided to divest out of the electric and gas utility business nationwide and focus only on telecom utilities. After a somewhat lengthy search for the right buyer, in 2002 Citizens sold Kauai Electric to newly-formed Kauai Island Utility Cooperative (KIUC), a federally-supported form of ownership especially for rural utilities under which the consumers (here the residents of Kauai) are the owners.

Cooperatives are a mixed blessing. On the positive side they don't operate from a pure profit motive, stay close to their customer-owners' concerns and can be more flexible and innovative under the right leadership. On the negative side the democratic process of electing the cooperative's board and leadership by a consumer-wide vote turns operations into a political event and does not always result in a qualified and diverse leadership group capable of navigating the complexities of running a utility. KIUC has seen a bit of both sides in its first quarter century, though it has survived as the only still-independent electric company in Hawaii not under Hawaiian Electric's monopoly elsewhere.

All that aside, our representation of Citizens Utilities and Kauai Electric came to an end on the sale. Citizens Utilities served Kauai well throughout that period and it was a mutually beneficial relationship for Carlsmith.

32. Rapid Expansion for Carlsmith

As I worked into the first half of my seventeen-year tenure as chair of Carlsmith's executive committee, our main task was not so much to maintain the momentum we had developed toward becoming a full service Hawaii firm – that almost had a life of its own - but correctly channeling it. It was quite a ride.

By the second half of the '60s several of the promising associates we had brought on in the late '50s and early '60s had become partners and were coming into their own as respected lawyers in their fields and as productive contributors to the firm. And the critical mass we were developing there as well as with our growing client base and reputation in turn attracted a new wave of promising associates. The one who would have the most impact on Carlsmith in time was Tom Van Winkle, who later would serve as chair of Carlsmith's executive committee for twenty years from 1985 to 2005.

Van Winkle grew up in California and Washington and graduated Phi Beta Kappa from Dartmouth College in New Hampshire before going on to Stanford Law School. He worked his way through law school in part as a law enforcement officer for Santa Clara County during summers. While at Stanford he met Marilyn Carlsmith, Merrill's daughter, who was a year behind him; they were married shortly after his graduation in 1963 and set their sights on careers in Hawaii.

Tom had joined the Army Reserve Officers' Training Corps at Dartmouth. After his Stanford graduation he owed the Army two years active duty, which he fulfilled as a Captain with the Army's Intelligence Corps (domestic counterintelligence).

In those days I did most of the interviewing and much of the deciding for new lawyer hires. One of our ticklish situations was how to treat Carlsmith-related applicants, of whom there were a fair number especially in that period. Our working rule was no preference, so much so that Merrill once half-jokingly remarked that the deck was actually stacked against Carlsmith-related applicants. No matter in Tom's case, for he was not only highly qualified on paper but right from the beginning gave off that air of practicality, ability, competence and judgment that was a solid predictor of success. I believe that, like Jim Boyle and some other of our very successful lawyers, his law enforcement and military service had already matured him and provided the tools of that success.

Tom joined Carlsmith in 1966 and was immediately thrown into his own introductory firestorm. His first job had him working doubletime for months to help close the Dillingham Honolulu wharves sale to the State. (This also enabled him to benefit early as had I from watching Wendell Carlsmith in action both at work and at play. As just one example, Wendell Carlsmith would sometimes invite his old and often bitter rival, Jack Hall of the ILWU, to Puuwaawaa Ranch to hunt by day and party by night. Tom listened on once as Wendell and Hall got rip-roaring drunk and traded tales on how they'd tried to outfox each other on a Maui labor organizing effort of decades earlier.)

Next up for Van Winkle was one of those threads that looked innocuous at the beginning but made much of his career early on and throughout. A woman I had grown up with on Kauai had married a man doing business in American Samoa. He was in a major dispute with the most prominent family there and she asked me to represent him. I was too busy and turned the job over to Tom. He went down to American Samoa and cleaned up against the family and their big firm mainland lawyers. The family was so impressed that they hired Tom for all of their work. Through that representation Tom impressed the Bank of Hawaii branch folks there, who then gave him their business and that of other bank Pacific branches like Guam. From that his reputation got back to the main branch in Honolulu and he took on more and more Bank of Hawaii work until he was the bank's go-to attorney especially on the more difficult, consequential engagements and the bank grew into one of Carlsmith's largest clients.

Tom became partner in 1969, the fastest anyone has made partner at Carlsmith, and he deserved it. He had much of Wendell in him, including that trait that all great lawyers have of believing that they can and will find a way to solve any problem for their clients. As he got into his career and his rhythm in the partnership he chafed at my leadership and the firm's direction, leading to some shall-we-say lively but healthy debates, and eventually our generation of firm leadership that had succeeded Wendell's gave way to Tom's and his generation. He grew into one of the most influential attorneys in Hawaii of that generation and certainly the most influential attorney for Carlsmith of the last three decades.

Along with growing our human capital, we were facing opportunities and decisions to expand our physical presence. One such opportunity which illustrated the various issues that come up when considering new locations arose in 1968 when Amfac asked us to open a Kauai office.

Amfac had used a very competent lawyer on Kauai for many years for matters which could be handled best by a Kauai lawyer, such as planning and zoning and some types of litigation. C. Brewer & Co. and other statewide organizations also used this lawyer. He had died.

We represented Amfac on some matters but wanted to grow the client. Amfac offered us that, if we opened a Kauai office, it would pay us a generous retainer for several years. It also suggested that other clients would also use us on Kauai and elsewhere once we opened up.

We thought that the proposal would give us an opportunity to expand on the islands of Kauai and Maui. But who would run the office? In our thinking it needed to be a solid lawyer who would be accepted in the community, knew how we worked, and could manage the office independently.

There was no Kauai lawyer who fit the bill. We concluded that it needed to be one of our existing lawyers. But we were swamped with work in Honolulu and the loss of just one lawyer from our Hilo office would hurt our established Big Island position. We decided that although we wanted to do it we couldn't staff it, and so reluctantly declined.

Lesson learned: Were we right? I think so. One of our top principles was to do the highest quality legal work and a corollary to that was to keep and grow existing clients by doing so. The Kauai expansion at that time and under those circumstances risked both. One shouldn't expand unless you have the resources to do it properly.

In 1974, though, we opened our third office, in Kailua-Kona. West Hawaii was growing, we had good existing and potential clients there, it had its own state circuit court, and some of our lawyers in Hilo and Honolulu were already spending a lot of time there. Bobby Carlsmith, Merrill's son who had joined us in Hilo in 1968, was willing to move over and manage the office. Timing and circumstances lined up.

By the early '70s we had already outgrown our Honolulu office space for ten attorneys in the City Bank building and were cobbling together space elsewhere in the building. It was not going to be a longterm solution and we looked elsewhere. But where and, most important, how much space? How much did we believe we would expand?

The Pacific Trade Center (now known as Pacific Tower) was then in development as the biggest and best office building in Honolulu and was leasing up. It was the perfect location for Carlsmith. We could be first in as an anchor tenant and could negotiate favorably for our new space, and the longer the lease and the more the space the better the overall terms.

We had long discussions about how much space and for how long. We were on a growth trajectory but would it last? How fast would or should we grow? How much of a chance were we willing to take with committing Carlsmith and its partners to legal obligations that might prove hard to meet?

In the end we decided that we didn't want to move again for a long time and we should, as we had previously, take a reasonable chance on our future. Jim Boyle negotiated a beautiful longterm lease under which we leased all of the 22nd floor and took successive options to lease half of the 21st floor, the other half of the 21st floor and some of the other floors so we could match rent and space to growth. Each floor had room for 28 lawyers and we moved in in 1973 with 18 (in addition to 8 in Hilo and one in Kona for a total of 27 lawyers). By a decade later we had filled two floors and were spilling over into the others.

33. The Taiwan Engagement

In early 1971 my old friend, architect Sam Chang, contacted me with an unusual and interesting proposition. He asked if I would join a Honolulu group he was assembling to offer suggestions to the government of Taiwan relating to the future use of a 65 acre parcel of property in the middle of downtown Taipei.

Taipei was a small city when the Kuomintang under Chiang Kai-Shek relocated to Taiwan from mainland China after their defeat by Mao Zedong and the Chinese Communists in 1949. The military department had been awarded this 65 acre parcel adjacent to the new government headquarters. By 1971 a rapidly growing Taipei business community had centered around the government and military properties. In short, the property was in the absolute center of government and business in Taipei and controlled by just one owner and thus highly valuable. The government had decided to move the entire military establishment to an area about forty miles out of Taipei. The question was: What should the government do with the 65 acres?

Sam and his family remained influential in Taiwan and Sam was acquainted with, and even had close personal relationships with, most of the Taiwan government. He knew the Vice President and almost all department heads personally.

The Minister of Economics contacted Sam Chang and asked him to put together a group of individuals with various skillsets to visit Taipei, study the issue, and give the Minister its advice on how to put this land to its highest and best use. The Minister had several important objectives: he wanted the plan to include room for modern, Western style hotels; he wanted office space for business; he wanted homes for residents; he wanted a good center for retail business; and he wanted to attract tourists from Japan, the United States and elsewhere.

In a traditional Chinese approach, the Minister told Sam that the government would pay all expenses of the members of the group but proposed that the members should not charge the normal fee for their services. The lure was, as the Minister suggested, that the members of the group would become known to important people in Taiwan, who would in the future use them for their own purposes at normal rates.

Chang put together a diverse group: Wes Hillendahl, chief economist for Bank of Hawaii; Sheridan Ing, a developer; an executive at Bank of Hawaii; an eminent contractor; a city planner; and me. The plan was that the group would spend a week in Taipei gathering information and then return to Hawaii and prepare a complete report containing a recommended development plan.

Sam had an extra request for me from the Ministry of Tourism, who wanted me to stay an extra week at the expense of the Tourism Bureau to assess the factors for tourism on the island and recommend what Taiwan could do to grow its tourism industry. The Minister of Tourism thought that Japan and the United States were probably the best markets. The People's Republic of China, hundreds of millions strong just one hundred miles across the Formosa Strait, was not then considered a source market as it was in virtual isolation and prohibited virtually all external travel.

I was apprehensive about doing all of this work without getting paid for my time. I questioned whether I would get legal business from Taiwan. However, I concluded (rationalized?) that it was possible, I would develop further expertise and credentials, and spending two weeks in Taipei with this elite group of Hawaii businessmen would give me an opportunity to develop closer relationships with them and the Hawaii business community.

Suzi and I had already planned a long-overdue vacation to Europe for that period, and she was not happy about my dropping our vacation for what I said was a business trip to Taiwan. So I proposed the following to Sam: that the government would pay for my wife's expenses as well as my own. I explained to Sam what he should tell the Taiwan government: that my wife was an inveterate traveler; that it would be very helpful for the Minister of Tourism to get the reactions and viewpoint of an American woman; in fact, that women were more apt than men to make the family decision on where to spend the next vacation. The Minister of Tourism agreed.

Our group landed in Taipei in mid-July 1971 in the early evening. The airport officials made sure that everything went smoothly and we arrived at a very modern downtown hotel. The next morning we awoke to read the early newspaper, which in glaring headlines announced that President Nixon would go to Beijing for the purpose of discussing the opening of formal relations between the United States and China.

This was not good news in Taiwan. What would this do to our assignment? At breakfast we all agreed that we would not discuss it with our hosts unless asked directly. All we would say would be: "We don't know anything about it. We're here to do our job in Taiwan." Our first meeting that morning was in the offices of the Minister of Economics. Nobody mentioned Nixon at all, neither at that meeting nor at any subsequent time during our stay in Taiwan. Perhaps they had just decided to act as if it had never happened.

We started off with a complete inspection of the 65 acre tract and the entire government complex, and then continued with various other business and residential areas in the vicinity and other fact-finding in the following days. We all met as a group at breakfast and at other times during the day. We had developed our tentative plan by just the end of the fourth day.

The 65 acre tract would be master planned as follows. Each of the four corners would be set aside for modern American style highrise hotels. High rise condominiums and highrise office buildings would be developed on the four perimeters. The entire interior would be developed as a park interspersed with street level small shops. We were unanimous in thinking that we had planned one of the most useful and beautiful inner cities in the world.

Our plan contemplated that a ministry of the government would continue to own the land and would lease lots out at normal percentage rent terms (payments of a percent of the revenues from the land, so that if the lessee does well so does the lessor) to hotels and on fixed rent terms for the remainder of the development. During the remainder of our stay each person in the group concentrated on checking out the plan to see if it would work from the perspective of his own expertise.

I spent several days at a big law firm. I read all of the statutes, paying particular attention to whether our plan for percentage leases would work. I found to my dismay that Taiwan had no experience with percentage rent leases. In fact, the law on leases was sparse; everybody bought their land. Small shops rented their spaces under simple verbal leases. I concluded that the government would have to pass some legislation before foreign investors would feel comfortable investing in leased land as was customary in Hawaii, the rest of the United States and elsewhere.

Other members of our team met with their Taiwan counterparts to discuss local law and customs: banker with bankers; architect with architects, etc. We usually met as a group with our counterparts for lunch and discussed the issues concerning us. We had no language problems; they all spoke fluent English.

The Taiwan group was uniformly well educated, most of them in the United States or Europe. One day we were having lunch at a private club in a large dining room. Across the room was a long table where lunch for about thirty people was being served. I asked my neighbor what the group might be. He said: "It is a luncheon put on by the University of Michigan Alumni Society. Michigan is a popular place for Chinese students to get a foreign education."

Our hosts usually took us out to dinner. I learned what a "Nine-Course Dinner" really meant. The courses would be served one at a time. Prior to eating a course everyone would drink a toast to the course with a good Scotch whiskey. Our hosts were holding their liquor very well. I asked Sam how that could be, considering how I felt. "Why, they are drinking a glass of cold tea; it just looks like Scotch".

Suzi was also invited to these dinners. Otherwise during the days she inspected the city, the world-class museum where the art treasures brought from the mainland were displayed, the beautiful hotel on the slopes of a hill, and the little shops everywhere. At some point she conceded that this wasn't such a bad vacation after all.

At the end of our first week everyone left for Hawaii except my wife and me. We were now hosted by Wellington Tsao, Minister of Tourism. Tsao explained further what he wanted from my week working for him: "We have certain tourism attributes, which we understand from the point of view of people who were raised in China. We think that our best market is Japan and the United States. I want to know what you think about these markets. Are there markets we haven't thought of? We have certain places on this island which we think are good magnets for tourists. You have worked in the tourism industry in Hawaii for a long time. Sam Chang had told me about your work in helping grow the tourism industry in Hawaii, particularly on the neighbor islands. I have arranged a guided tour for you which will show you what we think might attract Japanese and American tourists. At the end of your stay I want your frank advice on which attractions are most important and what we can do to enlarge our tourism industry. Your guides will pick you up at your hotel at 8:00 A.M. tomorrow morning."

It turned out that we had three guides for the entire week-long tour of Taiwan. First, we had a tour guide who was responsible for all arrangements and was in charge of the tour; second, we had a driver, who drove but seldom spoke; and third, we had an interpreter because our tour leader did not speak good English. Our interpreter was also the arranger for all events; let's call him the "front man" who took care of the details. Our itinerary went something like this:

Day One: We drove from Taipei to Sun Moon Lake. The countryside was beautiful. We passed from farmhouse to farmhouse with occasional small villages. Sun Moon Lake was beautiful; it lived up to its reputation. We visited an aboriginal village where descendants of the early inhabitants of Taiwan lived.

Day Two: We drove across the mountains to the eastern shore and up the Taroko Gorge to a high elevation. It was very picturesque.

Day Three: We drove into the high mountains – over 10,000 feet up. There was a small ski resort at Yushan. Could it be developed further into a resort that would attract tourists from the United States, Japan, Singapore or the Philippines? We stayed at Lishan, a beautiful mountain area where Chiang Kai-Shek maintained one of his guest houses. It had a haunting, Shangri-La feel to it.

Day Four: We drove to the southern end of the island which, on the same latitude as Kauai, is tropical. It had a few good beaches, but they were nothing like major beach resorts elsewhere in the world. Could it be developed into a seaside tourist resort?

Day Five: We drove to Kaohsiung, the second largest city on Taiwan located on the southwestern side of the island. It was quite modern in many ways and was surrounded by beautiful farmland and villages.

Day Seven: We returned to Taipei and toured various spots in Taipei that tourists might want to see. The National Museum was indeed a very impressive museum.

At the end of our trip I gave Wellington Tsao my verbal conclusions and followed them with a long memorandum when I returned to Hawaii. These were my thoughts in 1971:

(1) I agreed with Taiwan's thinking that its best tourism source markets were Japan and the United States. Mainland Chinese people were not yet travelling. The Southeast Asia world was still somewhat living in its own area. Europeans weren't travelling to the "Far East" in any numbers. Japan was probably the best market because Americans did not travel to Asia in great numbers; they went to Europe.

(2) The only beaches on the entire island were located on the south end of the island. There were just a few beaches and they weren't long, large, wide beaches. Guam had much better beaches and was easy to get to from Japan. The Japanese weren't travelling to Hawaii in large numbers then, but the rapid growth to come was already evident.

(3) I didn't think that their mountain ski resort could be improved and marketed. It wasn't a large area. Japan had far better skiing in Nagano and Hokkaido, and the U.S. had a large number of ski resorts far better than Taiwan could ever be.

(4) The best reason for Japan and American tourists to visit Taiwan was to experience what was essentially a Chinese environment without going to China, which could not then be done. The countryside was similar to China; the food was just as good; the museums were essentially Chinese and better than those in China at the time. I thought that Japan was the best market; it was close and China was of interest to Japanese. I didn't think that Americans would travel all the way to Asia in order to visit Taiwan, although certainly if they went to Japan they might broaden their trip to go to Taiwan.

(5) Another factor that Taiwan could try to market was the sheer beauty of the island and great variety of its natural resources. The basic countryside was beautiful; rolling hills, various crops, and quaint villages. Taroko Gorge was spectacular. The upper plateau was lyrical; no wonder that it was here that Chiang Kai-Shek made his home in his later years. The cities were all interesting. This attraction could be coupled with the Chinese aspect of the countryside.

6) I concluded by suggesting that Taiwan could best expand its economy by doing more of what it already did well: invest in industry and the manufacture of a variety of goods. It had a large number of very well educated businessmen who had the talent to expand their industries and market throughout the world. It had a large number of people who could work in those industries and earn a much better

living than they had at the time. Tourism had a role to play, but it would not be a major role.

Wellington Tsao was not happy with my report; after all, he was Minister of Tourism. However, he was gracious and we kept in touch from time to time.

What happened? Well first, of course, Taiwan did turn its attention to industry and manufacturing and developed one of the most successful economies and highest standards of living in the world.

Tourism did develop as a solid contributor to Taiwan's economy, though not on the scale of Hawaii or of the Hawaii beach resort brand type. Visitors to Taiwan grew from 500,000 in 1972 to over 10 million in 2016. Almost half of those 2016 visitors were what Taiwan refers to as "overseas Chinese", mainly from Hong Kong, Macau and Mainland China, which included a huge jump in Mainland Chinese after they were allowed to visit Taiwan in numbers in 2008). Of the other half, almost 2 million were from Japan, one million from Korea, 1.5 million from Southeast Asia, 500,000 from the United States and negligible numbers from Europe. Top tourist attractions are the culture and beauty of Taiwan. Tourism spending at US$15 billion accounts for about 5% of Taiwan's gross domestic product. (By remarkable comparison, in 2016 Hawaii tourism saw about 9 million visitors spending over $15 billion, though tourism accounts for a far greater share of Hawaii's economy than Taiwan's.)

As for the original trip purpose and recommendations, our group developed a beautiful master plan for the 65 acre parcel in the center of Taipei. The Minister of Economics and his staff were excited about what the plan could do for Taipei. The Minister took the report to the Premier, who decided not to pursue the plan. His reason was that Chinese never leased land. Instead, he caused the government to subdivide the 65 acre parcel up into many different parcels and sell them off. But in doing so the Premier did adopt the master-planned mix of uses we had recommended. It wasn't a bad result for Taipei, though it would have been far better if the government had retained overall ownership and control of the property.

Lessons learned:

(1) When working with foreigners in foreign countries, Americans in particular need to consider that foreigners do not necessarily have

the same vision as we have. In fact the same factual situation and set of challenges can create different and often surprising solutions in different cultures. Successful American companies make it work by using a system somewhat as follows: form a partnership with an established business enterprise in the country; let it be in the limelight; give great attention to its view on what will and won't work; and get the best law firm you can find in that country. In short, recognize that the people in these countries are indeed "foreign"; you have to consider that and work your way through it.

(2) In evaluating courses of action one must utilize a knowledge of the past and an assessment of the present to try to predict the future. My report to Tourism Minister Tsao incorporated predictions on the future, some of which came to pass and some of which didn't. In the latter category I did not accurately factor in the great transformation within China and with its relationship with the rest of the world, the rising economies of the Southeast Asian nations, and the great improvements in longrange travel.

Perhaps I could not have foreseen the latter two, but the essential historical fact staring us in the face our first day in Taipei was that Nixon was going to China. From that event one could have predicted that China would open up both inbound and outbound with a resulting major impact on Taiwan. Maybe we and our Taiwan hosts would have done each other and our task a better service by openly discussing the possible ramifications of one of the most dramatic events of the time.

The Taiwan engagement was well worth it. Even though I'm not sure it resulted in that much direct work, it enhanced my reputation, expanded my relationships, and if nothing more gave me dinner conversations for a lifetime. Our hosts were impressed with our work. They often came through Honolulu primarily to expand their markets in the mainland United States. Sam Chang always entertained them at the best Chinese restaurants Honolulu offered and always invited me. I learned not to drink a full glass of Scotch before every course.

34. The Australian Connection

The thread that began back in the 1930s when Wendell Carlsmith had retained accountant Ernest Cameron of Cameron Tennent & Dunn took an unexpected turn in the mid-'70s.

Cameron Tennent & Dunn had merged into international accounting firm Peat, Marwick Mitchell in 1960 and I had since done Peat Marwick's legal work in Hawaii and occasionally beyond. One of Peat Marwick's major clients in Australia was the Commonwealth Bank of Australia, then as now one of Australia's largest banks.

A U.S. law at the time, the Glass-Steagall Act of 1933 (a response to the Great Depression) said basically that banks couldn't invest in securities and other assets in addition to core banking and lending. (It was repealed in 1999 and some blame the Great Recession of 2008-2009 as a result since banks could and did take risky positions in investments.) There was no equivalent of Glass-Steagall in Australia and banks there were perfectly used to investing.

Commonwealth Bank had diversified from banking into real estate development. It had a very large development subsidiary headed by Fred Simms, an architect by training who had become a major developer of resort communities on Australia's Gold Coast.

The 1973 Arab oil embargo had led to a worldwide recession in 1974 and Australia was especially hard hit. Commonwealth Bank decided, perhaps secretly, that it needed to diversify out of Australia into overseas investments that would hedge the risks of further recession and of a decline in the Australian dollar against foreign currencies.

The bank, in consultation with Peat Marwick, decided that the United States was the best investment and that Hawaii was the best place in the U.S. to invest. It was close, the bank knew resort destinations and the real estate market looked stable.

Commonwealth Bank said to Peat Marwick: "We want to undertake a major land development in Hawaii. We are thinking about a residential condominium development in Waikiki. What law firm should we retain?" Peat Marwick said: "We checked with our folks in Honolulu and they say you should use Jim Case at Carlsmith." The bank retained me.

Fred Simms was assigned to come up and put the project together. He selected Wimberly Allison Tong & Goo, one of Hawaii's best architectural firms, as project architects. The firm, now known as WATG, was formed in Honolulu by George Wimberly who renovated the Royal Hawaiian Hotel in the 1940s. It grew into a highly successful international firm, a prime example of a local product made good worldwide. We had assembled a good project team.

Next Fred went looking for a location and found what he thought was a good one on both sides of Lewers Street in Waikiki close to the Ala Wai Canal. It was owned by Lum Yip Kee, Ltd. Lum Yip Kee had emigrated from China in the late 1880s and had gone into taro and rice farming along the streams that flowed from Manoa and Palolo Valleys through today's communities of Moiliili and McCully to Waikiki. The taro and rice farming was gone but the family had become major landowners and had transformed into a real estate investment and management company headed by third generation Tan Tek Lum.

Fred and I went to Tan Tek Lum to negotiate a master lease of the land. Lum's attorney was Asa Akinaka, who I knew because I had interviewed and almost hired him in the early 1960s; we had a good personal and professional relationship. Lum Yip Kee was in the business of leasing its land, they knew what they wanted and they knew how to negotiate for what they wanted. We were in the business of leasing their land, we knew what we wanted, and we knew how to negotiate for what we wanted. We completed a mutually satisfactory lease with no drama and in short order. (I later represented the owners of this and other Lum Yip Kee-leased condominiums in buying out the leases; it was always a straightforward and mutually satisfactory negotiation and agreement.)

Wimberly through Gerry Allison came up with a beautifully designed project, which was named Aloha Towers. Next up was construction financing. As is still true today, the banks wouldn't lend unless and until they were sure that there were enough buyers for the project to pay back the loan. They said: "We will give you the complete construction loan if you prove to us that you have [say] 75% of the units presold so that it'll cover your construction costs."

Well, I was a good client, so I told Fred: "OK, I'll sign up one of your very nice two bedroom units on the 10th floor looking up into Manoa Valley. That will help your presale requirement." I paid the 5% down payment. We got the necessary number of presold buyers and the construction financing and in 1975 started construction.

The real estate market fell apart in the middle of construction. Suddenly project units were overpriced. This meant that presold buyers could not get loans to complete their purchases, at least at any reasonable rate. It was cheaper for them to walk away from their 5% downpayments than to finance and close the purchase. That obviously put the project at great risk.

The Commonwealth Bank president decided to come to Honolulu to assess the situation personally. He brought along a young bank executive named Peter Currie, who was then assigned here fulltime to oversee completion of the project. Currie became my day-to-day client contact.

The bank president also brought his wife along, not the first person to find a reasonable domestic solution to a planned business trip to Hawaii. Suzi and I invited them to our house for dinner and, for being one of Australia's most famous, best-known executives and spouse, they turned out to be very down-to-earth. Suzi cooked up a fantastic dinner and then his wife insisted on going into the kitchen to personally make the famous Australian dessert pavlova. One thing about being a lawyer: you meet a lot of interesting people and learn a lot of interesting things, such as what is pavlova.

Commonwealth Bank finally decided that the only way to address the situation was to cut the prices for all Aloha Towers presold units by 10%. That held all presales and stabilized the project financing through construction and sale.

The bank came to me and said: "We're cutting the prices 10% on all presold units and your new price is this." I said: "No, I promised to buy it at the presale price and I'll buy it at that price." That was the honest thing to do and it made an impression on the bank. I bought the unit at full price. Then the bank said: "You know, this is a big complex and needs a resident manager. We'd like to rent your unit." So my good deed was rewarded by a good deed.

The project was completed in 1976. Then the real estate market turned again and the prices went way up. About two years after completion I asked if it was okay if I sold the apartment. The bank said yes and I did sell it for something like 25% more than I paid for it.

How did Commonwealth Bank come out on the Aloha Towers development as compared to its goals going in? The end result was very interesting. The bank had sent Australian money up to the United States to finance the development. Between that and the construction financing it lost money on the actual project. But when it returned its surplus money to Australia the exchange ratio had switched and the bank made a million dollars on the exchange rate. Was the bank lucky or smart? It correctly predicted what would happen on the value of the Australian dollar versus that of the United States dollar. The basic game plan turned out to be right.

Lesson learned: Sometimes it is wise to hedge your investments.

By that time we had an established relationship with Commonwealth Bank, Fred Simms and Peter Currie. The bank decided that it wanted to undertake another Hawaii condominium development and retained the same team.

Fred found an opportunity to buy a large parcel in Waialae Nui Valley, along the hillside on the Hawaii Kai side of the valley. The Wimberly firm designed a very nice project, which was named Kahala View Estates. Every condominium unit was one-story and designed with a view down the valley to the ocean. They were really like single-family houses but with the benefits of condominium ownership such as common areas and governance.

The Commonwealth Bank president approached his colleagues at the Darling Company in Melbourne, Australia to ask if they wanted to join in the investment. The Darling family was the most famous business name in Australia. They dominated business in Melbourne and were so well known throughout Australia that when one of the piers was built in Sydney Harbor across from the Royal Opera House it was called the Darling Pier.

The Darling family, perhaps three or four of them, came to Hawaii personally to review the potential investment and grilled me and the rest of the team. They decided to make the investment. The development went well and Kahala View Estates opened in 1978.

Although that was the end of Commonwealth Bank's and the Darling's Hawaii investments, the team they had assembled here stayed active on future opportunities and continued to retain me. Probably their best-known project was buying a group of very run-down cottages on the banks of Makiki Stream on the ocean side of Wilder Avenue near Punahou School and creating a beautiful residential condominium project named Punahou Cliffs, which opened in 1983.

My Australian connection continued on with Peter Currie, who had returned to Australia and become a very competent executive of Commonwealth Bank. Colonial Sugar Refining Company (today CSR Limited) was, like the bank and the Darlings, one of the largest, oldest and most storied businesses in Australia. Its base was in sugar throughout Australia and overseas especially in Fiji, though it had diversified into other businesses. Colonial Sugar was searching for a new chief executive to run sugar and its other agricultural enterprises, and hired Peter Currie, likely on the recommendation of Peat Marwick.

Just prior to Peter's hiring, Colonial Sugar had decided to diversify its agricultural operations (and perhaps its landholdings) and had bought a macadamia nut company in South Kona called MacFarms of Hawaii. I had helped start MacFarms in the late 1950s and probably knew more about macadamias than any other Hawaii lawyer from my representation of Honomalino Agricultural Company. With Peter's hiring, I suddenly became Colonial Sugar's Hawaii attorney for MacFarms.

A short time later Colonial Sugar entered into a partnership with the Campbell Soup company. The partnership involved two different joint ventures. The first venture was MacFarms and the second venture was an Australian company that was also a subsidiary of Colonial Sugar.

Peter Currie conceived a most interesting strategy. If macadamia nuts were cheap in the United States, MacFarms would send its nuts to Australia to be used in one of its subsidiaries, either a macadamia nut processing plant or the cookie company. If macadamia nuts were cheap in Australia, it would send them up to MacFarms for processing and then back down to Australia to make cookies.

This all worked fine for both Colonial Sugar and me until Colonial Sugar sold MacFarms. Suddenly our macadamia nut work stopped as the new owners of MacFarms retained other lawyers.

But Peter Currie and I were not finished. In the late 1980s my new client, Mauna Loa Macadamia Partners, was thinking of buying an Australian company which was Australia's largest processor of macadamia nuts. Peter Currie had just retired from Colonial Sugar. I recommended to Mauna Loa that they hire him as a consultant, which they did.

We worked up a negotiating strategy, Peter ran the negotiation and we made a solid offer to buy. However, a Singapore company arrived on the scene, made a much higher offer, and bought the company.

In 1990 I was back in Missouri for Suzi's high school reunion when I got a call from the Peat Marwick managing partner in Honolulu. He explained that Peat Marwick Australia had decided to put on a seminar there on investing in the United States and my name had come up. Would I travel to Australia (and Suzi could join me) to present a major speech on the opportunities and issues for Australian companies interested in U.S. investment? Of course I said yes, for all kinds of reasons, and came home to prepare a comprehensive speech on Australian investment into the United States. I even bought three new suits to look presentable. Then Peat Marwick called to say that they had cancelled the seminar due to lack of interest (I hope it was in the subject and not the presenter).

Thus, on a less-than-satisfactory note, ended my Australian connection. I haven't been able to get rid of the suits. Every time I open my closet I see my suits and think of the great speech I never delivered.

This thread began in 1930 and ended in 1990. It is not only one of the longest but probably the most convoluted of my stories. But it reinforces important lessons from my career.

First, it all starts with the quality of your work and the level of trust and confidence you engender in your clients. This thread started with and was sustained by that, and at any point the thread could have been broken by a failure to deliver quality, trust and confidence. Second, the best way to get business is still the old-fashioned word-of-mouth even if delivered at electronic hyperspeed as compared to the boat mail pace of my era. A recommendation from a trusted source is the gold standard. Third, personal as well as professional relationships are key. I took the time to get to know most of my best clients and counted some of them among my closest friends. And fourth: expect the unexpected.

35. Hawaii Energy Part Three: Kahuku Windfarms

Around 1978 Wayne Van Dyck, a California entrepreneur, called me up. He explained that his mission was to prove wind energy could work on a large scale and that he had formed a company, Windfarms, Ltd., to pursue that goal. He had determined that Hawaii was a perfect location for wind energy especially as it experienced steady trade winds about 70% of the time.

Van Dyck said that he was coming to Honolulu for the purpose of investigating the possibility of a wind farm project here and was interested in retaining a lawyer to assist. He noted that he had investigated various lawyers and law firms, that he understood I had represented Hilo Electric Light Company and was currently representing Kauai Electric Company, that Ishier Jacobson of Citizens Utilities Company had recommended me to him, and was I interested.

It was an interesting new and potentially profitable engagement where we could refine and broaden our expertise not only in public utility law generally but in the expanding area of alternative energy. I could see no conflict of interest. Any wind power produced would have to be sold to Hawaiian Electric Co. Ltd. since HECO had a virtually monopoly on distribution, and we had never represented HECO. It didn't seem likely that we would ever have to deal with existing clients or former clients. So we confirmed our retention by Windfarms and started immediately.

I had some experience with wind as I had sailed competitively all my life starting as a teen on Nawiliwili Bay and had to have a working knowledge of wind in my Navy service. I could talk somewhat intelligently on wind dynamics generally and was familiar with wind patterns throughout Hawaii. I knew, for example, that the most constant wind in Hawaii - and wind power requires the most constant year-round wind possible - was on windward shores and slopes close to the ocean where the cleanest wind is found. I knew that when wind hits a vertical object its preferred course is not up and over but sideways and around. I also knew that the best wind power turbine blades acted like sails or airplane wings in moving the wind efficiently over their surfaces.

The Site

When Van Dyck arrived we toured Oahu, focusing only there because of the large urban population and the fact that interisland power transmission lines were then not only economically but technically unfeasible. We reviewed various sites that might work and discussed related pros and cons, including the following:

(1) Makapuu Point. On the southeast corner of Oahu, it seemed perfect. The islands of Oahu and Maui channeled the northeast tradewinds down the Molokai Channel over the point. In addition, the winds which hit the Koolau Mountains between Makapuu Point and the Nuuanu Pali did not go over the mountains, but instead split to the sides across Makapuu Point and through the Nuuanu Pali. Thus, Makapuu Point had a perfect wind regime. But, and a big "but" it was: would the public accept wind turbines on Makapuu Point? I didn't think so and told Van Dyck.

(2) Nuuanu Pali. It was obviously a good site. The wind regime was terrific; everyone knew that the winds hitting the Koolau on either side of the Pali sweep through the Pali, to the enjoyment of visitors and residents alike. However, I was sure that the public would never allow the legendary Nuuanu Pali to be desecrated by a wind farm and told Van Dyck.

(3) Kahuku Point. Not only was it directly exposed to the northeast trades coming straight off the ocean, but the wind hitting the northern portion of the Koolau was diverted across Kahuku Point. Not only was it a good wind regime, but there was plenty of remote land in the hills behind Kahuku and Turtle Bay and away from any population where the wind farm could be built. The only real disadvantage was that the land, while owned by the Campbell Estate, was leased to the United States Army as part of the Army's field training program. While Campbell Estate was not opposed to its use for wind farms, we would have to get the Army to agree to a license to use its training grounds.

(4) Kaena Point. The tradewinds coming around Kahuku Point headed straight for Kaena Point on western Oahu at the end of the Waianae Mountains, more or less skipping the North Shore communities of Pupukea, Haleiwa and Waialua. There was a good paved road up to the top of the Kaena Point ridge. The military had a major communications station there, but a wind farm would not bother its operations. A project there would be more palatable to the public than Makapuu Point or Nuuanu Pali. It wasn't bad, but Kahuku was better.

(5) Palehua Ridge. This site was on the southeastern edge of the Waianaes overlooking central Oahu. There was a fairly good wind regime there because winds coming down through the middle of Oahu over Wahiawa and Schofield Barracks split east and west, with the western winds providing a pretty good windflow over Palehua. But there was an increasing population in that portion of the island which would likely lead to community opposition. The location was doable, but Kahuku and Kaena Point were better.

Windfarms decided that Kahuku was the most promising location overall and moved on to securing a site. It asked me to contact the Army to negotiate a license. After some due diligence I reached out to General Herbert E. Wolff, the senior officer in charge of the Army's Kahuku training grounds. I was told that a designated Colonel would be the person to contact.

The Colonel did not seem anxious to agree to anything like this, but at least was willing to listen. I explained that a large wind farm at Kahuku (80 Megawatts) would provide a good source of electricity for the entire North Shore and the north portion of Windward Oahu, accounting for close to ten percent of Oahu's total energy needs. It would be a good backup for Schofield Barracks, the main Army base in Hawaii. We didn't want to hinder any Army maneuvers and weren't asking for a lease. We merely wanted a license to build windmills on an area which I identified from our preliminary studies. We needed access along an existing road coming up from Turtle Bay, and would be a small nuisance during construction. Otherwise, our windmills would not hinder the Army's maneuvers. The Colonel assured me that he would speak with the General.

Much to my surprise and relief, he called up several days later and said that he had arranged an Army helicopter departing the Fort Shafter parade grounds at 8:00 A.M. sharp a few days hence for an aerial review of our proposed license site with General Wolff. I said that we also had a tentative plan to install transmission lines from the windmills to HECO's existing distribution systems and asked if we could also review the likely route on the way back; he said fine.

On the appointed day the General and we took off from Ft. Shafter and crossed the wild forests of Central Oahu to Kahuku. We inspected the proposed windmill site area which was on the edge of the Army's training grounds and relatively flat. An existing road came up from the main around-the-island road at Kawela Bay. It was obvious, to me at least, that there was plenty of room for windmills and that windmills and the Army could co-exist. On the way back we followed the line between the top of the sugar cane fields and the forest. It would be easy to construct a transmission line between the windmills and HECO's large substation near Wahiawa.

A few days later the Colonel called me up and said that the General thought the windmills might interfere with the Army's training. What to do? I called up the General's office and said that I would like to talk with the General in person. By this time they knew me. I was very pleased when they said that the General would give me a chance to change his mind. Of course, Army line of command: the Colonel would also be joining us.

I now had to somehow persuade the General that we could co-exist. I explained that I had been a Naval Officer during World War II and had been part of a contingent at the Fleet Training Base, San Clemente Island, California. Our group ran joint Navy- Marine training exercises preparing for the landings in the Pacific. We tried as hard as we could to simulate an actual landing. The Navy used *live* ammunition during this training. There were rare casualties, but the reality was that the Marines were prepared for real war when they landed on Pacific beaches and many more lives were saved as a result.

I told the General that our windmills would be an advantage to the Army. Army helicopters in realtime combat would have to fly into cities and between buildings, or through narrow gaps in forests or between mountains. They would get much better training if they had to fly around the windmills. I never said it, but I hoped that the Army General would carefully consider whether it was appropriate that Marines used live ammunition while he thought windmills would interfere with Army training.

The General himself called me up several days later and said that the Army would consent to a license of the windmill site under mutually agreeable conditions. With that we were able to conclude an overall lease with the Campbell Estate and the site was secured.

General Wolff eventually retired from the Army, went to work for First Hawaiian Bank and was a loyal contributor to the community. He bought a home on Waialae Iki, and later became my client when I represented the homeowners there in buying out their Bishop Estate leases.

Hawaiian Electric

Of course, Windfarms couldn't develop a windfarm unless HECO was willing to purchase its energy for distribution to consumers. We didn't expect to have a major problem here. The sugar plantations had produced electricity from bagasse and electric companies had purchased electricity from the plantations for decades, so these power purchase agreements (PPA) were common.

We needed an otherwise standard PPA but with a bit of a twist. All of our energy was "surplus energy", meaning that HECO bought it from us only as it was available and HECO had excess demand. We still needed a firm price for financing purposes. However, this price could be determined within somewhat known parameters which basically involved discounting the usual price for available energy to account for the times when the energy was not available or needed.

We negotiated a firm price with HECO fairly easily. We also agreed on the route of the transmission line from the windfarms to HECO's substation. In 1979 we executed a letter of intent with HECO to enter into a binding PPA once the rest of the project details were worked out.

Now opposition surfaced from an unexpected source. Environmental organizations had all pushed HECO to move toward alternative energy. But suddenly they opposed the project because transmission lines, rather than route along the highway or through inhabited areas (which they also opposed), might go through the lower edges of the forest owned by the State of Hawaii. We had not expected that a transmission line, which is a necessary tool in moving electricity, would be fought by these organizations. It seemed that they wanted electricity to be generated from alternative sources, but didn't want to provide the necessary mechanism to get it to consumers.

It took us some time to solve this problem. Fortunately, Waialua Sugar Company (a subsidiary of Castle & Cooke) owned sugar cane land up to the edge of the forest and was willing to lease an easement to us. Somehow we also found a way from the source of the windmills to the highway so that we could serve existing North Shore consumers. Now, we could move windfarm-generated electricity from a prime wind regime secured site through secured transmission lines to HECO and the consumer.

The Technology

The federal tax laws at the time had provisions which were designed to encourage the construction of windfarms. The maximum size of a windfarm which could obtain certain valuable benefits that would make the project economically viable was 80 Megawatts.

In 1980 Windfarms signed up Bechtel, one of the largest engineering and project management companies in the world, as its project engineer. Windfarms and Bechtel went to Hamilton Standard in Connecticut and asked it to design the appropriate windfarm and windmills.

Hamilton Standard was a very old company owned by a diversified parent called United Technologies. Hamilton Standard had been manufacturing propellers for airplanes for a long time. For example, it had designed the propeller for Charles Lindberg's plane, the Spirit of St. Louis, on his historic crossing of the Atlantic. Windmills use the same basic technology as propellers; they just operate in reverse. With propellers, fuel is used to turn the propeller, which then propels the plane forward, while with windmills, the wind causes the blades to rotate and create electricity.

Hamilton Standard designed a windfarm with twenty 4 Megawatt windmills. The blades would be 200 feet long so that the diameter of the windmill would be 400 feet. The blades would move twenty feet above the ground, leaving room for transit and use underneath the sweep of the blades. In 1981 Windfarms signed an agreement with Hamilton Standard to construct and supply the technology.

The Financing

Windfarms, Bechtel and Hamilton Standard worked to generate a total project cost for the initial development, technology, construction, loan interest during construction, initial operations, engineers and consultants, and all other expenses. It rounded out at close to $300,000,000.

We worked out a tentative financing structure as follows:

Start-up capital (Windfarms):	$ 3,000,000
Venture capital (other investors)	$ 27,000,000
Debt financing (loan)	$ 270,000,000
Total	$ 300,000,000

The project could work financially, justifying a good loan, under the assumption that the world price of fuel oil used by HECO was above $35 per barrel. At that level wind energy would be economically competitive with fossil fuel-generated energy. At the time the world price had been fairly stable for years at about $50 per barrel.

Windfarms persuaded Standard Oil Company of California that alternative energy such as windmills was going to be part of the world mix of fuels in the future and that Standard Oil should "get its feet wet" in this project. Standard Oil agreed to invest the $27,000,000 of equity for a share in the project.

Now it was up to the lenders to approve a loan for the remaining 90% of the project budget. There were several plusses: (1) United Technologies and Hamilton Standard were held in high regard in financial circles; (2) Standard Oil was willing to risk $27,000,000 in equity; and (3) the numbers seemed to pencil out. A group of lenders led by First Boston Corp. agreed in principle to make the loan if the details could be worked out.

At this point First Boston added a condition that eventually caused the collapse of the enterprise. There had never in world history been a windmill this large and if it didn't work the project could not succeed. United Technologies and its subsidiary Hamilton Standard must guarantee the performance of the windmills: if they broke, they had to fix them at their expense; if they didn't work as engineered, they had to replace them with something that did work at their expense; if nothing worked, they were liable for project costs.

This requirement put United Technologies and Hamilton Standard to the full test since they were asked to guarantee overall project success. The presidents of both United Technologies and Hamilton Standard and an entourage of their engineers and others visited Hawaii to review all aspects of the project. They inspected the site; it passed the test. They met with Carlsmith; we passed the test. They met with HECO and were satisfied with the PPA. In fact, the entire project was approved. They returned to Connecticut for what we assumed would be final approval.

Suspense for weeks. Then a bombshell! Hamilton Standard's engineers weren't sure the 400-foot diameter blades would stand up to the stress of a high wind or even a moderate tradewind. Their analysis when you heard it was so apparent that it was shocking nobody in the entire project course had thought about it.

The tip of a windmill blade moves faster than the base of the blade. The longer the blade the faster the blade tip moves both absolutely and relative to the base. Thus the longer the blade the more stress is placed on it at increasing wind speeds. With a 200 foot long blade, the tip would be moving at a tremendous speed even in moderate trades. The Hamilton Standard engineers could not assure themselves that their own windmill design would retain stability.

With that United Technologies and Hamilton Standard were not willing to guarantee their technology and First Boston was not willing to make the loan. The entire enterprise collapsed and Windfarms walked away from the project with the $3 million loss of its startup investment.

Subsequently engineers developed shorter blades that are more efficient in the production of wattage. The diameter of these windmills very rarely exceeds 200 feet although since they mostly produce less wattage than the 4 Megawatt blades would have produced it takes more of them. Windmills were eventually tried on the same site above Kahuku although not successfully, and another nearby site now hosts a substantial windfarm. The goal of renewable energy for Hawaii remains elusive.

Afterthoughts on the Windfarms engagement:

(a) Wayne Van Dyck and Windfarms did everything right. Van Dyck's plan was sound; he put up his own front money so that he could control events; he put together a great project team (including his lawyers!); he found Standard Oil to provide the remainder of comfortable equity; he found First Boston and lender participants willing to make a sizable loan; he hired the most qualified maker of propellers, and presumably windmills, in the country; and he made sure that its parent, United Technologies, was capable of assuring that the manufacturing and construction of the windmills was adequately managed and funded. He was a true entrepreneur and visionary.

(b) The Army carefully analyzed the project against its own needs and constraints and found a way that worked for it to contribute to the prospect of a better energy situation for Hawaii's military and civilian communities.

(c) HECO, in contrast to its later approach which began to view the independent development of alternative energy as a threat, entered into a fair PPA agreement to provide cheaper electricity rates for its customers and start the process of weaning away from fossil fuel energy sources.

(d) Standard Oil (now Chevron) looked way into its energy future and committed hard capital to get in on the ground floor of a new technology.

(e) First Boston and the lender consortium was willing to commit $270,000,000 to finance the project, but was brilliant in asking United Technology and Hamilton Standard to first guarantee the performance of a new technology.

(f) United Technologies was brilliant in questioning whether the technology of its own subsidiary would work and then pulling out rather than risk the company on being wrong.

(g) As for Hamilton Standard .... They were the best known experts in the business, but they failed miserably. They should have known earlier of the practical risks of a 400 foot diameter blade, and they could have been more conservative and used a tried-and-proven windmill of a smaller size. They were lucky not to have been sued by Windfarms and Van Dyck, as they most certainly would have been in today's far more litigious world.

I also think that Carlsmith did about as good a job as we could have. We persuaded the Army to give Windfarms a site license; we negotiated a reasonable PPA with Hawaiian Electric; we solved the transmission line problem; and we generally counseled Windfarms and oversaw and implemented its goals over the four years of the project. Now if only I had thought to ask the question on windmill tip speeds.

Aside from the satisfaction of doing a good job notwithstanding the result, Carlsmith profited enormously from the Windfarms engagement. First, our legal fees were substantial and helped sustained the rapid firm growth that was ongoing.

But more important in the long run, we were now more knowledgeable and had developed more and broader experience in the field of alternative energy than any other firm in Hawaii. This reputation fed on itself and helped us develop a deep bench of attorneys like Jerry Sumida who in time became the acknowledged leaders in this field. All of this added up to literally dozens of new clients and legal jobs in the area in the coming decades.

36. A Full Service Pacific Firm

In the mid-1970s, as I entered the second half of my tenure as Chair of the Executive Committee, Carlsmith was closing in on its goal of being a full service Hawaii firm. To that, with the work of Tom Van Winkle and others in other Pacific jurisdictions, we had implicitly added the goal of being a Pacific firm, by which we meant that we could provide full service to clients with interests outside Hawaii elsewhere in the Pacific. But to sustain the growth necessary to achieve our goal, we still needed to attract and retain quality clients with quality work, and we still needed to make sound decisions internally on how and where to grow.

Fortunately, by then we were in high demand by law school graduates as a preferred employer. We even had some real star power pass briefly through our doors, with John Roberts, later Chief Justice of the United States, and Ray Mabus, later Governor of Mississippi and Secretary of the Navy, taking turns as summer associates. I'm not sure if they were seriously checking us out or just on an interesting and pleasant interlude.

An entire new crop of high-quality associate attorneys with all the potential to become high-quality partners joined us. The most impactful of them on the future course of Carlsmith was Peter Starn.

Starn, originally from Missouri, was a combat-decorated Marine Captain who had flown CH-53 Sea Stallion helicopters in Vietnam. He went on to Stanford Law School and joined Carlsmith in 1972. Like Jim Boyle and Tom Van Winkle before him, his life experiences had matured him beyond his years and he sped through his associateship, making partner in 1976 and joining me, Charlie Wichman, Donn Carlsmith and by then Van Winkle on the Executive Committee in 1980. Starn's greatest strength and weakness was a supreme confidence in himself and his views and abilities. He deserved much of it for he was a first-rate lawyer from the get-go; clients flocked to him and his economic contributions to the firm multiplied. But internally he was divisive and advocated for decisions which cost the firm dearly.

We had always believed that the best way to grow the firm, especially at the partner level, was from within. Whether it was growing our Honolulu office or opening new offices, we felt that partners who had been trained and mentored by us to our quality standards and who shared our firm goals and values were most conducive to strengthening and continuing the "firm glue" that held us all together. Well into the 1970s the instances of lateral (external) partner hires were very few and far between. But we found that we could not keep up with demand and sustain our growth toward full service status from within alone; we just couldn't put enough associates into the pipeline and get them to partner level fast enough. We looked increasingly to lateral partners, with mixed results.

One example of a positive result was George Grubb. George was a national tax expert with a national firm in Ohio who had just one problem: he loved Hawaii and the ocean, especially body-surfing at Sandy Beach and Point Panic. He lateralled in as partner in 1971 and we instantly became one of the premier tax firms in the Pacific.

Another was Don Williams. Guam, just a few hours from Japan and the rest of Asia, was booming from a combination of defense spending and rapid visitor growth and we had both existing clients and a myriad of opportunities that created the foundations of an office there. Van Winkle had gotten to know Williams, then Attorney General of American Samoa, during his Samoan engagements. He lateralled in as partner in 1977 and we opened the Guam office, our first outside of Hawaii, in 1978, later absorbing a solid local firm as well. Saipan followed in much the same fashion in 1987.

We took a hybrid approach on Maui. We had wanted to open on Maui from back in the 1960s but could never find the right conditions, meaning an alliance of existing and future clients and a Carlsmith values partner to run the show. We did have one very strong client there, Maui Land and Pineapple Co., Ltd., dating back to Wendell Carlsmith's representation of the Hawaii sugar industry in the 1930s; Wendell and Charlie Wichman had helped form MLP when the Maui Baldwin/Cameron family spun it out of Alexander & Baldwin. Come the early 1980s MLP, which had moved into developing Kapalua, "suggested strongly" that we needed to open a Maui office, which we took to mean that if we didn't it would look elsewhere. We moved a mid-level partner and some associates over and opened in 1983. Later we merged with a well-respected local firm headed by Martin Luna and that office became a solid contributor to the firm.

Throughout the 1960s and into the 1970s, our biggest obstacle to full service status was the lack of a broadbased litigation/dispute resolution capability. We had some solid homegrown partners like Terry O'Toole but couldn't grow it fast or broad enough to meet client demand and opportunity. In 1975 we absorbed our largest lateral group to date when we brought in a top Honolulu litigation firm headed by Hod Greeley and Bernie Bays. That and the continued growth of our own hires gave us the right to call ourselves a top litigation firm.

In 1982, the same year that Wendell Carlsmith died while giving a presentation at Stanford Law School on the future of law, I turned over the reins as Chair of the Executive Committee to Charlie Wichman, who would serve until 1985 when Tom Van Winkle took over, completing Carlsmith's next generational transition. During that period we continued our growth, adding clients, attorneys and offices with mixed results, and Carlsmith faced a tumultuous decade ahead. But in 1985 we stood at 90 attorneys in six offices throughout Hawaii and stretching from Los Angeles to Guam, as compared to our two offices and 14 attorneys when I took over in 1965. Carlsmith was a full service Pacific law firm.

37. On Management

My time in active firm management spanned almost four decades, from 1951 when Wendell Carlsmith immediately started turning over management duties to me, through my seventeen years as firm Chair, and then continuing until 1990 when I stepped down from the Executive Committee at the age of 70. If practicing law well is as much art as science, managing law firms takes all that to another level.

First up is the nature of the beast. Law firms are by definition associations of lawyers, and lawyers are capable, strong-willed and competitive animals. When your first reaction to any situation is to control and advocate, that can certainly present obstacles to problemsolving and teambuilding. But once you realize that many lawyers just have to get through that initial reaction, a little patience and perseverance usually gets everyone to a more cooperative and constructive place.

Second, law firms are not strictly structured and good lawyers have choices, so attracting and retaining the best is an ongoing challenge. Of course compensation is a major ingredient, both amount and almost more importantly perceived fairness. But it is far more than that; it is the sense of shared values and a shared mission that holds the best firms together through good and bad, and that is hard to create and not so hard to mess up.

Third, law firms particularly thrive on strong teamwork and are particularly vulnerable if it is absent. Just one or two lone wolves, even if the best quality lawyers with the best clients, can destroy overall firm glue. In fact, we faced that specific scenario on more than one occasion and I'd like to think that we solved most the right way, by placing longterm firm continuity and success ahead of shortterm risk and reward.

Fourth and related, law firms function best through the establishment of sound and mutually agreed principles consistently and fairly applied over time. Both parts are critical and difficult. You would think that agreeing on sound principles might be pretty straightforward, but let's take a simple example: should older lawyers be paid more? There is no real right answer but there has to be agreement. And there never was a sound principle that didn't attract an arguably sound exception.

Remember as well that law firms are not just lawyers but whole communities of managers, paralegals, assistants, and other staff. They are in many ways like the lawyers, all of the same risks and rules apply to them, and what happens with the lawyers influences the staff and vice versa. It is a constant whole enterprise effort.

Further, the challenges of holding it all together and keeping it going forward in the best overall direction are magnified almost logarithmically the larger the firm grows. Managing one office of a few lawyers and staff in Hilo, where you could keep very close to what was going on and directly influence direction daily, was far different than doing so in a multi-office firm of dozens of different personalities.

My years in firm management, especially my seventeen years as Chair, were largely about the year-in, year-out logistics of hiring, training and compensating lawyers and staff, satisfying and growing clients, and making the best decisions possible on growth and other longer term issues. But my most important and valuable work and biggest challenge was ensuring that everyone got on the same page and stayed there.

That took many forms in many instances, some of which I've already described and some of which I will describe later. Just a few more examples here:

- Our secretaries were assigned to specific lawyers but the understanding was that they operated on a pool arrangement; if one secretary needed help for a rush job anyone else was available to help. There was one secretary assigned to one partner who did very good work for that partner but would not help anyone else. This grew into a major issue which not only impacted overall morale but risked the whole pool understanding. The principle was that team work was essential. I tried to get my partner to correct it himself but he reacted protectively and did nothing. So I waited until he went on vacation and then fired her.
- We had long followed the up-or-out model under which associates who did not make partner did not continue with the firm. To be fully fair to them and avoid overdependency on substandard associates or partners, we had taken it a step further and made an up-or-out call at

the two year and five year mark, before the normal partner decision at seven years. The principle was that we hired for a career and we wanted only lawyers who met or would likely meet our partner standard – the ability to deliver high quality legal service and to manage, retain and grow clients without supervision – to rise through the ranks to a productive career. This led to many disagreements with supervising partners who, although they conceded that the associate did not meet that test, had grown dependent on the associate for their own work. In at least a few such disagreements, the partner left the firm as result (though the larger related reason was an incompatibility with the firm's mission and goals.)

- We believed that practicing law, at least the way we wanted to, was a fulltime, in-office job. For one thing, most high quality law practice was and is highly personal, whether from a client contact basis or from the collaborative approach under which often the strongest results come from lawyers talking an issue through personally with each other. For another, the economic value of the attorney to the firm dropped far faster than any reduction in hours for those reasons and because we were still carrying associated overhead like offices, assistants and benefits. This led to various difficult situations.

One attorney was very high quality and promising but wanted to play by day and work by night for a fulltime salary. I explained that we could not continue his employment on that basis because we didn't want his fellow lawyers and clients having him available personally for just a few hours a day and because he wasn't worth a fulltime salary. He left to find an opportunity that fit his goals.

One attorney had a child and on returning from maternity leave asked to go on halftime status for halftime pay. The situation was complicated further by the fact that her father was the president of one of our clients. I explained that we did not want to deviate from our fulltime work policy and that in any event her halftime status translated into less than 20% of a fulltime salary. She left when an opportunity arose that fit her goals. This sounds raw in today's world and many law firms now make the allowances for broader social purposes; then we were consistently applying our principles of the time.

David Carey was a promising associate married to the daughter of the then-head of Outrigger, Dr. Richard Kelley; Outrigger and Kelley were good clients. Outrigger invested in a company and Richard wanted Carey to run it; he asked if we would let Carey work part-time at Carlsmith and part-time running the company. Same explanation. They weren't happy with the answer but understood it, and Carey continued fulltime before he left to run Outrigger for decades.

Looking back on it, most of my seventeen years were relatively smooth and there was not too much inner fighting among the partners. This was probably largely because most of the lawyers had started with us and come through the up-or-out process; we were all already on the same page. The stresses and strains started showing up more as we brought in laterals and grew beyond the management-by-walking-around level.

My biggest single challenge was managing the rise of Tom Van Winkle and later Peter Starn in a way that took full advantage of their talents and contributions yet did not harm or even risk the firm. By the early 1980s Van Winkle's billings matched my own atop the firm and he was clearly one of the best lawyers in Hawaii; Starn wasn't far behind. They were both highly ambitious and competitive and naturally aspired to firm leadership. They questioned my own leadership style and some of my decisions and thought they could do better. They were quite a thorn in my side.

I thought a lot about succession as I knew it was about time to turn it over. I thought Van Winkle had the ability to do it but questioned then whether, based on my experience with him to date, he had the style to pull it off. Starn was a great lawyer but there was no question he would not be a good firm leader, at least of Carlsmith. I thought Charlie Wichman was a unifying and stabilizing force and deserved a shot.

Charlie took over for me in 1982 and worked us through some very difficult decisions, but he never really wanted the job. By 1985 there was broad consensus that it was Van Winkle's time and he took over. Van Winkle remained Chair of the Executive Committee for two decades until Karl Kobayashi took over in 2005. As it turned out, he did grow into the strong and stable leader Carlsmith needed through a complicated period.

I made my share of mistakes during my tenure as Chair, but generally hope and believe that it was a productive tenure that moved Carlsmith forward and, as the saying goes, left it in better shape. I sometimes wonder why.

First, I had a secret weapon during those years: Janet Ginoza. Janet was my secretary for thirty years, and she was wonderful. First, she was highly organized and efficient, which took a huge load off of me I could then devote to focusing on doing high quality legal work and managing clients and lawyers. Second, she practiced what we preached; she was a true team player always available to help others when needed, as a result of which she always got the help she needed when she needed it. Third, she was genuinely nice and well-liked by all, from clients to attorneys and staff, which had the side benefit of my being able to keep a close and accurate ear to the ground. I was very lucky.

Aside from Janet, I think what it ultimately came down to was this: my fellow lawyers and staff trusted my judgment, but more importantly trusted that I would always put their interests and the interest of the firm ahead of my own. For example, in the annual split-up-the-profits compensation exercise, my share would often be less than what I thought I was truly worth, but far more important it was less than what my partners thought I was worth.

Management of Carlsmith was complicated and a burden. It was in addition to, not in replacement of, my fulltime law practice, and nobody that's ever managed a law firm has thought they were truly recognized for it. But it brought many rewards and I don't regret any of it. When I stepped out of firm management completely in 1990, the luster was long gone. I just wanted to go back to doing what I loved: practicing law and helping people.

Sheridan Ing (Men and Women of Hawaii 1972)

Tom Van Winkle (Carlsmith Ball)

Maui Surf ca. 1970s

Kona Surf ca. 1970s

With Charlie Wichman, 70th birthday, 1990

With Suzi and Janet Ginoza, 50th anniversary with Carlsmith Ball, 2001

J. W. A. (Doc) Buyers (ROD THOMPSON, HONOLULU STAR-BULLETIN)

Francis Swanzy (Frannie) Morgan

PART SIX

Ratoon Career
(1985-2012)

38. Taking Stock Again

Hawaiian sugarcane cultivation mostly utilized the ratoon method, under which an initial crop was harvested but the roots left in the ground to bear a later ratoon crop. The phrase passed into plantation slang as something that happens again later and usually unexpectedly.

Suzi and I had five children between 1950 and 1957. We thought that was it but then in 1963 we had not just one more but twins. That was a classic ratoon crop!

By the early 1980s I had already had a three decade career I only could have dreamed of starting out in 1949. Besides helping grow Carlsmith into a full practice Pacific firm, I had achieved my own success as a lawyer.

In 1979, the *Honolulu Star-Bulletin* had surveyed Hawaii attorneys to compile a list of their twenty peers who had had a significant impact on Hawaii since Statehood. Somehow I made the list along with legends Garner Anthony, Masaji Marumoto, Russell Cades, Dudley Pratt, Tom Waddoups, Nils Tavares, Charles Cassidy, O. P. Soares, Ernest Moore, Myer Symonds, Bert Kobayashi Sr., Marshall Goodsill, Art Reinwald, Walter Chuck, Wally Fujiyama, Dennis O'Connor, Bill Fleming, Martin Anderson and Fred Schutte. It was heady company and deeply humbling.

In 1981 Suzi and I celebrated empty nestdom when those ratoon twins went off to college. And about then I qualified for full Social Security payments!

I suppose I could have considered starting to ease off the pedal and "enjoying life". The problem was: despite the internal and external stresses of the practice I was thoroughly enjoying life already. There were longtime clients who depended on me to counsel them through major challenges, and unknown clients to come with new and fascinating challenges of their own. There was new leadership at Carlsmith who despite their self-assurance needed support and guidance.

I pushed on with hardly a thought, though if you had told me then I was only halfway through my career I would have laughed long and hard.

39. InterIsland Resort Part Four: Final Act

On April 9, 1982 I got an urgent call from my partner, Jim Boyle. It was no ordinary call as I was on a cruise ship between Turkey and Greece on a long-overdue vacation with Suzi and Charlie and Jeanne Wichman. We remember the exact day because we were docking in Athens the next day, my 62nd birthday, and we had planned a birthday dinner at a great restaurant overlooking the Acropolis. Boyle's message was only: "Please telephone me. Something important has come up."

When I finally arranged to talk with Boyle (it having been a little more complicated then than today), he said: "Dudley Child is afraid InterIsland Resorts is going under and he wants to know why you are in Turkey and Greece when he needs you here in Honolulu. I highly recommend that you come home immediately."

I talked it over with Charlie. We (or maybe just he) decided I had to go immediately. So the next morning, my birthday, I flew out of Athens, had my birthday dinner alone in an airport inn at Heathrow in London, and arrived back in Honolulu the next day. Meanwhile Suzi, Charlie and Jeanne had a great dinner at a restaurant overlooking the Acropolis and toasted my birthday over a bottle of good Greek wine.

Under Dudley Child, InterIsland had roared through the 1960s and 1970s and into the 1980s. It had assembled four great resort hotels (the Kauai Surf, Maui Surf, Kona Surf and Naniloa), complete statewide ownership of the Gray Line, a partnership with Bob MacGregor in Tradewind Tours and miscellaneous other tourism-related side businesses. But it had borrowed to the hilt to do so, was overleveraged and overexposed, and without further equity investment could not finance further growth.

The Child family was reluctant to allow any increase in current non-family ownership or bring in new investors do so because it did not want to lose control of the company. Wendell Carlsmith before me and then I had repeatedly advised the family that non-family equity was needed to get where they wanted to go and stay there and it could be structured so that control was never at risk. But Walter Child had strongly resisted that and Dudley Child, who was trustee of the family voting stock trust and so had full control of the company despite some limited outside investment, continued that position.

This left InterIsland Resorts at great risk of some combination of internal deficiencies and unforeseen external events. By 1982 a confluence of those events left the company in a precarious position.

Some were macro and had been developing for some time. Modern Hawaii tourism had been created by local companies like InterIsland and Outrigger, but now the national and international chains with their resources started coming into both Waikiki and the Neighbor Islands. Matson Lines sold the Royal Hawaiian, Princess Kaiulani, and Moana Surfrider to a Japanese company which hired Sheraton to manage them. Maui and Kaanapali grew, as did the Gold Coast on Hawaii Island which impacted both the Naniloa and Kona Surf.

Some were specific with far-reaching impacts. Continental Airlines was a partner with InterIsland in many of its ventures; a major crash of one of its planes caused a major dropoff in visitors to Hawaii and InterIsland hotels. Then the ILWU struck InterIsland; the strike lasted a long time and cause great financial harm to the company.

The Maui Surf was InterIsland's solid rock; it consistently made money and had carried the company. The Kauai Surf was a great property but Kauai tourism had not taken off like Maui. The Naniloa was in decline with the move of Big Island tourism from east to west, and although InterIsland did not have an equity stake in the Kona Surf it was not a successful venture dating back to the owner's decision to overbuild it.

Events caught up with the company pretty fast. First up was that the company, which had paid its shareholders regular annual dividends, could not do so and had to halve the dividend. Then, because there was no real cushion, cash flow started to become problematic.

Most if not all of this was known when I went on vacation in April 1982 and discussions were already ongoing on options. And there was no one precipitating event while I was on vacation. But you can't always predict how and when a client will come to a decision point, especially one that comes on urgently. Perhaps Dudley Child and his family just picked that time to face the facts.

When I arrived back the status quo was not an option and we revisited the various courses, including bringing in more private equity investors or taking the company public. The Child family just didn't want to do that. I think they concluded that there was nobody in the family willing and able to take the reins from Dudley as he had from Walter, they had had a good run, and the time was ripe to sell while the selling was good, turn the company over to new ownership and reinvest their sales proceeds elsewhere.

We decided to sell the whole company. We hired investment banker Lehman Brothers to run a national sale process because we thought the ideal buyer would be a national chain like Marriott or Hilton that would want to walk in on day one with beautiful resorts and related operations throughout the state and would pay a premium for that.

We decided in our own analysis that the whole business was worth around $16.50 per share. It was selling down at $2.00 a share based on current operations but we thought a buyer would look past that. Marriott looked at it and offered $10 a share. Somebody else looked at it and offered $10.50 a share. Amfac came and offered $11 a share but in Amfac stock, which we didn't want.

We walked away from a whole company sale and decided to sell off the individual assets of the company over time. We utilized a section of the Internal Revenue Code which provided for tax deferral if a company adopted and implemented a formal plan of liquidation: taxes would be due not twice when assets were sold and distributions were made to shareholders, but once on distributions which could then be spread over time.

A Hawaii real estate developer named Christopher Hemmeter was an old friend of Dudley from Cornell. Hemmeter bought the Maui Surf and Kauai Surf for $90 million as part of a rapid expansion of his hotel business into Hawaii's first real megaresorts that earned Hemmeter his own place in the inaugural class of the Hawaii Hospitality Hall of Fame. The Kona Surf owner bought out InterIsland's management contract and the Naniloa was sold to local investors. The statewide Gray Line franchise was sold to Art Woolaway who operated the Oahu Gray Line, and Bob MacGregor bought out InterIsland's interest in Tradewind Tours.

We spent about five years selling off all the assets of InterIsland Resorts. We made distributions to shareholders along the way so that, by the time we completed the liquidation, they were paid $16.50 per share net in total. The Child family's basis (original cost) in its shares was about fifty cents per share and many of the other shareholders had paid $2 per share. The Child family and the great majority of the other shareholders came out very well on the liquidation.

There are many lessons in InterIsland Resorts' history worth pondering for businesspeople and the lawyers that represent them. Just a few here:

(a) It is always important that a business have enough equity with which to grow and ride out the bad times. Initial owners, especially families, want to keep control, but it may be necessary to bring in additional equity just to get the venture up and running. The best time to invest sufficient equity is early in the game and before you desperately need the money.

(b) When the owners of a company decide to sell a company, there may be times when the sum of the parts may be worth more than the company as a whole.

Beyond the abstract lessons offered, the final days of InterIsland Resorts came with deep mixed feelings for the Child family and InterIsland's broad ohana. On the one hand we were all deeply sorry to see it go, but on the other hand we all felt that we had played a major role in the development of Hawaii tourism especially on the Neighbor Islands. For me, I had grown up with InterIsland from the very beginnings of my career and into my fifth decade and I felt gratitude for the opportunity, trust and friendship. Clients, like children, are not supposed to be favored, but I never quite had another client like InterIsland Resorts and Dudley Child.

40. Tipping Point for King Sugar: Hamakua Sugar

Back in the '60s I had negotiated the Honomalino Agricultural Company macadamia nut processing joint venture with Theo. H. Davies subsidiary Hawaiian Holiday with Francis Swanzy (Frannie) Morgan, Davies' representative and my Punahou classmate. And in 1968 I had travelled to London to assist the Dillinghams in their unsuccessful attempt to buy Davies, which the Davies family had instead sold to Hong Kong-based conglomerate Jardine Matheson. Now these two threads converged in the case of Hamakua Sugar.

Davies founder Theophilus H. Davies had hired a man named Francis Swanzy to manage his Hawaii investments. Swanzy turned out to be a fabulous entrepreneur. At some point he decided to start a sugar cane plantation in the Honokaa area of the Big Island which was called Honokaa Sugar Company. As time went on Davies through Swanzy acquired other sugar plantations up and down the Hamakua Coast like Laupahoehoe Sugar, Kaiwiki Sugar, Hamakua Sugar and Paauhau Sugar. Davies was the largest landowner and sugar grower on the coast.

Francis Swanzy married a daughter of Gerritt P. Judd, an early doctor in Hawaii who had later become an extremely important counselor to the Kings of Hawaii. In recognition of his services, Judd was awarded the ahupuaa of Kualoa in Windward Oahu at the time of the Great Mahele. What is today Kualoa Ranch devolved to Swanzy and then down through the generations to Frannie Morgan and his family.

Frannie Morgan had risen through the ranks at Davies to become senior vice president in charge of all Hawaii plantations. He knew sugar and Davies' plantations on the Hamakua Coast cold. But in 1984 Jardine Matheson, watching the overall decline of sugar in Hawaii, decided to close all of its plantations and sell off its lands.

Morgan was devastated. His family had generations invested in sugar and Davies, and he knew that if Hamakua Sugar ceased operations it might be the turning point for sugar in Hawaii.

Morgan had a further frustration. Jardine Matheson had many subsidiaries beyond Davies, and Davies had many operations beyond sugar. Morgan had felt for a long time that Davies had put its capital into other operations and had starved the plantations. The lack of maintenance, Morgan felt, had led in large part to their declining profitability. If capital and management interest could be focused on Hamakua Sugar, he believed, it could pull through and prosper again.

There was one description of Morgan that was universal: optimism. Morgan went to Davies and said that he would like to buy Hamakua Sugar. He would invest some of his own funds, ask Davies to finance a portion of the purchase price, and borrow most of the money from a commercial lender. At a defensible price it was a good deal for Davies because it could unload its whole sugar operation at one time rather than have to sell off the assets over years. Davies agreed in principle.

Morgan asked me to represent him in the purchase of Hamakua Sugar. He knew me and knew that I knew sugar, mergers and acquisitions, corporate finance and the Hamakua Coast. It was a wonderful new legal opportunity and challenge, and given my family's own history in sugar I wanted him to succeed.

Davies and Morgan settled pretty fast on an overall purchase price of $88,000,000. Morgan would put up $1 million and assume on the purchase $7 million of Davies' Hamakua Sugar-related liabilities. Davies would finance $20 million, meaning that it would treat that $20 million as a loan to Morgan (purchase money loan) and secure its loan with a mortgage on the company (purchase money mortgage). The remaining $60 million would come from a loan from a commercial lender.

The potential commercial lender we had identified was the Western Farm Credit Bank, then headquartered in Sacramento (now known as Farm Credit West headquartered in Kansas). The bank specialized in financing agricultural enterprises and was interested in principle in making the loan.

Morgan and I, the Davies executives (David Heenan, President, and Marty Jaskot, Treasurer) and two investment bankers from New York whom Davies had hired as advisers, met to negotiate the purchase details. Davies agreed that it would take a second mortgage behind the Western Farm Credit Bank. More importantly, Davies agreed that payments of interest and principal on its financing would only have to be made if Hamakua Sugar was generating positive operating cash flow sufficient for operations and the Western Farm Credit Bank's first mortgage. The basic concept was that if the plantation couldn't make that positive cash flow, then it wasn't worth $88 million.

It was obvious that the whole transaction depended on Morgan's ability to get the $60 million loan from the Western Farm Credit Bank. The parties agreed that Morgan and I would prepare a formal loan application and Davies would provide the financial data on plantation operations to back up the application. Further, I would draft a formal purchase agreement and Cades Schutte (the long-time law firm for Davies) would review it. If both sides could agree on everything, then Morgan would go to Sacramento to seek the Western Farm Credit Bank loan. The investment bankers recommended that I go with Morgan.

Morgan and I went to Sacramento. We explained the proposition to the bank and our pro forma financial projections for how the loan would be repaid from plantation operations. After negotiating through some details, the bank approved the loan in principle and its lawyers drafted a loan agreement including a first mortgage. I reviewed it with Morgan and we negotiated through some further details, and Morgan and the bank signed the loan agreement contingent on closing the purchase.

The final loan agreement also included a provision under which the Western Farm Credit Bank made available to Morgan a line of credit under which he could borrow up to an additional $10 million for short-term cash flow needs. The principal reason for this line of credit, which was not unlike the longtime operations of any other Hawaii sugar plantation, was to cover the annual gap between the plantation's costs of growing and harvesting the cane and payment for the cane after processing and sale to bulk purchasers like national bakery chains and beverage companies. Raw Hawaiian sugar was processed and sold by the California and Hawaiian Sugar Company (C&H) at a refinery in Crockett, California where the Sacramento River enters San Francisco Bay started up by the Big Five to break the monopoly on Hawaiian sugar refining then held by a few mainland companies. Every year the Hawaiian plantations would harvest and ship their sugar to C&H, who would process and sell it and then split up and send the various companies their share of distributions for the year. The Davies purchase included its share of C&H. Hamakua Sugar would draw down from the Western Farm Credit Bank line of credit the funds it needed every year to get through the harvest and then repay the drawdown later in the year from the C&H distributions.

Most important for Morgan, and it no doubt played into some of the high risks he took, none of these financing was guaranteed by Morgan or his family or were recourse loans. That meant that Morgan's downside if things went wrong was just losing Hamakua Sugar; he wouldn't also, for example, lose Kualoa Ranch. So his real risk, aside from the reputational and emotional consequences of things not working out, was his equity investment. Perhaps a lender today would not agree to a non-guaranteed, non-recourse loan under those circumstances, but those were the cards then.

As the overall deal started to fall into place, I went to Morgan with some concerns and recommendations that arose from the fact that the financing as structured only called for that equity investment by Morgan to be $1 million out of $88 million total ($98 million if the line of credit was fully drawn). That may instinctively look to some like a good deal for a buyer, especially if the loans are not guaranteed or recourse. But the fact was that it provided no equity safety net if the company hit a rough patch and could not pay its debt; the lenders would get some form of control pretty fast and no purchaser/borrower wants that.

I first suggested that Morgan contact some individuals who might inject more equity, but on the basis that Morgan would remain in control of the company. This was a non-starter for him: "Davies did not provide the financing necessary to keep the company going. My great-grandfather started this company, and I am personally interested in keeping it going. I want 100% control so that other shareholders don't stop me from saving this plantation."

I next suggested forming an ESOP (employee stock ownership plan) under which Hamakua Sugar's employees would invest in the company. It would provide needed equity, the employees would be involved in management and control, and they would have a greater interest in helping to keep the company afloat if things went bad. He didn't want to do this either. He wanted to make sure that he and his family would have sole ownership and control.

The deal closed later in 1984. For better or worse Frannie Morgan had doubled down on Hawaii sugar. Most of his friends and business associates and much of his family thought it was a mistake, but he set out to prove them wrong.

Morgan and I met shortly after closing to work out some post-closing details. He told me that in addition to keeping full family control of ownership he wanted his family involved in management. However, he said that he thought it would be beneficial to have one non-family member on Hamakua Sugar's board of directors to provide an independent perspective. Would I be that director?

Like most other comparable firms, Carlsmith required specific Executive Committee approval for an attorney to serve as an outside director on a client's board of directors. There was both a benefit, in terms of client relations, and risk, in terms of potential conflict, in doing so. In retrospect perhaps both I and the Executive Committee should have said no in this instance as the risk of potential conflict was more than minimal. But we all wanted Morgan to succeed and I thought I could contribute to that. The Executive Committee approved my service and I think I did contribute positively and constructively on the Hamakua Sugar, though I frequently disagreed with Morgan and it strained our professional and personal relationship.

There were five member of the Hamakua Sugar board. Besides Morgan and me they were daughter Patricia Morgan Poppe, who ran the land department and whose husband Jack Poppe was Hamakua Sugar manager; son John, who ran Kualoa Ranch for the family; and son David, who managed an agricultural park outside of Hilo. An important unseen influence was Frannie's wife, Margo; she had a keen business mind and perspective and Hamakua Sugar strained their relationship as well.

To his credit, Morgan took the board's responsibilities seriously. He always had regular board meetings at which issues were fully discussed. Besides the formalities, he wanted his children to learn about the company and industry from him, the business world and me, his dream being to hand off a successful plantation to the next generation. But he remained firmly and often stubbornly in charge. If an informal vote went 4-1 against him, he would invoke President Lincoln's famous Cabinet meeting example. At that meeting the vote had gone 6-1 against Lincoln's proposal. Lincoln announced: "The ayes have it."

Success of the venture depended on many factors, but by far the most important was the obvious one: the price Hamakua Sugar through C&H would be paid for its sugar. That in turn depended on various factors: consumer demand, competition on the world market and continued federal price support being the main ones.

Sugar had been selling for $385/ton for several years and that was the basis for Morgan's purchase price, loan repayment and operational projections. At that price, Hamakua Sugar could make a positive cash flow that would pay for operations, cover the Western Farm Credit Bank loan payments, and reduce the Davies debt. If the price went down to $365/ton, the company could still pay operations, cover the Western Farm Credit Bank loan, and pay something toward the Davies loan. At $345/ton, there would be no cash after operations and paying off Western Farm Credit Bank, and in fact there might be only enough cash for interest payments only. At $325/ton, there would not be enough cash flow to make any payments to the Western Farm Credit Bank.

Two adverse events occurred in the first year after closing. First, Coca-Cola, Pepsi Cola and other soft drink makers switched from cane and beet sugar to artificial flavors in their soft drinks. This major demand reduction obviously impacted the producers and refiners who had been their major suppliers.

Second, a growing number of other countries, with large government subsidies, started producing sugar and dumping it at depressed prices on the world market. This major supply increase caused a large reduction in the price of sugar on the world market. There were U.S. anti-dumping laws that protected domestic sugar to some extent, but they didn't address the consumer demand reduction.

The price for Hamakua Sugar's product declined to $365/ton. However, the Company still had positive cash flow for operations and the Western Farm Credit Bank debt and some left over for Davies.

Now Morgan looked for ways to increase cash flow and diversify out of sugar. Family operation Kualoa Ranch sold its cattle to Hawaii Meat Packers, which fattened, butchered and sold it to wholesalers. Morgan thought that Hawaii Meat Packers, which had a virtual monopoly in that space, was not paying Kualoa Ranch enough for its cattle and was not doing a good job.

Morgan had an expansion idea. Hamakua Sugar produced bagasse as a normal part of its operations and spent lots of money getting rid of the bagasse. Morgan thought that bagasse could be fed to cattle to fatten them up before butchering. This would mean that cattle feed did not have to be imported from the mainland at high prices. He believed that, in addition to Kualoa Ranch, ranchers on the Big Island and Maui would welcome an alternative to Hawaii Meat Packers and that Hamakua Sugar could provide that addition at lower cost.

Management prepared a business plan. The new Hamakua feed lot and processing plant would cost a sizeable amount. But the projections showed that Hamakua Sugar could fatten and process the cattle cheaper than Hawaii Meat Packers and thus should be able to undercut its prices and gain much of its existing business.

Here was the main problem: where would Hamakua Sugar get the money to build the plant and start up operations? Morgan was not going to invest further equity or seek outside equity, and further borrowings were not feasible. Management's answer was positive cash flow from cane operations and, if necessary, utilization of the Western Farm Credit Bank $10 million line of credit. It was risk on risk but Morgan and the Hamakua Sugar board forged ahead; they felt they had to grow cash flow and diversify or face the greater risk of further declines in sugar prices. The plant was built within forecasts and commenced operations and the business started coming in.

Now occurred what nobody had envisioned (in retrospect, why didn't we). Hawaii Meat Packers did not take this lightly and started a price war. Hamakua Sugar still fattened and processed the cattle cheaper than Hawaii Meat Packers but even with that there was a shortfall between costs and the price war prices Hamakua Sugar could charge. With positive cash flow from sugar tapped out, Hamakua Sugar drew on the line of credit not just for construction costs but to cover the operating shortfall through the war.

The situation was comparable to what occurred two decades later in the Hawaiian interisland air travel market. Go! Airlines entered the market, then dominated by two major carriers, Hawaiian Airlines and Aloha Airlines, by slashing its prices. Aloha felt it had to match Go! but that resulted in Aloha's eventual bankruptcy and Go! then pulled out. The only winner was Hawaiian Airlines which obtained and still enjoys a virtual monopoly.

Similarly, Hawaii Meat Packers could not sustain the combination of higher costs and lower prices and eventually closed down. But Hamakua Sugar, while it had "won" the war, was severely damaged by even greater risk exposure, mainly because it had had to utilize much of its $10 million line of credit for purposes other than intended and therefore had no real way if operating cash flow was low to cover the cash gap from cultivation to C&H distributions.

The overall risks were then compounded by a second well-intentioned but ultimately costly initiative.

Hamakua Sugar operated two sugar mills: one at Ookala (the old Kaiwiki Sugar mill) and one at Haina (the main mill), about 15 miles apart. Morgan reasoned that he could save costs by closing the Kaiwiki mill and doing all processing at Haina. Hamakua Sugar would haul cane from throughout the plantation to Haina and the Haina mill would shift to a seven days a week, 24 hours a day system. Management forecast the idea and concluded that, although it would cost $6 million to refurbish the Haina mill to the new processing schedule, Hamakua Sugar would make that up on the saved costs of operating the Kaiwiki mill.

Where would Hamakua Sugar get the money to refurbish the Haina mill and pay for any transition costs? Management's answer was that the forecast showed there would be immediate cost savings from closing the Kaiwiki mill that could be applied over to Haina mill refurbishment and that any short term shortfall could be covered from positive cash flow from cane operations or if needed drawing on the $10 million line of credit. The Hamakua Sugar board met and approved the project.

Now in implementation occurred what nobody had fully factored in (in retrospect, why didn't we?) First, while it was obvious that there would be more and longer hauls to just one mill, the full expense of more trucks and new driver hires and training had not been accounted for. Second, the Hamakua Sugar employees opposed the switch from a five-days-a-week to a seven-days-a-week schedule (no employee was being asked to work seven days but traditional schedules needed to be adjusted for the change) and the extra commute for many to Haina.

Two lessons for now from the Hamakua Sugar feedlot/processing plant (to go with some larger ones later):

(1) In standard corporate governance the role of a board of directors is to oversee management but not to substitute itself for management. When and to what extent should a director (or for that matter a lawyer) rely on forecasts or other submissions from management as opposed to question them? A board or a lawyer may be tempted to assume that management or the client has thought of everything, but they very rarely have. But then how can a board or lawyer know that and figure out where the questions are? There is no easy answer other than to say that the board and lawyer must apply their own independent experience and judgment to asking the questions that they

have until they are satisfied that all questions have been asked and answered. Here management's forecasts were wrong not so much on the numbers themselves but on the assumptions. This board generally and I personally should have asked more questions. Why didn't we?

(2) Short-term financing should rarely if ever be used to finance longterm projects. If positive cash flow from the longterm project is delayed, the short-term loan still comes due, and if longterm financing is not available for the longterm project that is usually a warning sign on the financial feasibility of the project. Doing so is sometimes justified if there is existing or potential equity available to cover any shortfall, but usually the reason the solution is considered in the first place is because there isn't. I knew all this but failed to dissuade Morgan and the board from this course of action; that was both of our failing.

Now, in the second half of the 1980s, Hamakua Sugar needed everything to go right. It didn't. The price of sugar went down from $365/ton to $345/ton and didn't recover. There was enough cash to cover ongoing operations but not to pay down the line of credit advances and the Western Farm Credit Bank loan, and in 1987 Hamakua Sugar went into technical default on the loan.

The Western Farm Credit Bank gave Hamakua Sugar plenty of time and flexibility to find a solution. We diligently worked through a whole range of options to do so, including further loan support from the State of Hawaii which saw it as a matter of state policy that the agricultural jobs and communities of the Hamakua Coast be preserved. However, it was virtually impossible to make any option work economically, especially one that would reasonably pay off Hamakua Sugar's lenders, if the end price of sugar would not support it.

Finally, the Western Farm Credit Bank lowered the boom. It ordered Hamakua Sugar to downsize by closing the less productive and higher cost sugar lands farther away from the Haina mill and to sell off those and other low-yield lands to pay down debt. We conducted a huge land sale process in both individual sales and through public auctions, but even that was not enough to sufficiently pay down debt and free up cash flow to maintain operations.

The pressure increased until it became questionable whether Hamakua Sugar could meet its payroll. Hawaii law requires that employers meet payroll and subjects them to criminal penalties if they don't. That risk combined with other events was just too great and Hamakua Sugar filed for bankruptcy. After 109 years Hamakua Sugar ceased operations in 1992 and began liquidation of its remaining assets. The largest beneficiary of that liquidation was the Kamehameha Schools/Bishop Estate which picked up a large portion of Hamakua Sugar's lands for a song.

The demise of Hamakua Sugar not only ended sugar and a lifestyle on the Hamakua Coast but presaged the final days of King Sugar in Hawaii, which has now occurred with the closing of Alexander & Baldwin's Hawaiian Commercial & Sugar plantations in Central Maui in late 2016. Frannie Morgan lost his $1 million equity investment; the Western Farm Credit Bank was paid its $10 million line of credit balance and recovered a good portion of its $60 million loan; Davies recovered only a portion of its $20 million second mortgage (although it probably considered in retrospect that the $44 million cash it did receive on purchase was a good deal); the State of Hawaii recovered only a portion of its loan; and general unsecured creditors lost everything.

What are my reflections?

(1) Hamakua Sugar's original forecasts of financial feasibility were sound, but they depended on the price of sugar staying at $385/ton or at least not going down as fast and far as they did. That didn't happen. It was probably impossible to forecast specifically that (a) soft drink processors would move to artificial flavorings, and (b) foreign governments including Europe would increase sugar subsidies and dump cheap sugar on the world market. Still, the forecasts clearly did not include a sufficient general contingency to account for overall risk.

(2) Morgan did not invest sufficient equity up front to cover results if less than forecasted, leaving him exposed to making risky decisions. His desire, insistence, that this be a 100% family owned and operated affair foreclosed external capital which could have been available without the loss of control. This is a common problem with family businesses which would play itself out again in the case of InterIsland Resorts and the Child family.

(3) Hamakua Sugar should not have used the Western Farm Credit Bank line of credit to fund the cattle feedlot/processing plant and the Haina mill move, as that left it highly exposed to the chain reaction that later occurred. Those investments should have been made with additional equity, and it's possible that the sequence of events which

occurred might not have been set in motion to start with.

(4) Could Morgan have pulled it off? Could he have succeeded if he had done everything right? Subsequent history would indicate no, though he and we didn't know that then.

(5) How did I feel when Hamakua Sugar shut down for good after having been my client in arguably my toughest all-around engagement for a decade? Of course I felt my client and I had not succeeded, but I also felt that we could have played our cards better to maximize the chances of success. I had to do the best job I could with what I was dealt.

(6) But did I do a good job for my client even though the enterprise didn't succeed, because after all just because you do your best job ever doesn't mean your client will succeed. I think I did a very good job in identifying and refining the issues and decisions to be made, in counseling my client on the various options and preferred courses, and implementing my client's decisions to my fullest ability. And my client trusted and depended on me even though he didn't always agree with me.

But I do think back to some of the decisions I joined in as a director of Hamakua Sugar, decisions that came back to haunt the enterprise. I was the sole independent director, charged with reasoned and informed knowledge and objectivity focused solely on the good of the enterprise and not of any one owner of or management. This was a tall order when the Frannie Morgan train was barreling down the tracks. Should I have asked more questions, questioned and challenged Frannie more vigorously, refused to agree even given an otherwise consensus? I thought I was doing so then but I wonder now.

I wonder whether I got caught up in my own personal history and desire to see my client succeed. After all my own roots were deep in Hawaii sugar and I wanted sugar to survive and prosper. Did I also lose my objectivity and critical view? A lawyer can never do that. You can pour yourself heart and soul into achieving your client's goals, but not at the expense of your objectivity. A client depends on you for that.

Frannie Morgan, my good friend and client, died in 1999. I can still see the twinkle in his eye, the slight hitch in his stride, and above all his boundless belief and optimism. He deserves to be remembered for that and for trying.

41. Family Heritage: Rolling the Boulder Uphill

By the 1980s Theo H. Davies was not the only Big Five company seriously looking to get out of sugar and Frannie Morgan was not the only kamaaina with a heritage in Hawaii sugar and the goal of further chapters for sugar in Hawaii. I represented such a family in two such attempts, only it was my own family.

Hilo Sugar Company

Hilo Sugar was a C. Brewer & Co. company of about 18,000 acres located along the Hamakua Coast just outside of Hilo. Hawaii Island was a Brewer stronghold, not only in sugar but in macadamia nuts through Mauna Loa Macadamia Nut Corporation and in other diversified agriculture, and Brewer's web spread not only through agricultural but related businesses. Brewer owned a trucking company, stevedoring company and chemical and fertilizer company that serviced the whole island, but their success all rested on sugar.

Brewer was the oldest of the Big Five. In the mid-1970s, after 150 years of operation, it was acquired by Philadelphia-based International Utilities Corporation (later known as IU International), a holding company for various diverse businesses.

IU sent one of its mid career executives, J.W.A. "Doc" Buyers, out to Hawaii to take over as President and CEO of Brewer. Buyers had gone to Princeton University and played on the Tigers' championship football team; the "Doc" was reportedly tagged on him by his teammates after Doc Blanchard, the All-American West Point running back. Marv Tilker was Executive Vice President.

By the early '80s my brother, Bill Case, was closing in on four decades in the sugar industry, all of which he had spent with Brewer. He had started at the bottom, agricultural trainee, before working his way through the well-worn rungs of a true Hawaii sugar man's career: cultivation superintendent at Hilo Sugar; field superintendent at Kilauea Sugar and Hutchinson Sugar; manager at Paauhau Sugar and Mauna Kea Sugar; and vice president, sugar operations. Probably his most interesting posting was as head of Brewer subsidiary Hawaiian Agronomics, which exported Hawaii's state-of-the-art-agronomical expertise to countries such as Iran and Indonesia. He was now senior vice president, agricultural production, in charge of all of Brewer's sugar, macadamia nut and other agricultural interests, reporting to Tilker.

Along the way Buyers had evidently formed the view that sugar was not going to survive and that he needed to get Brewer out of sugar. This was easier said than done due to the close relationship between sugar and Brewer's other interests. Bill disagreed with Buyers and that, with Buyers' I-know-best dictatorial style, made for an often-difficult working relationship.

Brewer had earlier acquired Mauna Loa Macadamia Nut Corporation that processed and marketed macadamia nuts grown by others. In 1983 it had become the largest producer of macadamia nuts in the world. Brewer next decided to start growing macadamia nuts for its own account, particularly in Kau. Sugar cane needs a lot of rainfall while macadamia nuts need less. Brewer owned Kau Sugar and so took the lower elevation, lower rainfall lands just makai of its prime sugar lands and planted them in macadamia nuts. You can see them today along Mamalahoa Highway on both sides of the Pahala turnoff.

Doc Buyers called a meeting with my brother:

Doc: "We're doing great over there in Kau but I need more macadamia nuts for Mauna Loa. I want you to take your best sugar land in the middle central part of Hilo Sugar and put it into macadamia nuts."

Bill: "Well, you know, sugar is a marginal cost operation. If you already have your mill and equipment then if you add land that's marginal income and profit, but if you take out land you lose your profit. The land you want is our most valuable sugar land. You take our best land out of sugar, you're taking all our marginal profit, we can't continue in sugar."

Doc: "Hey Bill, who's running this company."

Bill: "You are, Doc."

Doc: "Put it in macadamia nuts."

Bill: "You know, it's not a good place for macadamia nuts. It's too wet out there. You can't mechanical harvest out there like you can down in Keaau, where they have good ground, or Kau which is dry. It's a terrible, muddy place, the wettest land on the island."

Doc: "Who are you, you haven't heard me. Do it."

So Bill went and did it. They had a terrible job planting the macadamia nut trees; everything was mud. He took hundreds of acres out of sugar.

So the next year, 1984, Buyers said: "Bill, here's the Hilo Sugar reports. I told you sugar was no good."

Bill said: "Doc, you made it that way."

Doc said: "I didn't make it that way. You just can't grow sugar."

I had to agree with Bill. I knew myself, from working with sugar plantations all my life, that if you have your base costs covered, then you can expand your production and you only have farming costs, and that additional land becomes very productive and profitable. And for Buyers who had no experience in agriculture much less sugar to question forty years of experience and success was at best arrogant.

Bill was deeply disappointed and so mad that he couldn't help talking about it, at least privately to me because Buyers did not brook anything said against him. He came down to Honolulu and asked me and our brother Dan Case, by then senior partner of the prominent firm Case, Kay & Lynch, out to lunch.

Bill told us: "I think that Doc Buyers intends to close down all of Brewer's sugar plantations, and I think that's a mistake. We couldn't afford to buy the whole works, but what if we put together a family hui and buy Hilo Sugar from Brewer. If Brewer is going to close down sugar, it is going to have so much land that it will not know what to do with it. Maybe we can make an offer at a reasonable price to give Brewer some money now and keep Hilo Sugar going. I think we can make money if we run it as a sugar plantation and run it well, but if it doesn't work out we can sell the land for other purposes."

The three of us agreed in principle and on a tentative equity-debt structuring. We put together an offer to buy all of the stock of Hilo Sugar Company for $23,000,000, and went to see Marv Tilker to present our proposal.

Tilker took it back to Buyers. Buyers said: "I think we can make more money selling the land." Tilker called Bill in:

"Bill, I would rather see you guys buy it, because I think we've got so much land that it's going to be a big job to sell all of it. But Doc told me to say no. He thinks he can make more money selling the land. Sorry! But don't leave us, Bill, we want you to stay on the job."

That was the end of the Case family's attempt to buy Hilo Sugar. Bill stayed on the job. Hilo Sugar continued in some form of operation until 1995. Kau Sugar closed the next year, ending sugar cultivation on Hawaii Island.

Waialua Sugar Company

Waialua Sugar was a Castle & Cooke company which had about 15,000 acres in sugar cultivation on Oahu's North Shore stretching from Waimea Valley and above Haleiwa to the mill town of Waialua and beyond to Mokuleia. About half its land was owned by Castle & Cooke and about half leased from the Bishop Estate. It was exceptionally productive land with plentiful water and had been in continuous cultivation since the late 1800s when Castle & Cooke had bought the plantation.

While the other Big Five had focused mostly on Neighbor Island sugar, Castle & Cooke had mostly stayed on Oahu. Besides Waialua Sugar, it owned Oahu Sugar which included the former Ewa Plantation and milled its sugar out of its Waipahu mill. Castle & Cooke had also acquired James Dole's Hawaiian Pineapple Company (later Dole Food Company) and thus owned and operated the world's most productive pineapple lands in Central Oahu around Wahiawa and Whitmore Village and flowing down to Waialua Sugar's North Shore lands, along with Iwilei (a.k.a. Dole) Cannery near the Honolulu docks. It also owned the island of Lanai, then a pineapple plantation.

By 1985 Hawaiian sugar and pineapple were facing severe international headwinds and an uncompetitively high cost of labor and production in Hawaii. Castle & Cooke was in financial difficulty and a Los Angeles entrepreneur, David H. Murdock, acquired a controlling interest. Murdock was not interested in the company as a going agricultural concern; his interest was in the land for residential and commercial development (though after exiting Hawaii pineapple he did turn Dole Food into the world's largest producer of fruits and vegetables).

Oahu sugar was now down to just two plantations: Oahu Sugar/Ewa Plantation and Waialua Sugar. This lower critical mass of Hawaii sugar placed at risk the California and Hawaiian Sugar Company, the joint enterprise of Hawaii sugar companies to collectively refine and sell their sugar. Most of the refining especially for Neighbor Island sugar was at C&H's Crockett, California refinery and sold on the mainland. But Oahu's sugar was refined at the former Honolulu Plantation's Aiea refinery and sold in Hawaii. If either Oahu Sugar or Waialua Sugar shut down, that refinery would close and, as it was not economical to ship the remaining plantation's sugar up to Crockett, the other plantation would have to close also.

When Francis Morgan acquired Hamakua Sugar in 1984 he also acquired an ownership interest in C&H. The board of directors of C&H consisted of officers of Hawaii's sugar companies. The board set up a legal committee and Morgan assigned me to that committee. As a result, I was hired as C&H's lawyer in Hawaii (under a conflict of interest arrangement covering situations in which Hamakua Sugar and C&H may have divergent interests). Harold Somerset, C&H's president, came down to Hawaii once a quarter for board meetings, at which I was responsible for reporting on legal affairs affecting C&H and sugar in Hawaii. I got to know Somerset very well.

In 1987 Murdock announced that Castle & Cooke would shut down Waialua Sugar in 1989. The question for C&H and Hawaii sugar was whether it could be acquired and continued in operation. We discussed various options, one of which was for Frannie Morgan to buy it. I advised him that he personally shouldn't and couldn't do it, that he needed all his attention and resources focused on Hamakua Sugar; he agreed.

As I considered who else might acquire Waialua Sugar, I turned for advice once again to someone whose expertise and judgment I trusted: my brother, Bill Case. Like with Hilo Sugar, Bill still felt sugar could survive in Hawaii, understood that the loss of any more plantations would make it harder to do so, knew Waialua was a good plantation, and thought the right owners with the right approach could make a go of it.

As we discussed options, we asked again: can our family do it. Bill would run the company and plantation, I would be the company lawyer, and we'd put together a family hui (joint venture) to come up with beginning equity and creatively raise and finance the rest. We went to our brother Dan, sister Mary Ellen (Casey) Beck, and stepmother Marie Case, our father Hib's second wife. They were all willing to give it a ride.

I next went back to an idea I had tried unsuccessfully to get Frannie Morgan to adopt at Hamakua Sugar: an employee stock ownership plan. Not only would an ESOP offer the upwards of 2,000 Waialua Sugar employees a chance to own their company and continue their heritage, but a well-tailored ESOP could serve as part of our financing.

Next I went to Jack Hewettson, manager of Waialua Sugar. Hewettson had taken over for the legendary Bill Paty, my Punahou schoolmate, in 1984. I knew Jack, knew he shared Bill's views, and knew that the Hawaii sugar men were a tightknit group regardless of what company they worked for. I said: "Could you put together a group of managers, particularly at Waialua Sugar but anybody else, to join our hui and put up some equity?" Hewettson wanted in and thought others would as well.

So now we had at least on paper Case family equity, ESOP equity and borrowing power, and management equity, to go with existing management that wanted the enterprise to succeed. But we still didn't have enough money; we had to borrow the rest.

Bill, Danny and I worked with Hewettson to refine our forecasts on how much revenue Waialua Sugar could reasonably generate and so how much we could reasonably borrow and pay for the plantation. We worked up a credible financial plan inclusive of price and loan. The challenge, besides whether Castle & Cooke would sell at the price, was whether anyone would make the loan to us given the state of Hawaii sugar. Of the potential lenders, I thought Bank of Hawaii was most likely but its risks needed to be substantially reduced.

I went to see C&H president Harold Somerset in Crockett and said: "Look, Castle & Cooke has announced that it is going to close down Waialua. When that happens, your Aiea refinery will be worthless because you won't have enough sugar to refine." Somerset said: "That's right, we can't survive, we'll have to close it down." I said: "Well, that's a big loss for C&H and a big loss for Hawaii. If I went to the Bank of Hawaii and got a loan to buy Waialua Sugar, would C&H guarantee the loan? If it does, I am pretty sure that Bank of Hawaii will give us the loan." He said he'd think it over and call me back. He called back the following week and said: "We will guarantee the loan as long as it has normal terms, which we think it will."

I had still not gone to either Castle & Cooke or Bank of Hawaii, and I needed to get Bank of Hawaii lined up before presenting the complete package to Castle & Cooke. I thought this was such a touchy loan that I didn't want to go through ordinary bank channels that would just apply standard loan criteria and decline right off. So I called up Bank of Hawaii president Frank Manaut, and asked if I could come see him personally on a large and unusual loan. I had known Frank for a long time dating back to the somewhat infamous days of the Waikiki boarding house called "Red Hale" where young bachelors like Frank, Charlie Wichman and my brother Dan had started off. "Frank", I said: "I have an important loan prospect and I wanted to see you personally because I don't want to go any further with it unless you think it's going to be okay." So I laid the whole story out to Manaut and asked to borrow our projected amount with which, counting equity, we could make a sound offer to Castle & Cooke for Waialua Sugar. Manaut said: "Well, C&H is a client of ours and they're backed by the Big Five. You say C&H is going to guarantee the loan? Who have you talked to?" I said: "Harold Somerset and he assured me that C&H will guarantee your loan." Frank mused: "Harold would not have done that without clearance from the Big Five so it must be true. Well," he said, "I'd like to save Waialua Sugar, so if it's going to be guaranteed by C&H, we'll do it. Now, we've got to go back through channels. You go and see our usual lending officer and explain the whole thing to him, and then you tell him that you have already talked to me and we'll make the loan."

There was one last piece of the puzzle to fit in before going to Castle & Cooke. We had determined that Murdock was unlikely to sell the Waialua Sugar lands in fee and we didn't think we could pull that off pricewise anyway, so our plan called for Castle & Cooke to give us a longterm lease on the land. But Castle & Cooke only owned half the land; the Bishop Estate lease on the other half only had another five or so years left on it and we needed the same longterm lease there. I went to Bishop Estate's Oahu land manager, Jim Wriston, Jr., explained the whole package, and said: "What we need you to do is to give us an extension of that lease; we don't want to buy this company and lose our land in five years." After a very short period Wriston responded: "We will extend the lease for thirty years after you close except that we want to pull out this piece of land overlooking Waimea Valley which is in sugar now but we have other longrange plans for it." That was fine with us.

We had our equity, loan, land and management. Some may think why go to so much effort without first asking Castle & Cooke whether it would be willing to consider an offer. The answer is simple: because without all the effort to develop a package the offer would have lacked credibility and the answer would have been no. We now had a credible offer and were ready to approach Castle & Cooke. But how? In such an enterprise the details of each and every step deserve careful consideration.

I decided to go see Bill Mills, who was Castle & Cooke's Hawaii manager and handled all operations for Murdock who was largely an absentee boss. Mills was amazed that we had pulled the whole proposal together and gave it careful consideration. He said: "I don't think Murdock is going to want to do it. But, on the other hand, we really don't have a plan for Waialua Sugar right now and we have our hands full with Dole Food and Lanai [which Murdock was busy turning into a resort destination]. This will give us some time but I don't know about thirty years." I told him: "We're not going to do this for less than a thirty year lease; we need that before we will risk all of our money on it." He said: "Well, give me your formal offer and I will recommend it to Murdock because I think we have enough land in Central Oahu, especially the Dole lands, to handle our needs for the foreseeable future."

Murdock responded through Mills: "Look, I don't want to sell it. I'm not sure I want to go thirty years, but if the guys will take ten years, I'll do it." I told Mills: "We can't do that; we can't make this work based on a lease for only ten years." Mills said: "I will report back to Murdock and suggest that he consider it further."

Then an unexpected obstacle arose. The real estate boom of 1988-90 referred to as the Japanese bubble came roaring in as Japanese money flooded Hawaii and drove up land prices. A favored investment was raw land for high-end golf courses and surrounding residential developments, anywhere and everywhere. Murdock reversed course: "I'm definitely not selling the Waialua Sugar lands and I don't even want to do a lease. I've decided not to do anything except that I want to look at a possible golf course development." He instructed Bill Mills to discontinue further discussions with us.

That was the end of the Case family's attempt to buy Waialua Sugar. The plantation was given a reprieve while Murdock investigated bubble options but the bubble burst in the early 1990s. Waialua Sugar closed in 1996, a year after Oahu Sugar closed. C&H shut down its Aiea refinery. It was the end of sugar on Oahu. The Castle & Cooke Waialua lands were not redeveloped but are now being sold off for smaller scale agricultural and gentleman farmer uses.

Reflections:

(1) On Hilo Sugar, I think that Doc Buyers was right on two scores: (a) sugar did not have a bright future; and (b) the Hilo Sugar lands were valuable.

(2) I think that our effort to buy Hilo Sugar would have worked out. The difference was that our offer included buying the lands owned by Hilo Sugar. We probably would have eventually been required to close down the sugar operations because of world sugar markets, but we would have recaptured our investments from the sale of the lands.

(3) We probably would have eventually had to close Waialua Sugar. In that case fee title to the land was not part of the deal and so we had no good exit strategy. Our investment and that of the other equity investors would have been lost. Bank of Hawaii would have called the C&H guarantee and C&H would have ended up with the biggest loss. But then C&H had the most to gain from success and the most to lose if Waialua Sugar closed.

(4) An obvious last question looking back is why, knowing all that we did know about Hawaii sugar in the mid-1980s, were my family and I prepared to invest our own money in its future. With the benefit of hindsight the answer is multifaceted. First, although sugar was facing headwinds it had only been two decades since its peak production year of 1966 and its future was still somewhat within the industry's control. Second, we believed that Hawaiian sugar with all its advantages and with some changes such as employee ownership could still survive and prosper, especially at the right purchase price and debt level. Third, as we had structured the transactions we did not stand to lose more than we had invested and so were not risking all of our family's assets on the outcome. Fourth, at least with Hilo Sugar, our exit strategy of land sales was sound. But fifth and perhaps most instructive, like Frannie Morgan it was our heritage and we felt an obligation to it which may well have clouded our overall judgment.

Isn't it true that change is often hard to see and harder to accept even when it is staring you in the face.

42. Hawaii Land Reform

"To reduce the perceived social and economic evils of a land oligopoly traceable to the early high chiefs of the Hawaiian Islands, the Hawaii Legislature enacted the Land Reform Act of 1967, which created a land condemnation scheme whereby title to real property is taken from lessors and transferred to lessees in order to reduce the concentration of land ownership."

Thus commenced the May 30, 1984 decision of the Supreme Court of the United States in the case of *Hawaii Housing Authority v. Midkiff,* 467 U.S. 229. The decision also resolved the companion cases of *Portlock Community Association (Maunalua Beach) v. Midkiff* and *Kahala Community Association, Inc. v. Midkiff*; I represented the Kahala Community Association. In that decision the Supreme Court ruled unanimously in favor of the Hawaii Housing Authority and community associations in deciding that the Hawaii Land Reform Act was constitutional. It was truly a landmark decision that would remake much of Hawaii and would fully occupy Carlsmith and me for well over a decade.

Land in Hawaii

To understand that impact, one must step back and take on the difficult task of reviewing the history of land in Hawaii. What makes that undertaking especially difficult is that it is a highly politically and emotionally charged subject that especially over the half century has been too often romanticized and subjected to revisionist forces making objective study and discussion problematic. For anyone interested in getting to the truth of the matter, I urge reviewing the source material or books taken directly from such material. Foremost among them are *Exalted Sits the Chief* by Ross Cordy, *Ruling Chiefs of Hawaii* and other works by Samuel Kamakau, *Ancient History of the Hawaiian People* by Abraham Fornander, the works of John Papa Ii and David Malo, and John Chinen's *Original Land Titles in Hawaii.*

This is how the U. S. Supreme Court summarized matters in its Midkiff decision:

"The Hawaiian Islands were originally settled by Polynesian immigrants from the western Pacific. These settlers developed an economy around a feudal land tenure system in which one island high chief, the alii nui, controlled the land and assigned it for development to certain subchiefs. The subchiefs would then reassign the land to other lower-ranking chiefs, who would administer the land and govern the farmers and other tenants working it. All land was held at the will of the alii nui and eventually had to be returned to his trust. There was no private ownership of land.

"Beginning in the early 1800s, Hawaiian leaders and American settlers repeatedly attempted to divide the lands of the kingdom among the crown, the chiefs and the common people. These efforts proved largely unsuccessful, however, and the land remained in the hands of a few. In the mid-1960s, after extensive hearings, the Hawaii Legislature discovered that while the State and Federal governments owned almost 49% of the State's land, another 47% was in the hands of only 72 private landowners. The legislature further found that 18 landholders, with tracts of 21,000 acres or more, owned more than 40% of this land and that on Oahu, the most urbanized of the islands, 22 landowners owned 72.5% of the fee simple titles. The legislature concluded that concentrated land ownership was responsible for skewing the State's residential fee simple market, inflating land prices, and injuring the public tranquility and welfare."

What complicated matters further was that the large central residential landowners were not the Big Five sugar-based companies but the alii trusts which still held much of the lands granted to the chiefs in the Great Mahele of the 1840s (contrary to popular understanding, not the division of lands between Hawaiians and foreigners but between the king and his chiefs). Foremost among them was the Estate of Bernice Pauahi Bishop, the beneficiary of which was the Kamehameha Schools dedicated to the education of ethnically Hawaiian children. The Estate was led by a board of trustees who were then and still are among the most influential figures in Hawaii (see *Broken Trust* by Randall Roth and Samuel P. King). The senior trustee of the Bishop Estate in the 1970s was Frank E. Midkiff, the father of my client and friend Robert Midkiff.

By the 1960s Bishop Estate alone owned close to ten percent of all land in Hawaii. Although much of its landholdings were in unpopulated or sparsely populated areas of the Neighbor Islands, it also owned large portions of Oahu in urban residential use. These included much of East Honolulu, Aiea/Pearl City, Kailua and Kaneohe. It did not sell these lands but had instead entered into longterm leases with residential lessees.

The societal conflict between highly centralized land ownership and the yearning of people to own their own land was nothing new to the human condition. It was the case in many countries, especially those like England and France that had highly rigid aristocracies descended from feudal systems, and the failure to remedy it had been a driving force in social discord up to and including revolution and war.

The main reason for our own country's immigrant heritage lay not just in freedom but in the promise of owning your own land without obligation to the local lord. The Northern Ireland branch of my own family was just one example, as attested by a letter still in our possession to my great-great grandfather back in the old country from his brother in the new country: "Move to the United States. You may be one of the richest farmers in the Belfast area but you'll never own your own land as long as you stay in Northern Ireland. So come to the United States." Which he did.

The Hawaii Land Reform Act

Similarly, land reform was a central social goal to broaden ownership beyond historical result in many states and countries. In Hawaii it was a central platform item for the Democratic Revolution of 1954, and the legislature had come very close to passing the Maryland version of land reform in the early 1960s.

Picking back up with the U. S. Supreme Court's Midkiff decision:

"To remedy these problems, the legislature decided to compel the large landowners to break up their estates. The legislature considered requiring large landowners to sell lands which they were leasing to homeowners. However, the landowners strongly resisted this scheme, pointing out the significant federal tax liabilities they would incur. Indeed, the landowners claimed that the federal tax laws were the primary reason they previously had chosen to lease, and not sell, their lands. Therefore to accommodate the needs of both lessors and lessees, the Hawaii Legislature enacted the Land Reform Act of 1967, which created a mechanism for condemning resident tracts and for transferring ownership of the condemned fee simple to existing lessees. By condemning the land in question, the Hawaii Legislature intended to make the land sales involuntary, thereby making the federal tax consequences less severe while still facilitating the redistribution of fee simple."

The Hawaii Land Reform Act set up a mechanism under which, if a certain minimum number of lessees in a residential tract petitioned the State, through its Hawaii Housing Authority (HHA), to acquire their land, HHA would hold a public hearing to determine whether the acquisition met the public purposes of the Act and, if so, initiate an action to acquire the land using the government power of eminent domain. The prices were to be set by negotiation between the lessor and lessees or, if they could not reach agreement, by a judge or jury determining the fair market value of the land. Although HHA technically acquired the land, it was essentially required to resell it to the lessee without any markup on the price. And as things worked out, usually lands were transferred directly from the lessor to lessee in a negotiated settlement.

The Act also contained another important provision that triggered the sequence of events leading to the U. S. Supreme Court's decision. The standard land lease provided for a fixed lease rent for some initial period and then for the rent to be renegotiated to then-fair rent value for further periods of the lease. A basic Bishop Estate lease was for 55 years, with lease rent fixed for the first thirty years and then renegotiated for a subsequent two ten years and the last five years of the lease. The Act said that, in any such renegotiation, the lessor could not charge more than 4% of the overall value of the land, in effect a form of rent control.

Although the Act was enacted in 1967, it took some years for the administrative procedures to be set up through the HHA. And during that period there was no real pressure on the lessees since the earliest leases entered into shortly after the War were still running out their initial thirty year fixed rent terms. That changed in 1976 as the first Waialae Kahala leases with the Bishop Estate came up on the thirty year mark and the lessees faced drastically increased rents.

Enter again, like so many other points of my career, unexpected threads from my earlier life (or in this situation my ancestors'). The Kahala Community Association consisted of the Waialae Kahala lessees and they had determined correctly that their best course was to act jointly on this challenge. The association president was Lois Bruce, who happened to be the daughter of the couple who had moved into my grandparents' longtime home in Haliimaile, Maui when they moved out in the 1940s. We also attended the same church. Lois knew me as a lawyer, but we also had that personal connection that persuaded her to seek my counsel for the association. She came to see me and I took on the representation of the Kahala Community Association. Not only was it a fascinating challenge, but I knew that its result would set a precedent for similar situations that would face thousands of other residential lessees in the coming years.

The Bishop Estate's longtime attorneys were the Honolulu law firm of Ashford & Wriston. Clinton "Tink" Ashford was their senior lawyer. I knew Tink dating back to our days as contemporaries at Punahou; he was as fine a land lawyer and person as they came and a formidable adversary in a negotiation or courtroom.

I went to see Ashford and told him that the Kahala Community Association lessees were prepared to renegotiate their lease rents under the Hawaii Land Reform Act. I said that we were willing to agree to the maximum 4% of the fair market value of the land as specified in the Act and so all we needed to discuss was how to agree to the fair market value. But Bishop Estate had other ideas. Ashford responded: "The law is unconstitutional and we're not going to negotiate with the association on that basis".

In early 1977 we triggered the Act's condemnation procedures with the HHA. The Bishop Estate and Ashford objected again on the basis that the use of the government's power of eminent domain under these circumstances lacked a sufficient public purpose and was therefore unconstitutional.

To make a long story short, everything ended up in court. To its credit the state through the HHA committed fully to defending the Act and was a full partner in the litigation all the way to the end. There was a parallel action going on with the Portlock (Maunalua Beach) Community Association also against Bishop Estate and that was eventually consolidated with ours.

I was in charge of the litigation in the sense that I had the direct client contact and had the responsibility to strategize with the client how we should proceed. But Bernie Bays, who had come over to Carlsmith in 1976 with Hod Greeley, was our chief litigator and he did a masterful job. The trial court ruled in our favor: the law had a legitimate public purpose and was constitutional.

Bishop Estate appealed. The case bounced back and forth between the federal and Hawaii courts for a few more years until in 1983 the U.S. Circuit Court of Appeals for the Ninth Circuit (the last level below the U. S. Supreme Court) ruled in favor of Bishop Estate. It concluded on a 2-1 opinion that the Act was no more than "a naked attempt on the part of the State of Hawaii to take the private property of A and transfer it to B solely for B's private use and benefit."

Our last and only option was the Supreme Court of the United States and we appealed to it. Contrary to what most believe, in the great majority of appeals to the U. S. Supreme Court it is up to the Court whether to take the case and the Court declines to consider the great majority of such appeals. But the Court accepted our appeal, which gave us some hope that we might yet prevail.

We convened with our fellow attorneys for the HHA and Portlock Community Association and made a decision that perhaps was against our instincts but turned out to be the right one. We decided that despite whatever opinion we might have of our legal capabilities and although the dream of every American lawyer is to argue a case before the U. S. Supreme Court, we were out of our league and needed to find an expert. We agreed that HHA would take the lead and engage a U.S. constitutional law expert who would represent all of us. Harvard Law School Professor Laurence Tribe took on the engagement. He was the preeminent constitutional law expert of his era; he not only taught constitutional law but read every decision of the U. S. Supreme Court and studied how each Justice thought about a wide range of issues.

We had drafted our appellate brief for filing with the Court which focused on procedural issues. But Professor Tribe ignominiously threw our work out: "You're missing the point. The issue here is rent control which has been approved by the Court over the ages. Furthermore, condemnation law says that a government may condemn land for a proper public purpose, but who decides what is a proper public purpose? I think that the Court will decide that it cannot referee every single decision as to a legitimate public purpose, and will generally leave it to government to determine whether a particular condemnation is an appropriate public purpose."

We all started over on that page. Professor Tribe argued our case to the Supreme Court and Tink Ashford argued it for Bishop Estate. My son Ed, who by then had joined Carlsmith and was on the case with

Bernie Bays and me, attended the oral argument in person and the post argument gathering with Tribe, who told him he thought we'd get a unanimous favorable decision.

And so we did. From the Court's decision: "The Hawaii Legislature enacted its Land Reform Act not to benefit a particular class of identifiable individuals, but to attack certain perceive evils of concentrated property ownership in Hawaii – a legitimate public purpose."

Of many lessons learned: Don't think you know everything. Get help from experts when you are entering into unfamiliar territory.

Implementing Land Reform

With the Supreme Court's Midkiff decision, the Hawaii Land Reform Act was fully enforceable as to both rent caps and fee acquisitions. Initially we focused on the rent renegotiations but as those dragged I told my clients I thought they should just pursue acquisition. I said: "Let's just go straight to the core; let's use the Act to buy your land."

We promptly did exactly that, not just for the Kahala Community Association but for other Bishop Estate residential lessee communities and then for other communities leasing residential land from other larger landowners. Once we started these actions Carlsmith was the instant expert on the Hawaii Land Reform Act and helping lessees to acquire their land and the clients came. (It always helps to be first in some new area of law.) As a few examples we took on representing the lessees of the Queen Emma Foundation in Foster Village and of Castle Ranch in Kailua. In all we took on somewhere close to thirty community associations over the years.

We developed a rhythm in which we tried to settle directly with the landowners first at a fair price. If that didn't work, we began the formal proceedings under the Hawaii Land Reform Act through to a trial on the fair market value to be paid for the land. Often we settled on the eve of trial but sometimes we had to try the case to a verdict.

Most of the early cases were with the Bishop Estate and it fought us the whole way. In one of the first cases, Kamiloiki and Kamilonui in Hawaii Kai, the jury split the baby between the lessee and the lessor represented still by Tink Ashford. In Kahala the jury gave Ashford a clear and probably deserved win on value.

These early cases gave everyone a good picture of what a judge and jury were likely to do; that and the cost and effort of a full litigation incentivized early and mutually fair settlements. We reached a point where we could get into a productive negotiation with the Bishop Estate right away and could agree very quickly on fair market value and how we would structure the land sales. The same was true of other large landowners.

In fact, most of the large landowners concluded that they preferred to get out of the residential leasehold business if they could get a fair price. Administering thousands of lessees and leaseholds, especially when you were proposing to increase their lease rents by ten times or more, was complicated and unpleasant. They could take the proceeds of those sales and reinvest them in other lands, such as commercial shopping centers or industrial warehouses here and on the mainland, and make a far better return. And they earned a distinct tax advantage if those sales were considered to be under threat of condemnation, a technical term of art in the tax world.

In the course of all of this we represented the lessees of some very large tracts of land. In Enchanted Lakes in Kailua there were fifteen hundred homes under lease; we negotiated a settlement of the entire Enchanted Lakes subdivision. We negotiated settlements of almost every subdivision between Diamond Head and Hawaii Kai, such as Waialae Golf Course, Waialae Nui, Waialae Iki, as well as subdivisions in Leeward Oahu such as Kaonohi (Pearl) Ridge and Windward Oahu such as Heeia.

One of the most unusual cases involved Niu Valley, where through Tom Van Winkle we represented the owner, lessor Pflueger Trust. The trust had leased its land out to residential lessee on longterm leases under which it was earning only about a 1% return on its land values. Van Winkle advised the trust that if it could arrange to trigger the Hawaii Land Reform Act it could negotiate fee sales with its lessees under threat of condemnation, defer its tax gains and reinvest the sales proceeds at a much higher return.

Van Winkle and the trustees contacted some community leaders and suggested that they form a community association to initiate fee purchase negotiations under the Hawaii Land Reform Act. They did, and the trust and association then negotiated out a fair price and closed the sales. The lessees got their land and the trust took its tax-deferred proceeds and reinvested in other higher return investments. Everybody won.

For Carlsmith and me the Hawaii Land Reform Act cases occupied a huge portion of our time for well over a decade. They were administratively difficult and not especially economically rewarding. But they were personally rewarding as we were able to help somewhere in the range I would guess of 6,000 clients acquire their land, and 6,000 people and their families and friends now knew that Carlsmith and I had represented them successfully on a matter of great personal importance.

Although the Hawaii Land Reform Act technically remains on the books, the era of largescale residential leasing of land by a few landowners in Hawaii is largely over. In that the Hawaii Land Reform Act achieved its purpose. Considering the escalation in land prices since and the failure to advance the rate of home ownership in Hawaii and especially in Honolulu over the last decade, it is tempting to argue as some do that the Act failed. But then the real question is where would Hawaii be today if the Act had never been passed, defended and implemented to start with.

The Next Frontier of Land Reform: Residential Condominiums

Like single family residential land, Hawaii had evolved a system of disproportionately large numbers of residential leasehold cooperative and condominium apartments in urban Honolulu (and Hawaii had virtually invented condos with one of the earliest condominium laws in the early 1960s). And like single family residential land, the fee ownership of these leasehold apartments was centralized in the larger landowners. This created conditions and issues similar to those of the Hawaii Land Reform Act.

Our work on the Hawaii Land Reform Act led coop and condo associations and their lessee members to us as clients with the similar goal of acquiring their fee interests. But there was no authorizing legislation for City and County of Honolulu coop and condo lessees similar to the Act for single family residential. Key members of the City Council supported such legislation and we worked with them to gain its enactment in 1991.

We became instant experts on fee conversions of leasehold coop and condo apartments and the clients came. The underlying public purpose of the ordinance was the same as with the Hawaii Land Reform Act and the *Midkiff* case had essentially settled its constitutionality so we did not have to repeat all of that step. And like the Act many landowners saw the benefits to them of negotiating sales at a fair price with the associated tax benefits and reinvesting their proceeds in higher return properties.

As an example, I negotiated successfully with Lum Yip Kee Ltd through Tan Tek Lum and Asa Akinaka, with whom I had negotiated the Aloha Towers development back in the 1970s, for fee conversion of a number of their leasehold condominium properties in Waikiki and Moiliili; they took their proceeds and formed Twin Trees Land Company, a no-doubt prosperous commercial real estate investment company.

Over the next decade we negotiated many successful fee conversions throughout Oahu. But in the late 1990s some of the larger owners of leasehold condominiums led by the Bishop Estate mounted an effort to repeal the Honolulu ordinance. Their basic argument was that there was a difference between single family homes and residential apartments.

The issues came to a head in 2005. We opposed repeal on behalf of many leasehold owners who still wanted to buy their units, and I and others briefed our supporters on the Council. It was very hotly contested and strongly lobbied.

At the lengthy public hearing on the repeal proposal, I remember in particular the testimony of Eric Yeaman, then Chief Financial Officer of the Bishop Estate. Councilmember Duke Bainum, our strong supporter, did a beautiful cross examination of Yeaman, something like this:

Bainum: "How many condominium units were on Bishop Estate land before the Honolulu Fee Conversion Act was passed?"

Yeaman: "About 20,000".

Bainum: "As I understand it, the Bishop Estate has fought the conversion to fee simple for condominiums and co-ops. Is that right?"

Yeaman: "Yes".

Bainum: "Now, you said that the Bishop Estate did not want to convert condominiums and co-ops. Did you sell any of your condominium and co-op units during the period you were fighting this matter all the way up to the Ninth Circuit, saying you didn't want to sell?"

Yeaman: "Yes we did."

Bainum: "How many do you now own?"

Yeaman: "About 6,000."

Bainum: "So all the time you fought the Act, you were selling as fast as you could. Is that right?"

Yeaman: "Yes."

Bainum: "What do you intend to do with the 6,000?"

Yeaman: "We intend to sell them all, except for the Kahala Beach Apartments, the condominium next to the Kahala Hilton."

Bainum: "Why is that?"

Yeaman: "We hope to build a hotel on that property someday."

Bainum: "Do you know that when the Kahala Hilton was built the Bishop Estate trustees agreed with the City and County of Honolulu that if the City granted this zoning for the Kahala Hilton, the Bishop Estate would keep Kahala Beach and the entire area from Diamond Head to the Kahala Hilton in fee simple forever, and not develop hotels there?"

Yeaman: "Yes, we are aware of that but we hope to change people's minds."

At the very end the ordinance was repealed on a 5 - 4 vote of the Council and then-Mayor Mufi Hannemann signed the repeal. Since then, leasehold coop and condo owners have not had the same rights as single family residential lessees to acquire their fee interests at a fair price. This doesn't mean that fee owners won't sell, just that the lessees have no leverage in gaining a fair price. I once called up the Bishop Estate's chief negotiator and said: "This condominium has come to me and we'd like to try to negotiate a fair price". He replied: "My orders, Jim, are not to negotiate at all with you or with any association. We will set the price, and they can take it or leave it."

The overall percentage of leasehold condos in Honolulu is significantly down from a few decades back as many owners desired to convert and new condos are far more marketable as fee rather than leaseholds, so the ordinance and basic market forces had some effect. Still there are thousands of leasehold condos coming up for rent increases or the end of their leases, and it will be interesting to see whether they create the same forces for land reform as occurred with the Hawaii Land Reform Act and the first time around for the Honolulu ordinance.

Luck in Law and Life

I remain proud of my role in this chapter of Hawaii's history. Land reform in Hawaii and indeed throughout the country and world is unfinished business but we made a pretty good dent in it in our corner and time. And I was gratified recently when my daughter-in-law, studying constitutional law in law school, read *Midkiff* as a still-seminal case in condemnation law and saw my name; she became an instant star in class when she said she knew that lawyer!

But I marvel at how I got into it all in the first place. After all, in 1976 I hardly knew that we had a Hawaii Land Reform Act, much less had any expertise in it.

You can be a great lawyer and have great expertise and that'll get you clients and work a lot of the time. But that's not how I got all of this work that sustained Carlsmith and me for a good two decades.

I got it because I knew the president of a community association. She had grown up in my grandparents' house and we went to the same church. She needed help and knew I was a lawyer and from all formed some initial impression that she could trust me to either do the work or find someone that could.

That was just luck. Luck is essential in the games of bridge and poker and it has a role in the practice of law. A lot of life is luck, isn't it? But the thing about luck, like opportunity, is you don't exactly know when it'll come along but you can open the door to let it in when it does. When that work happened along I had assembled the tools to do it.

43. Growing Pains for Carlsmith

In the first half of the 1980s, as Donn Carlsmith, Charlie Wichman and I transitioned the firm reins over to Tom Van Winkle, Peter Starn and their generation, Carlsmith wrestled with an almost existential question: what next? We had succeeded beyond our dreams in growing this little three-lawyer Hilo firm into a full service Pacific firm, one of the most prominent (of course we thought the most prominent) in Hawaii and the Pacific Basin, inside a generation. But what should you do, what must you do, after you've succeeded?

A long range planning effort was convened to look at the big picture. The first and foremost choice was whether to continue to grow or stabilize. Perhaps that basic question should have been considered more deeply as it had widespread ramifications as soon became apparent, but the answer then was almost a foregone conclusion. Growth and the willingness and courage to take calculated risks for longterm gain despite the naysayers were now three generations deep in Carlsmith's DNA, and the next generation especially had its own dreams and was going to take its own shot at success. And there was a strong sense that, with the legal profession becoming increasingly competitive and consolidated, the best if not only defense was a good offense.

The next decision was where and how to grow. The answer was on one level simple: where our present and future clients were and would be. But then it got more complicated. In Hawaii proper, the established clients were mostly spoken for by the top firms who were usually smart enough not to give their clients cause to leave, and the new clients such as the inbound Japanese investment that was rapidly accelerating were hotly pursued. We had already solidified our position in the Western Pacific in Guam. The only other real locations for possible growth were Japan (which was highly protective and made little economic sense) and the West Coast (which could make sense under the right circumstances).

To that were added the same limitations on growth from within that we had faced in the 1970s. We couldn't do it by just hiring more new associates; we had to lateral in proven partners and their firms with existing clients and practice niches. Under the right circumstances this could work well (as in our lateral expansions in Guam, Saipan and Maui), but it carried real risk of disrupting existing firm culture, productivity and compensation expectations and thus the departure of valued attorneys and staff if the fit was wrong.

Two key decisions in 1984 would illustrate the hazards of growth and trigger a decade-plus of challenge for Carlsmith. The first was to absorb eight attorneys from the Honolulu firm of Mukai, Ichiki, Raffetto & MacMillan.

The firm was built around Stanley Mukai and Andy Ichiki. Mukai was a Harvard Law School graduate specializing in tax and business law, while Ichiki was a Harvard/University of Washington Law School graduate and business lawyer whose community contributions were already legendary. Other firm members included Stan's brother Frank and Karl Kobayashi.

The firm had focused for decades on inbound Japanese investment and it had an A list of Japanese clients. On paper it was a good fit: Mukai Ichiki had outgrown its current partnership and was looking for large firm support; it had more and more sophisticated work than it could handle and we had high quality lawyers who could do the work; and we saw the opportunity to grow in a productive and promising niche market in which we did not have a significant presence. They joined us, the firm was renamed Carlsmith, Wichman, Case, Mukai & Ichiki, and Stan Mukai went straight onto the Executive Committee.

The problem was compatibility. Not of most of the Mukai Ichiki lawyers: Andy Ichiki was a collaborative, productive and beloved partner from the beginning until his untimely death in 1997; and Karl Kobayashi grew into an excellent lawyer and respected firm leader. The problem pure and simple was Stan Mukai and to a lesser extent Frank.

Mukai's style and approach was the antithesis of the Carlsmith way. He demonstrated this by 10:00 A.M. on his first day by trying to fire our longtime receptionist for not escorting his client to his office contrary to our practice of having the attorney or secretary come out. He alienated the associates inside of a few months by giving many of them the same assignment without telling them in order to test them out (as if associates don't compare notes). He disagreed with us on associate training and investment and on partner compensation.

But these were all indicative of a broader issue: we simply were incompatible in style and substance. That played itself out in the countless issues and decisions a firm or any other business faces day to day, big and small. This went on in a form of stalemate for a full decade before the Mukais left for another firm. It was deeply disruptive and costly to Carlsmith at a key point in our development.

One would fairly ask: if it wasn't working out why didn't we part ways much earlier? The answer: we had become mutually dependent on each other and there were real consequences to doing so, consequences that we both feared worse than tolerating and working around a problematic situation. But we should have nonetheless, because the damage done ended up being far worse than had we cut our losses and taken our hit earlier. That's one lesson, but the more important one, which in our desire to grow we didn't fully heed, is: don't underestimate the importance of fit when making the decision to start with.

The second key decision of 1984 was to open a Los Angeles office from scratch. If we had decided to continue growing, and if growth out of Hawaii was the only practical option, Los Angeles and its greater Hawaii-Pacific Basin focus (as opposed to San Francisco and its establishment California focus) was the logical choice.

The argument went that no other Hawaii firm had offices on the mainland, offices in L.A. would distinguish us and add credibility, we could better service and attract L.A.-based clients with interests in Hawaii and throughout the Pacific, and by doing aggressive high quality work in these big leagues we could expand our work and client base to more than just Hawaii and the Pacific. After all the roadmap was there – we had already done it in going from Hilo to statewide and beyond – just a little larger scale. On paper it could work and work well, if we followed the basics of an existing client beachhead, a trusted administrative partner, nice offices and a reasoned financial investment in success.

Peter Starn led the charge in the Executive Committee. He and his best friend in the partnership, litigator Terry O'Toole, had succeeded at a young age and had their sights set on broader horizons. Starn came to the committee with a plan: he had a major L.A. business who had promised to give us all of its work if we opened in L.A.; he would locate and build out nice office space; and he and O'Toole would staff the office.

It was a tough decision. It had the ingredients of success if everything worked and we wanted to keep two of our best partners fully engaged. But it was a huge investment both financially and in the time and energy of key partners, and we were taking a big chance on the promised beachhead client. I wanted to support the next generation as I had with the Mukai Ichiki merger and I agreed with an L.A. office in principle, but I concluded this particular proposal was too risky all around. Charlie Wichman and I voted against it in the Executive Committee but the proposal carried by one vote and we all exited the meeting in full support of the L.A. move.

It did not get off to a smooth start. First, Starn spent extravagantly on the new office, which not only drained firm resources but was not received well in the other offices that were being asked to restrict compensation and capital spending to fund growth. Second, the promised client did not materialize, which pushed Starn and O'Toole into a broader business development rather than practicing/billing lawyer role. We slowly added some clients and additional lawyers, but the financial and human costs were far greater than projected.

The Mukai Ichiki merger and L.A. office were just two specific events that stretched the fabric of the firm in the first half of the 1980s. Those and overall rapid growth especially in lateral hirings and generational leadership change all risked the invaluable firm glue that had always held us together.

An early warning sign came in 1984 when respected partners Joe Kiefer and Alan Oshima left with some other attorneys to form their own firm. It was not all that unusual for attorneys to come and go, but it was unusual for established and loyal partners to leave together. Kiefer said later: "It got a little too aggressive for me." (Kiefer would go on to serve as Bank of Hawaii's chief counsel and a major referral source for its business back to Tom Van Winkle who built the bank into one of Carlsmith's largest clients.)

Carlsmith held an annual retreat in the fall of each year at which we brought all of our partners from all offices together to strengthen personal and professional relationships and generally try to keep the glue strong. The 1985 retreat at Kuilima Resort on Oahu's North Shore was especially significant given all that had occurred over the past year.

I had flown in from the mainland and come straight to the retreat. Charlie Wichman met me and said: "Hod Greeley just announced that he is leaving with Susan Walker to form his own firm." This was a shock, as Hod was our senior litigator and a member of the Executive Committee, where he had just voted with the rest of us to exercise our lease option on the 23rd floor of our building. I believe that for Hod it was mostly about feeling left out of the change taking place and wanting to control his own destiny.

We didn't know then that three of our most promising litigators had decided independently to leave and form their own firm because, as one said, "it's not the same firm as when I started". Hod's departure shook litigator Bernie Bays, who had come in with Hod; he and another litigator soon joined forces with the group of three and they all left to start the firm now known as Bays Lung Rose & Holma. With that and Hod's departure we had lost the bulk of our Honolulu litigation capacity.

We moved forward as best we could into the second half of the 1980s. We were still a top (we still thought the best) full service Pacific firm with an A list of clients and deep expertise and capacity in many general areas and several niche areas, and were still able to attract high quality new clients and attorneys. We slowly but surely built back a competent litigation department and continued our growth strategy.

In all this we were especially fortunate that the economic boom of the time sparked by Japanese investment carried us through financially and masked our weaknesses. This was a double-edged sword, though, because it allowed us to avoid remedying those weaknesses toward the day when we would not have such a cushion.

L.A. continued as a challenge throughout. In 1988 we followed the lateral hire formula by absorbing an established Southern California firm whose specialty was cross-border transactions with Mexico; this led later to us opening an office in Mexico City. There was not much connection back to our Pacific Basin strategy but our focus was on sustainable critical mass in Southern California.

By this point we had grown to around 120 attorneys. Then, in 1990, we took our biggest gulp yet when we merged with a Southern California firm headed by legendary attorney Joseph Ball.

Ball, then in the twilight of his career, fully deserved his legend status. Probably best known for his role as senior counsel to the Warren Commission that investigated the assassination of President Kennedy, Ball was widely regarded as one of the leading trial lawyers of his generation. He had built a diverse firm of about 60 attorneys around him which included other luminaries like former California Governor Edmund (Pat) Brown out of offices in Ball's hometown of Long Beach as well as Los Angeles and Beverly Hills.

The possibility had arisen in 1989 when we asked Ball's partner Tony Murray to bring his L.A. litigation practice into the firm. Murray had declined but said a whole-firm merger might be possible. Tom Van Winkle had led a yearlong discussion with Joe Ball and his firm to consider the possibility.

Again, on paper, it was promising. For Carlsmith it could be instant critical mass and credibility in Southern California and beyond and true litigation capacity. The attraction for the Ball firm was less clear but on the face of it was about projecting itself beyond Southern California into the Pacific and about marrying up with national commercial, real estate and transactional expertise. The merger closed in 1990 and the firm name changed (in true law firm egalitarian style; nothing like lawyers negotiating over firm names) to Carlsmith, Ball, Wichman, Murray, Case, Mukai & Ichiki ...!

By the early 1990s Carlsmith had reached its apex at close to 200 lawyers in eleven offices stretching from Washington, D.C. (where one of our partners had moved) to the Western Pacific. But then the Japanese bubble, heavily invested in Southern California, Hawaii and the Western Pacific, burst spectacularly and those economies tanked. There was simply not enough activity and clients to sustain a close-to-200 lawyer firm in the principally affected economies and we were forced to embark on a very painful and highly disruptive process of downsizing and office closing to preserve the firm.

By the mid-1990s Carlsmith (by then mercifully renamed Carlsmith Ball, by which it is still known) was back down to closer to 100 attorneys throughout Hawaii, the Western Pacific and L.A. Peter Starn had left to found his own firm, joined later by Terry O'Toole. We were still a top full service Pacific firm with many challenges and successes to come, but the era of growth that had begun in earnest under Wendell Carlsmith a half century earlier was over.

44. Macadamia Nuts Part Two: Mauna Loa Macadamia Partners

IU International had bought C. Brewer in the mid-1970s and had sent Doc Buyers out to take charge of the investment. But by the mid-1980s IU was divesting many of its assets and Brewer was one of them. Buyers pulled together a hui (Hawaiian slang for joint venture) consisting of many of his old Princeton Tigers teammates and friends along with Hawaii business leaders and third party investors to purchase Brewer from IU in a $200 million leveraged buyout. The 1986 deal left Brewer deeply in debt and Buyers set out to reduce that debt.

One of Brewer's subsidiaries was Mauna Loa Macadamia Nut Corporation, which then both grew macadamia nuts at its orchards in Hilo and Kau and processed and marketed them and nuts grown elsewhere out of its Keaau plant. It was one of the largest growers and the largest processor of macadamia nuts in the world.

As part of financing the transaction, Buyers and his bankers decided to separate ownership of the orchards and production facilities on the one hand and the processing and marketing facilities on the other. Mauna Loa Macadamia Nut Corporation retained direct ownership and operation of the processing and marketing side, but the orchard and production side was transferred to Mauna Loa Macadamia Partners, L.P., a master limited partnership. This syndicated the orchards, meaning that Brewer could now sell limited partnership interests in the entity to passive investors to raise money while retaining overall control through the entity's general partner, Mauna Loa Resources Inc., a Brewer subsidiary, much like we had done almost three decades earlier with Honomalino Agricultural Company.

Mauna Loa Macadamia Partners was listed on the New York Stock Exchange and its limited partnership interests were publicly traded there. This meant it had to comply fully with all federal securities laws and regulations including public disclosures of all material information and required corporate governance provisions. This also meant that, while both grower Mauna Loa Macadamia Partners and processor Mauna Loa Macadamia Nut Corporation were commonly controlled by Brewer, they had to operate at arms length as if they were completely separately owned and managed, meaning that, for example, they had to enter into macadamia nut purchase agreements under which the latter would buy and process the former's nuts on market terms.

One of the federal securities requirements was that the board of directors of Mauna Loa Macadamia Partners general partner Mauna Loa Resources Inc. had to have a certain minimum number of independent (outside) directors who were not officers, directors, employees or shareholders of any of the entities or their affiliates. These independent directors had the same responsibility as company directors to oversee company management except with the added value of perspective.

But the independents had another function as they constituted a Conflicts Committee to periodically review the managing partner's management of Mauna Loa Macadamia Partners and any conflicts of interest that may have arisen as a result of the relationship among them. This was meant primarily to safeguard the limited partners' passive investments against any inside trading among Brewer and its affiliates. If the Conflicts Committee raised an issue the full board could technically overrule it, but then that action would have to be disclosed publicly which was a powerful disincentive against disagreeing with the Conflicts Committee.

Jim Andrasick, Brewer's executive vice president and chief financial officer, called me up in 1986 and asked if he could come over to see me. I was surprised and didn't know what to expect as we were not then representing Brewer and I had no reason to think that they would consider leaving their longtime regular counsel, the Goodsill firm. But Andrasick's reason was to ask that I join the Mauna Loa Resources, Inc. board of directors as one of their three independents and chair the Conflicts Committee. My fellow independents and committee members would be Robert Hughes, a retired Brewer executive, and Dr. Ralph C. Hook, Jr., Dean of the University of Hawaii's College of Business Administration. We would join Brewer executives Andrasick, Tilker, Buyers and Kent Lucien.

Carlsmith's policy had remained, for conflicts and risk management purposes, that partners could not join the boards of directors of for-profit companies without advance permission of the Executive Committee. Further, approval should not be provided unless there was some clear advantage present or future to the firm in doing so.

I discussed the matter with Tom Van Winkle, by then Chair of the Executive Committee. We considered that I had expertise and experience in macadamia nuts: I would be a valuable addition to the Mauna Loa Resources board and would gain visibility for the firm as a director of a publicly traded Hawaii company. Equally if not more important, I would be meeting with the top executives of Brewer which we had not represented for many years, and this relationship might produce legal work for us if Brewer's regular firm Goodsill was conflicted out or the executives thought I would do a better job. Van Winkle agreed that the opportunities outweighed the risks of my service and so I accepted.

Despite all I thought I knew, it was still a steep learning curve. My real expertise to date lay mainly in the orchard development and production side from my Honomalino days and just a little about processing from my brief involvement with Hawaiian Holiday. But Mauna Loa was a far larger and more complex total operation not only in scale but in diversity, everything from land acquisition and lease to planting through international trade disputes and adjustment assistance to the end consumer. It was quite a crash course beginning at the age of 66.

Interestingly, our Conflicts Committee was put to the test early on over the interpretation and administration of a nut purchase contract between grower/seller Mauna Loa Macadamia Partners and processor/buyer Mauna Loa Macadamia Nut Corporation. The contract set the terms of crop purchase and price. The issue was whether low quality or "unusable" nuts were covered by the contract. Our Conflicts Committee read the contract to say that buyer had to buy all of seller's macadamia nut harvest, which made sense when you considered that it was a whole harvest that was contracted and sold. The Brewer executives for processor/seller didn't want to buy and pay for the unusable nuts and things got a little tense.

I went to Jim Andrasick and said: "Look, our view is that the contract requires you to buy. But rather than us saying that to you directly, I propose that you authorize me to retain an outside law firm to provide a third party opinion. This will be a protection for not only us but you as well as you want us to give you an answer that we think is wrong and we're not going to do that." Andrasick agreed.

I wanted a good lawyer, one whose opinion Brewer would have to accept. I engaged Hugh Shearer at Goodsill; though one of our top competitors it was a very good firm, not to mention Brewer's own firm, and Hugh was a well-respected attorney. Hugh reviewed everything and agreed with our interpretation. Brewer just said okay, though it did renegotiate subsequent purchase contracts to adjust for the unusable nuts contingency.

During my whole service as Chair of the Conflicts Committee, there was hardly ever a time that the inside directors overruled us. Partly it was the public disclosure factor, but mostly it was that we just had a very good committee. We would talk things over from all angles and almost always agree among ourselves before we went to the full board. I also in time served variously as Chair of the Audit Committee (overseeing financial and operational risks, reviews and disclosures), Nominating Committee (proposing new directors), Compensation Committee (determining top executive compensation) and Governance Committee (overall corporate governance to include leadership succession). This all gave me a lot of influence every bit of which I would need to address some very tough issues down the road.

At some point after many years Mauna Loa Macadamia Partners wanted to buy some new orchards and wanted to raise the money to do so through a public offering of its limited partnership interests. By then I think that the Brewer executives had formed a favorable opinion of me and the partnership hired me to represent them in gaining Securities & Exchange Commission approval of the offering. We worked with a San Francisco investment banking firm, the SEC approved the offering, the offering was successful and the orchards were purchased. From then on Carlsmith represented the partnership on its legal matters, fulfilling one of the purposes of approving my service as a director.

In 1998 Buyers announced summarily that he was moving Brewer's headquarters from downtown Honolulu to Hilo. This was represented publicly as a move by Brewer back to its agricultural roots, but the reason was at least equally that Buyers' girlfriend, actress and former Miss Hawaii Elizabeth Lindsey, lived there; she became his second wife in 1999. The move made little economic or business sense for Brewer, was highly disruptive to the executive team, and was very costly as Buyers spent lavishly on a new Brewer headquarters overlooking Hilo Bay. It all set off alarm bells with Buyers' Brewer co-investors, the Brewer executives and employees, and the directors of Brewer's various subsidiaries including Mauna Loa Macadamia Partners.

In 2000 Brewer sold Mauna Loa Macadamia Nut Corporation and its nut processing and marketing facilities and operations to the Shansby Group, a private equity investment partnership out of San Francisco. Now Brewer was just in the macadamia nut growing business through Mauna Loa Macadamia Partners and that entity's relationship with Shansby's newly acquired processor was truly arms length.

Shansby turned out to be very difficult, some of the most difficult, deceptive and untrustworthy people I ever met. I think they figured out what I thought of them, because when they wanted to discuss or negotiate anything they would call up Doc Buyers and say: "Doc, we don't want to deal with Dennis Simonis [by then president of Mauna Loa Macadamia Partners] or your lawyers. Let's just you and us talk." Doc loved that and it lasted until we later had to make sure that Dennis was included in all meetings.

Shansby soon decided to buy the other main Hawaii Island macadamia nut processor, Mac Farms. A purchase of Mac Farms would give Shansby control of 85% of island processing capacity. Since there would be no effective competition, most growers including Mauna Loa Macadamia Partners would have no choice but to sell their macadamia nut harvests to Shansby at whatever price Shansby set.

I met with the Hawaii Attorney General and explained the whole operation of the macadamia industry and how the Shansby purchase was anti-competitive in violation of federal and state antitrust laws. He agreed and said he'd support us if the issue went to court.

I met with the Shansby executives and told them their purchase of Mac Farms would violate antitrust law and we were prepared to go to court. They rejected our argument and plowed ahead, so we sued them to stop the acquisition.

Shansby now sought a meeting with us to try to settle the lawsuit. They hired Honolulu attorney Marjorie Bronster, a former Carlsmith partner who had gone on to serve as Hawaii Attorney General before returning to private practice.

The meeting was held in the Mauna Loa Macadamia Partners' board room in Hilo. We set up place cards for everybody. We put Dennis Simonis and me in the middle on one side, and Shansby's Hawaii head and

Marjorie Bronster facing us on the other side and the local head of the processor right opposite Dennis and me. We put Doc Buyers way off at one end of the table and the Shansby president way off on the other end so they couldn't talk to each other. But whenever our middle of the table would talk to the other side, the Shansby president would start talking down the whole length of the table to Buyers on the other end. It was almost comical.

No surprise, nothing happened and the meeting ended. We went back to court and won the lawsuit. Shansby did not buy Mac Farms but resold Mauna Loa Macadamia Nut Corporation four years later to Hershey Foods at a huge profit. Hershey resold the company in 2015 to local company Hawaiian Host, Inc.

In 2001, over Doc Buyers' strenuous objections, his co-owners of Brewer voted to liquidate the company (sell all its assets, distribute proceeds to owners and dissolve the company), of which more later. As part of that process, Buyers personally acquired all of the ownership interests in Mauna Loa Resources, Inc., the general partner of Mauna Loa Macadamia Partners. So I was now serving on the board of a company owned 100% by Buyers, which led me in my early eighties into probably my most difficult single legal job.

Shortly after the transaction I began to worry that Buyers was suffering from Alzheimer's disease. I felt he had made a series of questionable decisions dating back to moving Brewer's headquarters to Hilo in 1998 and his demeanor and behavior had become more difficult. I disagreed with many of his decisions and did not especially like our dealings, but he was not the first corporate leader to make controversial decisions and be less than well-liked, and it was generally up to me to help him make the best decisions possible and to get along with him or get out. This, though, was different; I now questioned his basic mental capacity to make decisions and run the company.

I wasn't just a company employee or lawyer; I was on the board of directors and further the chair of the Audit and other committees. Mauna Loa Macadamia Partners was a public company of some 3,000 limited partners traded on the New York Stock Exchange and regulated by the Securities & Exchange Commission. I had undertaken obligations as a fiduciary which were owed not to Buyers but to the company and its owners, and I had undertaken potential liability to the owners and SEC if I did not fulfill those obligations.

But what did that all actually mean in this circumstance? I thought an owner of a company might want to know if its investment was being managed by an executive with Alzheimer's disease. But did Buyers? I was no doctor and it was possible my own judgment was clouded by my disagreement with him on the merits. Did I have a duty at this point to advise my fellow directors, other company executives, the SEC or the general public and if so who and when? Who could or should I talk to: my fellow Audit Committee members (who would then have their own obligations based on my questions); the other directors who were inside directors beholden to Buyers; company head Dennis Simonis; Buyers' wife Elizabeth Lindsey? Throughout my career and even in my most difficult engagements I usually got a good sleep; after all, what could I do while I was sleeping. But this one kept me up at night.

I finally decided to start with Elizabeth Lindsey. I had met her but scarcely knew her. I told her of my observations and said: "I'm just calling to see whether you've made any similar observations and, if not, I wish you would look into it very carefully because it's very important."

Lindsey replied: She said: "Well Jim, I've been going out of my wits, because I think you're right. In fact Doc and I went to San Francisco to see some eminent doctors at the Stanford Hospital who are specialists in Alzheimer's and aging. They told him that he has Alzheimer's, he should retire from all business, and he shouldn't drive anymore. But I can't get him to do it. He thinks all doctors are stupid and he's the only guy in the world that knows what's going on and what's good, and we're having hell in our household. Every day he goes to the office and I'm worried about it."

I asked: "Do you know whether Dennis Simonis knows about this?" She said: "I think he suspects this and I think you should call him."

I called up Simonis and told him of my conversation with Lindsey. He said: "Jim, you're absolutely right. He cannot think straight. Do you know he doesn't answer his letters anymore? No matter how important the letter, he tells his secretary to write the answer." I said: "Does his receptionist know all this?" He said: "Yes, she and I talk with each other. She is almost ready to go to the hospital herself because she doesn't know what to do. She needs the job. She really needs the job."

By this time I had involved Ralph Hook, my fellow independent director and Conflicts Committee member. Our first and most immediate concern while we sorted out exactly what to do was that Buyers, as sole owner, would make a deal with someone that would seriously harm the company and its owners. We knew that Buyers thought he knew better than anyone else what to do and didn't think he needed anyone's help to cut a deal and we feared he would act precipitously. I made an arrangement with Simonis and Buyers' secretary: the secretary would not let anyone see Buyers alone on Mauna Loa Macadamia Partners business, but would call Simonis who would sit in on all business meetings.

Could we now get Buyers to sell out altogether and avoid what surely would become necessary if he continued as owner and president? I went to see my brother Dan, whose son, Steve Case, had acquired control of Maui Land & Pineapple Company, then still a large agricultural grower and processor. I told Dan: "Doc Buyers is getting ready to retire and there's nobody really to take over for him. Would MLP consider buying out Buyers?" Dan got Steve's permission to take a look at it.

The next time I went to Hilo I had lunch with Buyers. I said: "Doc, you're about 75 years old. It is my duty as Chair of the Governance Committee to plan for transition in case you or Simonis retires or dies. We also don't know who will end up owning your interest in the company. The best solution may be for you to sell your interest now. Maui Land & Pineapple would be a good buyer and they're interested in discussing a purchase with you."

Buyers said: "Well, Jim, I like owning and running my company." I said: "If you don't like MLP, Doc, then I think I can find another company like Alexander & Baldwin who is already in agriculture and would be a very good owner and manager." Doc said very simply: "Jim, I don't want to sell."

Now what should I do? I had an idea: could the partnership itself (Mauna Loa Macadamia Partners) buy out Buyers' 100% ownership interest in its general partner (Mauna Loa Resources Inc.)? It was unusual for a partnership to own its general partner which in turn manages the partnership, and it would take the action of our board of directors, on which Buyers sat, to approve the purchase. But it could be done fast and without a possibly public search for an external buyer. We researched the question and determined it could be done.

I went back to Buyers: "Doc, we're still looking for a smooth transition. Why don't you let the partnership buy you out for a fair amount. You would leave the company and our limited partners in good hands since all our people already know how to run the business." Buyers said:

"Jim, I already told you, I just like owning and running the business."

To that point I had never confronted Buyers with his Alzheimer's and had hoped we could find another way out of the quandary, but now I had no choice. I spoke directly to Buyers: "Doc: I know, and I know your wife knows, and I know Dennis Simonis knows, and I know your secretary knows, that your doctors have told you that you have Alzheimer's and that you are no longer capable of running this business, so we need to find a way out of this." Doc said: "They're all wrong! It will stay the way it is".

I called a meeting of the entire board of directors except Buyers and advised them of everything. We voted unanimously to remove Buyers as chief executive officer of Mauna Loa Resources Inc. if he did not resign and scheduled a meeting for a few days hence in Hilo at 10:00 A.M. to formalize his removal in that event.

Here was the problem. Buyers was not only chief executive but sole owner of the company and as such he could fire his board of directors on short notice and install a replacement board that would avoid this result and do what he wanted. We assessed that once Buyers knew what was afoot, he would consider and might well pursue that possibility, to the detriment, we had concluded, of the company and the 3,000 or so limited partners in the partnership.

I prepared two press releases. The first one said that J.W.A. (Doc) Buyers, Chief Executive Officer of Mauna Loa Macadamia Partners since 1986, has decided to retire, and recited his many positive accomplishments. The second one said that Mauna Loa's board of directors had regrettably voted to remove Doc Buyers as CEO of the company on the basis that he was no longer capable of discharging his duties.

I called up Buyers' secretary and asked her to schedule a meeting with Buyers for 9:30 A.M. the morning of the board meeting. I chose 9:30 A.M. so he wouldn't have any time to consider the possibility of removing the board before the meeting. I told the secretary it was a private meeting with just me, though we had decided my fellow Conflicts Committee member Ralph Hook would accompany me as a witness. I didn't tell the secretary what the meeting was about though I'm sure she knew; she was very good.

We met at 9:30 A.M. and I told Buyers: "Doc, the board has unanimously lost confidence in you and wants you to resign as chief executive officer and board member at our meeting shortly. We also want you to sell your ownership to the partnership for $750,000." (That had to be part of the deal since otherwise Buyers could undo everything later. He had paid $450,000 for it so that was a good profit for him.)

Buyers said: "Well, I don't want to resign from either and I don't want to sell."

I said: "Doc, we must have a transition in the general partner and the board intends to accomplish that now."

He said: "Well Jim, you're older than I am, why don't you resign?" Then he turned to Hook: "Ralph, you're older than I am too. What's the matter with you two guys?"

I gave Buyers the two press releases: "Doc, we're going to issue one of these press releases right after our board meeting. Which one do you want us to issue?"

After an awkward silence as he considered his position, he said: "Okay, I'll retire and sell. But I want you two to retire from the board today also." That caught me off guard as it was a win for the company. But I said: "We can't do that, Doc, because the board needs stability through this transition. But I promise you that if you do retire and sell now then if it is ok with Ralph he will retire from the board in a year and I will retire in two years." Ralph said okay and Doc said okay.

Buyers went into the board meeting and resigned his CEO and board positions. We released the first press release. Buyers sold his ownership interests to the partnership. I continued to do Mauna Loa's legal work until my retirement in 2012. Ralph Hook and I resigned our board positions as and when promised, though the board invited me to every board meeting as if I was a director until my retirement. When I retired the board gave me a beautiful koa bowl in recognition of my quarter century of service to Mauna Loa.

There are many lessons in my involvement with Mauna Loa, especially our challenges with Doc Buyers. But rather than me relate what I think they are, what do you think? What would you have done in my shoes?

45. Hawaii Energy Part Four: Biofuels

The energy thread that had started with Hilo Electric Light Company in the 1950s and run through Kauai Electric and Windfarms had continued on. Most notably Jerry Sumida, now a renewable energy expert in his own right, represented Puna Geothermal Venture which had pioneered geothermal energy harnessing Hawaii Island's volcanic steam commencing operations in 1993.

Now in the early 2000s a new client retained us to pursue another generation in development of a long-sought largescale renewable energy source for Hawaii, an island state uniquely dependent on imported fossil fuel. That Hawaii had allowed ourselves to become so dependent on fossil fuels and so exposed to the vagaries of world oil prices and shipping disruptions approached tragic as we had some of the best and most diverse renewable energy sources in the world, so these engagements had become for us more than just legal challenges.

The client was Energy Investors Funds. Founded in 1987, EIF was the first national private equity fund devoted exclusively to the independent power and electric utility industry and had raised billions of dollars to deploy in energy-related investments. It was a serious player with the expertise and resources to conceive and manage an alternative energy project and the finances to see it through to stable operations. EIF's Hawaii project was managed by William Garnett.

The project was biofuel-generated power, meaning here the production of energy from the burning of organic mass such as trees and plants. Biofuel as an energy source was not new to Hawaii: the sugar plantations had each generated their own power through the burning of bagasse, the residue after the extraction of juice from sugar cane. What was different with EIF was the scale of the project.

The project started out as a 20 Megawatt power generating plant at Honokaa on Hawaii Island's Hamakua Coast. This was somewhere in the range of a quarter of the island's total energy demand at the time. The attraction of Honokaa was a planted eucalyptus forest of over 10,000 acres just down the coast. Eucalyptus is an optimum biofuel source because the trees grow fast, about seven years to harvest, thus enabling sustainable crop rotation on a large-enough plantation, and burn well.

The forest was on land Bishop Estate had purchased out of the Hamakua Sugar bankruptcy and the trees were coming up on first harvest. EIF aimed to buy the land (which was not going to happen) or lease it from Bishop Estate. EIF would harvest one seventh of the forest every year and replant it; the harvested timber would be trucked to the plant for power generation. Bishop Estate was open to such a lease.

EIF calculated that the new power plant would be by far the lowest cost producer of electricity on the island. Not only was the fuel readily available and sustainable, but the plant was large and modern enough to lend significant economies of scale. There were other independent power generators such as Hamakua Energy Partners' 60 Megawatt plant also at Honokaa which burned naphtha, but EIF's would be the largest.

Like anywhere else in the state except Kauai, Hawaiian Electric held the monopoly on power transmission and distribution to the consumer. A power generator no matter how efficient (perhaps especially if efficient, as it challenged the Hawaiian Electric fossil fuel program), could not operate without an affordable power purchase agreement with, in this case, Hawaiian Electric subsidiary Hawaii Electric Light Company (formerly my prior client Hilo Electric).

HELCO stonewalled us the whole way. Its position was: "We don't need your electricity." HELCO had invested in a new fossil fuel generating plant in Kona and said it wanted to build that up rather than take the EIF power. It kicked us up to Hawaiian Electric.

HECO's president and key operational executives refused to meet with us. They kicked us over to Robert Alm, who was in charge of planning and public affairs. Alm said all the right things: "We think in our planning office that it is a good idea and will recommend it to the executives upstairs."

I'm sure upstairs never intended for this project to see the light of day as it was too threatening to the overall business model and instructed HELCO to continue stonewalling us. Finally the head of HELCO said: "We'll enter into a PPA with you if you build us a transmission line from Honokaa to Kona at a cost of $50 million." That sunk the project financials. EIF had much better uses for its funds in localities that actually wanted renewable energy to work and it pulled the plug. How sad!

EIF still thought the model could work in Hawaii and it turned its attention to Kauai which was not under the thumb of HECO. All but one of its sugar plantations had shut down and there was plentiful available land. Eucalyptus, a remarkably diverse and resilient tree, could grow well there. The overall business plan was the same as on Hawaii Island only on a smaller scale given Kauai's smaller population (and the fact that Kauai already had tapped alternative energy sources like hydro to a greater extent than the other islands). We would buy or lease enough land to plant a seven-year rotation eucalyptus forest, build and operate a 25 Megawatt plant, the most efficient on the island, and sell the power to Kauai Electric.

Kauai Electric, probably on reflection due largely to the individual motivations of individual directors, was pursuing a different model of a whole bunch of mini 3 Megawatt hydro or 2 Megawatt something else here and there throughout the island. This made no real sense given the alternative of a larger and more stable power generation source. But rather than tell us no straight out, they said: "You don't have any land for your forest. Buy or lease the land and we'll talk with you."

By then Grove Farm had purchased the Lihue Sugar lands from Amfac so it was practically the only game in town for the acreage we needed. It had thousands and thousands of acres lying idle.

We made Grove Farm a very good offer to lease. Besides a greater economic return than it was getting or could reasonably hope to get during the lease term (at least for agricultural uses, which was the land's classification and thus permitted use), we said: "As long as we have a certain minimum acreage to start with and can maintain that minimum, you can take land out of the lease anytime you want for any reason including residential or commercial if you can get the zoning."

Grove Farm's president, Warren Haruki, stonewalled us, saying: "I can't do it; we don't have any land available." We researched the former Lihue Sugar lands which were almost 6,000 acres: title was completely clear as there were no outstanding leases and Grove Farm did have land available.

Why did Grove Farm decline the leases and perhaps worse give us an inaccurate reason? I never did fully find out. Perhaps the island ties between Grove Farm and the directors of Kauai Electric were too strong.

But we did learn later that Grove Farm had given out one year revocable permits on much of its land to many different permittees including business and government leaders (meaning they could utilize the land on a year-to-year basis unless and until Grove Farm terminated that use). Grove Farm must have calculated that it was safer to continue the status quo than to lease its land to EIF for a major source of alternative energy for Kauai.

Without land for a eucalyptus forest there was no project and EIF pulled the plug. It had much better uses for its funds in supportive localities. How sad!

EIF did remain interested in Hawaii and in 2004 acquired Hamakua Energy Partners and its existing PPA with HELCO. It grew into a fund with around $4 billion in assets but did not further consider largescale investment in Hawaii renewable energy.

Observations:

(1) Throughout the decades of our representation of renewable energy companies (partially enabled fortuitously by never representing Hawaiian Electric), renewable energy in Hawaii has grown but slowly and often painfully. Today we stand at close to a quarter of all energy production being renewables. Kauai Electric has in fact done better than the Hawaiian Electric companies at about 42%, and HELCO is at over 50% though only because Puna Geothermal Venture itself produces a quarter of Hawaii Island's power. Wind is now at about 6% and biomass at about 3%. I wish I could regard this as solid progress, but I look back mostly on lost opportunities that foundered mainly on Hawaiian Electric's rearguard action funded by millions expended on lobbying and public relations efforts. While I generally think businesses know best what's good for their future and how to get there, this is one case in which change can only really come from government and the community.

(2) How many times in the course of history does the first inventor, investor, innovator fail, only to have the next generation succeed? I had many first-timers in many endeavors as clients throughout my career, some of whom did succeed but many of whom did not. Hopefully I gave each my best effort regardless of chances or outcome, and in any event each such engagement gave me the opportunity to become the expert that the next generations would consider engaging as well.

46. Just for the Love of It: Waimea Valley

The ahupuaa of Waimea on the north tip of Oahu is one of the greatest in all the islands. From Puu Kainapuaa at elevation 2,400 feet on the Koolau summit above Laie and Hauula, Waimea sweeps west almost ten miles as the crow flies through three separate stream valleys in the most remote and wildest part of the island. The streams, spilling over waterfalls, converge into two and then one, Waimea River, on the fertile flatlands near the coast before flowing into Waimea Bay with its world-famous beach and big wave surfing site. The surrounding bluffs offer spectacular views over the North Shore and Pacific Ocean.

In ancient times Waimea was a classic ahupuaa, from its mauka forests through its lowland agriculture to its fishery. From the 11th century on it was known as the Valley of the Priests as it had been awarded to the kahuna nui (high priests) of the Paao line. Kamehameha the Great had confirmed its status when, on conquering Oahu in 1797, he awarded the ahupuaa to Hewahewa, his top spiritual adviser and the last kahuna nui of the line. Hewahewa was at Kamehameha's side when he died in Kona in 1819. He later renounced the religion of old and converted to Christianity, moving back to Waimea where he died in 1837 and is buried.

Waimea is thus a place not only of great physical beauty and natural abundance but of deep history and spiritual power. Ownership of most of the ahupuaa was awarded to Hewahewa's granddaughter at the time of the Great Mahele but, like so many others of her time, she borrowed heavily against it and eventually lost ownership in the late 1800s. Castle & Cooke acquired the entire 5,600 acre ahupuaa in the early 1900s and still through Dole Food owns the mauka 3,700 acres which form part of the U.S. Army's training range.

The makai and more accessible 1,900 acres of Waimea Valley remained intact and were utilized for ranching and farming until 1971, when Castle & Cooke sold it to Charles Pietsch III, a local developer. Pietsch owned a Hawaii company called Attractions Hawaii which had opened Sea Life Park at Makapuu Point in the 1960s. Pietsch envisioned a similar operation for Waimea called Waimea Valley Adventure Park. His business plan was to: (a) build a restaurant near the shoreline road, a road up to beautiful Waimea Falls and a railroad farther up into the valley; (b) protect ancient cultural sites; (c) develop a world-class botanical garden with native and imported plants; and (d) subdivide the land and sell off lots throughout the valley and on the bluffs for luxury vacation homes.

Enter, with particular relevance to this story, the Hawaii Land Use Act, a revolutionary and still-one-of-its-kind law enacted in 1963. Under the law all land in Hawaii was and is classified into four categories: Urban, Rural, Agriculture and Conservation. County zoning can specify the details of land use but must generally comply with the state land use designations which match their descriptions. The law was and is administered by the State Land Use Commission, one of the real levers of power in Hawaii especially as land use reclassifications can instantaneously turn lower value lands as in Conservation or Agriculture into extremely valuable land as in Urban. (The reclassification of the former sugar lands of Oahu's Ewa Plain to residential and commercial uses is perhaps the best example.)

Virtually all of Attractions Hawaii's Waimea land, like Castle & Cooke's mauka portion, was classified Conservation. This brought it under the jurisdiction of the Hawaii State Department of Land and Natural Resources. As administered by DLNR there were very limited conservation-related uses that could be made of the land. Further, there could be only one single family residential dwelling per Conservation-classified zoning lot. Virtually all of Attractions Hawaii's Waimea land had survived from the Mahele award as just one lot, and subdivision of existing zoning lots was strictly controlled by DLNR. In short, the permissible uses of the land were limited and the options few, all of which added up to a lower value.

Attractions Hawaii got some limited exceptions that allowed it to open the restaurant, and it built the road to Waimea Falls, protected some cultural sites and developed a fine botanical garden. With that it opened Waimea Valley Adventure Park in 1975 which by the 1980s had grown into one of Oahu's top rated attractions. But the business declined in the 1990s and Attractions Hawaii never received the necessary approvals to build the railroad or subdivide and reclassify the land to allow for luxury residential homes.

By 1996 Attractions Hawaii was in serious financial trouble with a substantial loan owing to Bank of Hawaii and declining revenues. When the bank moved to foreclose, Pietsch declared bankruptcy. Christian Wolffer, a New York investment banker and venture capitalist, bought the company from Pietsch and paid down a good chunk of the bank loan. Wolffer's basic intent with Waimea Valley was to pursue Pietsch's business plan of an adventure park and luxury home development. But he didn't get the development approvals either and with the park continuing to lose money, Wolffer tried to sell Waimea Valley for first $25 million and then $19 million. When there were no takers, Wolffer again put Attractions Hawaii into bankruptcy.

As the attempts to develop and/or sell Waimea Valley continued, they were strongly opposed by a coalition of North Shore community groups who wanted to "Keep the Country", environmental, preservation and naturalist groups who wanted to preserve the natural resources of the valley, and native Hawaiian groups who wanted to protect the cultural heritage of the ahupuaa. They turned to political advocacy and in 2001 succeeded in getting the City and County of Honolulu to initiate a formal court action to acquire Waimea Valley by eminent domain (condemnation) for permanent natural park and preservation purposes.

There are only two basic questions in an eminent domain action. The first is whether the proposed taking is for a legitimate public use. That had been the heart of the dispute in the Hawaii Land Reform Act case we had earlier taken to the U. S. Supreme Court, but a taking for park purposes was such a classic public use that this question was never in dispute.

The second question is how much the government entity must pay the owner for the condemned property. The answer is fair market value, meaning the price a reasonable buyer and reasonable seller both motivated to achieve the transaction and acting at arms length would agree to pay as of the date the condemnation action is filed. But there is a crucial qualification when determining fair market value, which is that value is calculated according to the actual legally permissible uses of the property at that point, not what the buyer might be able to do in the future if it was able to get approvals to expand the permissible uses. What that meant at Waimea was that Attractions Hawaii was entitled to the value of the land as one zoning lot classified conservation, not as if it were subdivided into many lots and classified for more expansive use.

In condemnation actions, the condemning authority (here the City and

County) is entitled to take immediate possession of the land if there is no dispute over public use if it deposits its good faith estimate of fair market value into court pending the final determination of fair market value payable to the owner. The City and County estimated the fair market value of Waimea Valley at $5.2 million based on the independent conclusion of a professional appraiser, deposited that amount into court, took possession of the land and leased it out to the Audubon Society for operation.

The court case wound through various steps and issues for four years. Attractions Hawaii and Wolffer were represented by well-respected and well-connected Honolulu attorney Bill McCorriston, whose firm the Mukai brothers had joined when they left Carlsmith. The City was represented by its Corporation Counsel; then-Mayor Mufi Hannemann was heavily involved. The judge ordered confidential mediation and finally scheduled trial on fair market value for the end of 2005.

In preparation for trial the City obtained two other professional appraisals to go with the earlier $5 million appraisal; they came in at $8 million and $3 million. The owner, however, never got a real appraisal; he only got a value projection based on the assumption that the land would be reclassified to Urban and subdivided and that the resulting luxury houselots would sell for a high price. His projection came in at $18 million. This projection was not an appraisal that would have been allowed to be considered at trial because it calculated fair market value not as the land was but as the owner hoped it would be in the future.

In November 2005 Mayor Hannemann and his Corporation Counsel announced to the City Council that they had reached a confidential tentative settlement with Wolffer. City Council approval was required and requested, and a committee of the whole (all Councilmembers) met behind closed doors and voted 5-4 to recommend the settlement to the full Council for final approval.

When details of the recommended settlement were made public, the community groups and much of the general public were outraged. For the settlement called for the City and County to acquire the makai portion of Waimea Valley at minimal cost in return for Wolffer reacquiring the mauka portion for development. Clearly Wolffer and McCorriston had succeeded in scaring the City and County into believing it would be required to pay an exorbitant amount for the land which it could not afford if the matter went to trial, and then offered to fix the manufactured problem for them. Hannemann himself had apparently advised the City Council that the potential liability the City faced at trial was far more than even the owner's $18 million projection. It appeared that either Hannemann and his lawyer had been outmaneuvered or worse had been coopted.

University of Hawaii Law School professor Denise Antolini headed the Stewards of Waimea Valley, the umbrella community organization. She knew of my work on the Hawaii Land Reform Act and asked me to represent the Stewards in opposing the proposed settlement. I took on the engagement pro bono (literally for the public good), meaning essentially at no charge because I too thought they were right, I too wanted Waimea Valley preserved, and I felt I could help.

The Stewards' first instinct was to contest the proposed settlement in court. But, I explained, that would be highly difficult if not impossible as if the court-appointed mediator recommended a settlement that all parties supported and the City Council had approved it would be very unlikely the judge would turn it down. I argued that the solution was political, that we had a far better chance of persuading the Council majority to change their votes if they understood the breadth and depth of community opposition and further that the Mayor and his lawyer were dead wrong on the law and the City exposure and thus on the City's negotiating position. The Stewards agreed.

The Council scheduled a special meeting for final consideration for December 7, 2005 and we went to work on presenting our case. Dozens of supporters showed up on the hearing day, all wearing the Stewards' bright red tee shirts. We had developed about ten basic arguments against the settlement and these were apportioned out among the testifiers.

The hearing started on an unusual albeit auspicious note. Normal practice for a legislative body such as the Council when discussing sensitive legal issues is to go into executive session, meaning the public is kicked out and the Council talks privately with its lawyers. The Corporation Counsel requested executive session and one Councilmember made the necessary formal motion. But not one other Council member even seconded the motion; it thus failed and the proceedings remained fully open and public.

The testimony commenced. In all some 75 members of the public testified personally and a further 160 submitted written testimony opposing the settlement. In my concluding personal testimony I told the council: "Mayor Hannemann is telling you that if you don't settle this now and instead go to trial you might end up having to pay much more even than the owner's $18 million projection. But he's wrong because first the maximum will be the owner's projected $18 million and second the judge will likely throw even that out since it does not comply with the rules. Don't let them scare you; you have a winning hand and should just say no and take it to trial. Chances are they'll settle on more reasonable terms rather than take a chance on the trial."

One by one the Councilmembers spoke in opposition to the proposed settlement. When the final vote was called the five members who had previously supported the settlement switched their votes; the final vote was 9-0 against and the settlement was rejected. We had won! The fair market value would now be set by either trial or another negotiated settlement, but Wolffer would not be able to acquire and develop any portion of Waimea Valley.

Mayor Hannemann, backtracking and probably trying to save face, now told the Council that he would undertake the further negotiations. I don't know why the Council trusted him to do that and didn't instead say they'd do it themselves or retain their own lawyer to do so, but they turned it back over to him.

A month later a settlement was reached under which Wolffer was paid $14.1 million for Waimea Valley. In all likelihood Wolffer and McCorriston secretly thought this was a very good price under the circumstances.

Payment was orchestrated not by Hannemann but by the Trust for Public Land, a private nonprofit dedicated to "creating parks and protecting land for people". It came from the City and County of Honolulu (the $5.1 million already paid), the U. S. Army ($3.5 million in federal funds linked back to training impacts), the DLNR ($1.6 million in state preservation funds), the Audubon Society ($1 million) and the Office of Hawaiian Affairs, a constitutionally-mandated autonomous state agency charged with improving the wellbeing of native Hawaiians. OHA had long sought to purchase Waimea Valley and took over ownership, with the Audubon Society continuing its management role. The settlement also granted the City and County a conservation and preservation easement over the valley, protecting it permanently.

Waimea Valley was saved. OHA took over full management in 2008 and has stewarded it since. It was a good cause and a good result.

Lesson One: A lawyer's job is to figure out how to turn what seems improbable into the possible. Lesson Two: A lawyer must develop and utilize whatever tools are in the tool kit to make the improbable possible. Lesson Three: Law is a wonderful profession to utilize in achievement of the public good.

47. Full Circle: The Dissolution of C. Brewer

C. Brewer & Co., Ltd., the original member of the Big Five, was founded by Captain James Hunnewell in 1826, just 38 years after the "discovery" of Hawaii by Captain James Cook and 16 years after Kamehameha the Great united the islands under his rule. Its original business was the sandalwood trade with China. Captain Charles Brewer joined as a partner in 1835 and, as sandalwood was harvested close to extinction, moved the company into whaling ship supply and general merchandise.

As whaling in turn ran its course and sugar commenced its century-and-a-half run, Brewer, like the other Big Five, became agent for the small plantations that cropped up across Hawaii before moving into ownership and consolidation. By the 1920s Brewer handled a quarter of all Hawaii sugar and was one of Hawaii's largest landowners.

In the late 1950s Brewer diversified into macadamia nuts and in the next few decades grew into one of the world's top producers and processors. As sugar faded it sought to diversify further into various Hawaii products and to export its tropical agricultural expertise around the world.

The careers and lives of generations of Hawaii's people were intertwined with Brewer, from downtown Honolulu throughout communities stretching from Naalehu at the southernmost point of Hawaii Island to Kilauea at the northernmost point of Kauai. They ranged from immigrant fieldworkers whose children and grandchildren became the leaders of Hawaii to the true sugar men like my brother Bill and up to the senior executive corps.

This was true of Carlsmith as well, dating back to Brewer's acquisition of Carlsmith founder David Hitchcock's Hilo Coast sugar plantation in the late 1800s. Carl Carlsmith and Wendell Carlsmith after him represented the sugar companies through much of the first half of the twentieth century and beyond. I did the same on various occasions throughout my own, and later in my career commenced a quarter century of service to Brewer subsidiary Mauna Loa Macadamia Partners. And our own family made a run at acquiring Brewer's sugar operations.

Doc Buyers and his hui of Princeton Tiger and local investors bought out IU in 1986. Now in late 2000 Buyers' co-investors had gone close to fifteen years without any distributions or other returns on their investments as virtually all profit had been plowed back into debt reduction and their patience was running out. They may well have begun to question Buyers' capacity to lead Brewer as was then similarly occurring to me. They decided to sell out to convert their investments into greater liquidity elsewhere and retained me to assist.

Buyers fought it all the way. At one point the Brewer board found a buyer with ready funds to buy out all investors at a fair purchase price and we entered into a purchase and sale agreement to that effect. Buyers sabotaged the deal and the prospective purchaser filed a lawsuit for breach of contract against Brewer which we had to settle unfavorably.

This led a majority of the board and investors to a major decision. Rather than further pursue a sale of the whole company, they would dissolve it. This meant that its individual parts would be sold off over time to pay off debts and then for final distributions to owners, and when all of that was concluded, all assets sold, debts paid, other liabilities removed and profits distributed, the company would cease to exist. They knew as did I from the dissolution of InterIsland Resorts that the sale of parts rather than the whole could prove much more profitable properly implemented.

The board charged me with preparing a plan of dissolution for a formal vote. At Brewer I worked with general counsel Alan Kugle and chief financial officer Kent Lucien. Buyers was aware of the effort but was not in charge. At Carlsmith I was ably assisted by Joe Goldcamp, who was both a lawyer and a certified public accountant. He had spent his career on the accounting side with Price Waterhouse and had done all of Brewer's tax work for decades. An archaic Price Waterhouse policy which was not uncommon with the accounting firms of the time had required him to retire at age sixty and he had joined Carlsmith. We all worked with the major Brewer investors, most of whom were on the East Coast.

We prepared a full set of dissolution documents, the major element of which was a complete plan of dissolution laying out in detail how it would all be achieved. The plan called for an executive committee of four directors to supervise day-to-day company operations during the liquidation. Buyers would no longer be President and Chief Executive Officer of Brewer; he would continue as Chair of the Board without executive authority, and would retire as an executive and commence earning generous retirement pay.

A formal board meeting to approve the plan and the dissolution of Brewer was set for May 2, 2001. All fifteen or so directors attended, including Buyers and his daughter Jane, an executive at investment banker Morgan Stanley. I outlined the proposed plan and the accountants spelled out the financial implications further.

I wondered what Buyers would say and what Jane Buyers would do. The vote was unanimous and Kugle and Lucien were appointed joint chief executive officers. I believe Buyers' old Princeton friends and perhaps Jane also had persuaded him that the board would vote for dissolution and he was better off accepting the inevitable. No doubt there were many in the room who believed it was time to close the Brewer/Buyers chapter. I still had the Mauna Loa Macadamia Partners chapter with Buyers recounted above to close.

Doc Buyers died in 2006 and was buried back home in Pennsylvania. He was lauded by many as a champion of diversified agriculture who wisely steered Brewer out of its sugar age and as a visionary in many areas, and he clearly mentored and influenced many people who went on to their own careers of accomplishment. He deserved all of that. But among many complex people I worked with throughout my career he was one of the most complex, and I saw and had to deal with another side which I have tried to portray fairly. The real purpose of doing so is the lesson to be learned: it is always possible for any one person to have some good and some bad traits, and in fact that is the case with most of us.

From the 2001 dissolution vote on until my retirement in 2012 I represented Brewer on virtually all matters except dissolution-related litigation. It was a huge and complex undertaking.

Brewer still had major holdings across Hawaii and beyond in diverse industries. There were about twelve subsidiaries including sugar, macadamia nuts, diversified agriculture, transportation and trucking, chemicals and fertilizers, stevedoring and water, plus various landholdings, an interest in C&H Sugar and other assets. There were also various liabilities to be resolved, ranging from bank debt to employee retirement obligations to open workers compensation awards to pending and threatened litigation.

We got to work. We either sold the subsidiaries or merged them back into Brewer. We sold off the land, perhaps 400 separate transactions of various sizes in all. We bought annuities to assure employee retirement benefits. We negotiated and settled contracts, brought and defended litigation to close out claims, and paid off debts. It was messy and took much longer than anticipated.

We got most of it done before I retired. Alan Kugle continued on as the sole Brewer employee responsible for completing the dissolution. Periodic distributions were made to owners over the years as reasonably available and as Kugle worked through resolution of a few last disputes. In July 2017 Kugle resolved the disputes, paid final expenses and made final distributions to owners, enough for them to make a decent return on their investments. The dissolution was complete and Brewer passed into history.

That (to go with the last shipment of Hawaiian sugar which arrived at C&H Sugar in Crockett, California in January 2017 from Hawaii's last sugar plantation) truly marks the end of an era. Perhaps it is appropriate that it also marked the end of my own long career.

48. Closing the Door

The Carlsmith partnership agreement required that once partners turned seventy their fellow partners had to vote by a two-thirds majority annually (and anonymously) to continue them for another year or else they would have to leave the partnership. Although not as extreme as the straight sixty-and-out policy of some of the accounting firms of the time, the provision had the same well-intentioned purpose of a safety check against partners who had overstayed their welcome or were no longer up to the job.

I don't recall whether I drafted that provision into the original Carlsmith partnership agreement back in 1959 at the age of 39. But if I did, 1990 when I turned seventy would have been a case of being hoisted on my own petard. Luckily my partners voted that year to continue me as a partner for another year, and continued to vote me back annually for another decade and a half. It became a running joke, as my partners would come up to me after every annual partnership meeting first expressing sincere but concerned best wishes for a successful vote and then great relief that I had made it again.

As already somewhat recounted, the years after seventy brought some of the most complicated and intense challenges and some of the sweetest successes of my career. They were also some of my most lucrative as I was responsible for major clients and major engagements. So my partners were continuing me not just out of charity but because I remained a major income generator for the firm.

In 2004, as part of a national program administered by the Administration on Aging, I received Hawaii's Senior Citizen of the Year Award. I travelled to Washington, D.C. to join fellow awardees from around the country in both celebrating our awards and making the point that citizens can continue lives of contribution and fulfillment deep into their senior years. I was graciously received by Hawaii's Congressional delegation, and one of them, U.S. Congressman Ed Case, even took me on a personal tour of the Capitol and came to my award dinner.

Why was I able to continue my own career so deep into my senior years? Part of it may have been basic genetics, for I did not face any major illnesses or other debilitating circumstances throughout. But aside from that there were two major factors.

The first was that, dating back to my readings of the ancient Greeks on my Navy destroyer in the Western Pacific in World War Two, I strove throughout to live a life of balance. Their lesson, which I sought to follow, was that the ideal life is one of diverse interests nourishing mind and body. My time and energy went into my work, my family, my community and myself, the latter meaning regular physical and mental exercise. As one example, throughout those decades I kept up a regular weekly paddle tennis game and sailed competitively out of the Kaneohe Yacht Club. While the stereotype of success is the hard-charging, work-obsessed, 24-7 professional, the real secret to success over time is balance.

The second was simply that I loved my work and wanted to get up every day and get to it again. The classic idea of retirement was not appealing.

By the mid-2000s my body started to catch up with me. All those decades of tennis, pounding around the sailboat and other physical activity had taken their toll and I just wasn't able to move around as well. And in my mid-eighties I didn't have the same overall energy level as prior decades.

In mid-2006 I resigned from the partnership and became Of Counsel to the firm (meaning essentially an employee rather than owner). I felt that I could continue on productively if I moved to an expectation of halftime work, and as I had established and administered the rule that partners and associates needed to work fulltime I couldn't very well ask to go to part-time and remain a partner.

I made Carlsmith an offer they couldn't refuse: I would move to Of Counsel status; I would come in every morning and be available whether or not I had work; I would work beyond the morning if and when needed by my clients or the firm; they would pay me a salary which was less than a beginning associate; and they would give me a bonus after every year was over if they felt I'd earned extra. Karl Kobayashi, who was then taking over as Carlsmith's seventh Chair of the Executive Committee, graciously accepted, and even threw in that I could stay in my beautiful corner office of over three decades.

It turned out to be a good deal all around. I remained pretty busy and often worked past mid-day. I also remained a substantial income generator for the firm though usually without an annual bonus so they did well on me. I guess I could have gotten upset over that but it wasn't worth it: I was doing what I wanted to do, and what was I going to do, lateral somewhere else or go out on my own?

Much of my time was in transitioning my cases and clients over to Carlsmith partners. I would usually get the partner up to speed on the engagement and involved with the client before ceasing direct client contact and remaining available for questions. Perhaps most rewarding, besides not having to go to any more partnership meetings or attend to firm management, was the opportunity to train up a whole new generation of lawyers, who humored and maybe even really listened to my "Well, I had a similar problem back in the 50s …" responses to their questions.

There was no special timetable for full retirement. After a few years I had virtually all of my clients transitioned over and was hearing less and less from the clients and partners. I suppose I was trying to finish my last big job, the dissolution of C. Brewer, but that dragged on longer than expected. Finally my body had had enough as it became too difficult to walk between my parking and the office and just around the place. Perhaps I could have been picked up and dropped off every day and kept going, but it was just time to go.

I retired from Carlsmith Ball at the age of 92 on December 31, 2012, sixty three years after I had received my Hawaii license and sixty-one years after I had joined Carlsmith in Hilo. As a retirement gift my Carlsmith ohana gave me an exquisitely crafted marine sextant to be sure I could keep fixing my position and continuing on course. I closed the door and went home.

INDEX

A

Walter Ackerman 58
Admiral Thomas 149
American Samoa 156, 194
Asa Akinaka 178, 241
Ala Moana Shopping Center 82-84
Alexander & Baldwin (A&B) 24, 41, 151, 158-161, 194, 221, 257
William P. Alexander 7
Alexander Young Hotel 114
Gerry Allison 178
Robert Alm 261
Aloha Airlines 113, 149, 218
Aloha Towers 178-180, 241
American Factors (Amfac) 7-8, 24, 41, 98-100, 141-142, 144, 151, 158-162, 167, 210, 262
Page Anderson 8, 10
Martin Anderson 206
Anderson, Wrenn & Jenks 2, 7-8, 20, 48
Jim Andrasick 251-252
Julie Andrews 109
Ann-Margret 109
Garner Anthony 206
Denise Antolini 268
Architects Hawaii 146
Clinton (Tink) Ashford 236-238
Ashford & Wriston 236
Association of Owners of Makaha Towers 80
Charles and Minnie Merriam Atherton 2
Attractions Hawaii 264-267
Audubon Society 267, 269

B

Duke Bainum 241-242
Baldwin/Cameron Family 194
Joseph Ball 248-249
Bank of America 99
Bank of England 86-87, 153

Bank of Hawaii 8, 57-58, 94, 97-99, 142, 166, 170, 228-229, 231, 247, 266
Bank of Maui 57
Bernie Bays 195, 236, 238, 248
Bays Lung Rose & Holma 248
Bechtel 188
Mary Ellen (Casey) Beck 227
Cora A. Benneson 19
Beverly Hills, California 249
Big Five 24-25, 38-39, 42, 48, 53-55, 70, 98, 150-151, 158, 214, 223, 226, 229, 233, 271
Bishop Estate (Estate of Bernice Pauahi Bishop/Kamehameha Schools) 102, 105, 144, 146, 187, 221, 226, 229, 233, 235-239, 241-242, 253, 261
Biltmore Hotel 73
Blaisdell Hotel 72
Boston, Massachusetts 5-6
James W. Boyle 80, 135, 166, 168, 193, 208
Charles Brewer 271
Harry Bridges 39
Edward Broadbent 7
Brobeck Phleger and Harrison 38
Marjorie Bronster 254-255
Brooklyn Navy Yard, New York 4
Edmund (Pat) Brown 248-249
Brown Family Investment Group 109
Lois Bruce 235
Robert Bunn 144-145
John A. Burns 51-52, 144
Jane Buyers 273
J.W.A. (Doc) Buyers 204, 223, 226, 231, 250-251, 253-259, 272-273

C

Russell Cades 206
Cades Schutte 7, 41, 55, 66, 110, 144, 214
California & Hawaiian Sugar Company (C&H) 55, 214-216, 218, 227-228, 230-231, 273-274
Ernest R. Cameron 48, 59, 62, 73, 75, 127, 177
Cameron Tennent & Dunn 59-60, 73, 107, 115, 177

Campbell Estate 184, 187
Captain Cook Coffee Company 61, 106
David Carey 198-199
Carlsmith Ball (Carlsmith) x, passim
Carlsmith & Carlsmith 21, 35
Carlsmith, Carlsmith & Cox 9, 11, 41
Carlsmith, Carlsmith, Wichman & Case 114, 116
Carlsmith, Wichman, Case, Mukai & Ichiki 245
Carlsmith, Ball, Wichman, Murray, Case, Mukai & Ichiki 249
Carl S. Carlsmith (Carl Schurz Smith) 2, 20-22, 25, 30-31, 34-36, 53, 75, 124, 271
Donn W. Carlsmith 112-114, 116-117, 119, 124, 131, 135, 244
Marilyn Carlsmith 165
Merrill L. Carlsmith 9, 21-22, 34-36, 41, 44, 51, 67, 112-116, 119, 124, 165, 167
Nelle Wood Carlsmith 20, 30, 34, 36
Robert (Bobby) Carlsmith 167
C. Wendell Carlsmith 9-11, 21-22, 25, 34-44, 48-55, 59-62, 65-66, 73-76, 85-87, 93-99, 103, 105, 112-116, 119-121, 124, 126, 131, 134-139, 151-155, 157, 162, 166-167, 177, 194-196, 208, 249, 271
C. Brewer & Co., Ltd. (Brewer) 8, 24, 45, 106, 162, 166, 223, 250-254, 271-274, 277
Catholic Church 49-50
Aderial Hebard (Hib) Case 2, 7, 13, 74, 228
A.H and Lucia O. Case 12
Case & Case 2
Daniel Hebard Case 2, 4, 9, 12, 20, 57
Daniel Hibbard (Dan) Case 3, 7, 13, 225, 227, 229, 257
Ed Case 15, 136-137, 237, 275
Elizabeth (Betty) McConnell Case 3, 13
John Case 15, 136-137
Kathryn Merriam Case 2
Case Kay & Lynch 225
Case Lombardi & Pettit 7
Marie Case 227
Russell Case 15, 136
Steve Case 257
Suzanne Catherine Espenett (Suzi) Case 6, 11, 14-15, 91-93, 109, 121- 122, 136-137, 170, 172, 179, 182, 203, 206, 208

Suzanne D. Case 15, 136-138
William B. (Bill) Case 3, 5, 13, 162, 223, 227-228, 271
Charles Cassidy 206
Castle & Cooke 8, 24, 65-66, 106, 151, 188, 226-230, 264-265
Castle Ranch 238
Centex Corporation 104
Sam Chang 88-89, 127, 141, 143, 148, 169-170, 172, 176
Chiang Kai-shek 88, 169, 173-174
Debbie Child 93
Walter D. Child, Sr. 72-77, 93-94, 96-98, 128, 139, 209
Walter D. (Dudley) Child, Jr. 93-99, 129, 139-141, 143-145, 148, 208-211
John Chinen 232
Citizens Utilities 158-161, 163-164, 183
City and County of Honolulu 80, 102, 240, 242, 266-269
City Bank Building 168
Charles E. Clapp 5, 109
Walter Chuck 206
Coco Palms 94-95, 158
Colonial Sugar Refining Company (CSR Limited) 181
Commonwealth Bank of Australia 177, 179-180
Connecticut General Life Insurance Company 142-143
Continental Airlines 209
James Cook 271
Cornell University 2
Cornell University School of Hotel Administration 93, 210
County of Hawaii 79-80
Gilbert E. Cox 41, 54-55, 135
Crockett, California 55, 214, 227, 274
Peter Currie 179-180

D

Darling Company/Family 180-181
Dartmouth College 165
Geoffrey Clive Davies 150-152, 155-156
Theophilus (Theo) H. Davies 150, 212
Dean Witter (Morgan Stanley) 66, 273
Paul and Anita De Domenico 110-111
Democratic Revolution 51, 54, 234

C. W. Dickey 139
Dillinghams 48-50, 52, 61, 78, 85, 119-120, 138, 150-152, 154-157, 166, 212
Dillingham Entities 48-50, 61, 82-83, 101-104, 113, 120, 137,
Benjamin Franklin Dillingham 48
Benjamin F. Dillingham II 48, 50, 102-104
Lowell S. Dillingham 48, 50, 102, 120-121, 125, 151-152, 154
Walter F. Dillingham 48, 104, 125
Nelson Doi 54-55
Dole Food Company 226, 229, 264
James Dole 226
Herb Dunn 59

E

Edgewater Hotel 139
Troy Elmore 151
Energy Investors Funds 260-263
Evanston, Illinois 3
Ewa Plantation 226-227

F

John B. Fernandes 160-161
Finance Factors 148
First Bank of Hilo 57
First Boston Corp. 189-191
First Hawaiian Bank 187
First National Bank of Wailuku 57
Bill Fleming 206
Hiram Fong 148
Abraham Fornander 232
4-H Farmers of America 72
Freshfields 86-87, 152-153, 155-156
Fujimoto Brothers 112
Wally Fujiyama 206

G

Guy Gadbois 109
William Garnett 260
Janet Ginoza 200, 203

Glass-Steagall Act of 1933 177
Go! Airlines 218
Joe Goldcamp 272
Gold Coast, Australia 177
Goodsill Anderson Quinn and Stifel (Goodsill Anderson) 2, 7, 20, 48, 58, 67, 82, 85, 103, 251-253
Marshall Goodsill 137, 206
Government of Japan 21
Don Graham 82-84
Grand Hyatt Hotel 73
Gray Line 75, 95, 208, 210
Great Mahele 23, 96, 212, 233, 264
Hod Greeley 195, 236, 247
Greenwell Family 144-146
Grove Farm Plantation 2-3, 7-8, 23, 64, 74, 162, 262-263
George Grubb 194
Guam 166, 174, 194-195, 244-245
Guantanamo Bay, Cuba 4
Guenoc Winery 113

H

Halekulani Hotel 96
Jack Hall 39-40, 51-52, 126, 166
Hakalau Sugar 62, 108
Hamakua Energy Partners 261, 263
Hamakua Sugar 110, 212-222, 227-228, 261
Hamilton Standard 188-191
Hana Sugar 108
Mufi Hannemann 242, 267-269
Warren Haruki 262
Harvard Law School 5,-6, 8-9, 82, 109, 112, 163
Harvard Business School 5, 148
Willard C. Hatch 80-81
Hawaii Hospitality Hall of Fame 140-141, 210
Hawaii Housing Authority 232, 235-237
Hawaii Land Reform Act 232, 234-236, 238-240, 243, 266, 268
Hawaii Land Use Act 265
Hawaii Meat Packers 217-218
Hawaii Planing Mill (HPM) 113

Hawaii State Department of Commerce and Consumer Affairs 66, 76, 98
Hawaii State Department of Land and Natural Resources 265, 269
Hawaii State Employees Retirement System 62
Hawaii State Office of Hawaiian Affairs 269
Hawaii State Public Utilities Commission (PUC) 67-68, 158-161
Hawaiian Airlines 71, 73-74, 218
Hawaiian Commercial & Sugar (HC&S) 221
Hawaiian Agronomics 224
Hawaiian Dredging & Construction Company 48, 85-86, 141, 146, 152
Hawaiian Electric (HECO) 8, 64, 68-69, 75, 160, 162-164, 183, 187-191, 261-263
Hawaiian Holiday 110, 212, 252
Hawaiian Host, Inc. 255
Hawaiian Pineapple Company 11, 120, 151, 226
Hawaiian Telephone 8
Hawaiian Trust Co., Ltd. 134
Dr. Guy Haywood 137-138
David Heenan 213
Christopher Hemmeter 210
Helen Henderson 65
Jack Henderson 65
James (Jim or Kimo) Henderson 65
"Babe" Henshaw 3
Robert (Bob) Herkes 93-94
Hershey Foods 255
Hewahewa 264
Jack Hewettson 228
William H. (Doc) Hill 65, 68
Wes Hillendahl 170
Hilo Electric Light Company (HELCO) 41, 64-69, 76, 78, 137, 158, 183, 260-261, 263
Hilo Gas Company 91
Hilo High School 34, 112
Hilo Hotel 71
Hilo Iron Works 36
Hilo Sugar 65, 223-227, 231
Hilo Womens Club 91
Hilo Yacht Club 88

Hilton 210
Hilton Hawaiian Village 141
Hind-Clarke Dairy 61
Robert Hind 61, 104-105
Robert Hind Estate, Limited 61-63, 79, 104-107
Robert Robson Hind 61
Robson Hind 61
Hitchcock & Hitchcock 19, 28
Hitchcock & Smith 20, 28
Hitchcock & Co. Sugar Plantation 24, 271
Almeda E. Hitchcock 19, 27-28, 134
David H. Hitchcock 18, 20-21, 24, 26, 28, 35, 271
D. Howard Hitchcock 18
Edward G. Hitchcock 24
Harvey R. Hitchcock 18
Don Ho 141
Jack Hoffman 10
Hollywood, California 108
Hollywood, Florida 4
Holualoa Ranch 61
Honokaa Sugar Company 110, 212
Honolulu City Council 102-104, 240, 242, 267-269
Honolulu Gas Company 91
Honolulu Plantation 227
Honomalino Agricultural Company 105, 107, 110-111, 181, 212, 250
Honomalino Ranch 61, 105, 107
Ralph C. Hook, Jr. 251, 256, 258
Hoomau Ranch 109
Herbert Hoover 20
George Houghtailing 102-103
Robert Hughes 251
James Hunnewell 271
Hutchinson Sugar 224

I

Andy Ichiki 245
John Papa Ii 232
Sheridan Ing 147-149, 170, 201
Tom Ingledue 69

InterIsland Resorts 70, 72-76, 78, 93-100, 137, 139-140, 142, 144-148, 158, 208-211, 221, 272
Inter-Island Steam Navigation Company 71-74
Inter-Island Travel Service 73-75, 94
International Longshore and Warehouse Union (ILWU) 39-40, 51-52, 166, 209
International Market Place 102
International Utilities Corporation (IU International) 223, 250
Iolani School 113
Ishier (Ish) Jacobson 160-163, 183
Island of Hawaii xv, passim
  Gold Coast 144, 147, 209
  Haina 61-63, 79, 105, 107, 219-221
  Hamakua Coast 24, 45, 65, 110, 212, 223, 260
  Hilo 2, passim
  Holualoa 61
  Honokaa 66, 71, 111, 212, 260, 261
  Honomalino 36, 105, 181, 250, 252
  Hookena 71
  Hoopuloa 71
  Honuapo 71
  Hualalai 61
  Kahaluu Bay 144
  Kailua-Kona 61, 71-72, 76, 128, 144, 167
  Kaiwiki 219
  Kalakaua Park 18
  Kapua 105, 108
  Kau 65, 224-225, 250
  Kawaihae 144
  Keaau 106, 225, 250
  Keahole 144
  Keauhou 144, 146
  Keaukaha 67, 93, 122
  Kohala 57-58, 61, 65
  Kona 57-58, 61, 66-67, 89, 93, 105-106, 111, 143-144, 168, 181, 261, 264
  Kukaiau 71
  Kukuihaele 71
  Mamalahoa Highway 106, 109, 224

Mauka Kea 73, 91
Mauna Loa 91, 105
Naalehu 271
Napoopoo 71
Ookala 219
Onomea 21, 24, 65
Pahala 224
Papaikou 24
Puna 66
Punaluu 71
Puuanahulu 61
Puuwaawaa 61, 119
Queen Kaahumanu Highway 144
South Kona 36, 61, 105, 181
Volcano 66, 73
Waiakea 25, 67
Waianuenue Avenue 21, 28-30, 34, 55, 78, 87, 124
Wailoa River 31, 64, 67
Wailuku River 31, 78, 79
Waimea 19
Wainaku 79
West Hawaii 61, 139, 144, 147, 167
Island of Kauai vi, xiv, passim
   Grove Farm 2, 3, 7-9, 13, 23, 64, 74, 162, 262-263
   Hanalei 96
   Huleia River 64
   Kalapaki Beach 96-97, 130
   Koloa 8, 23
   Kilauea 271
   Lihue 2, 3, 96, 262
   Nawiliwili Bay 72, 96, 183
   Port Allen 158, 161
   Waimea Canyon 96
Island of Lanai 72, 226, 230
Island of Maui xv, passim
   Black Rock 98-99, 130, 141-142
   Central Maui 221
   Haleakala 136
   Haliimaile 236

    Holua 136-138
    Kapalaoa 136
    Kaanapali 98-99, 130, 141-144, 209
    Kapalua 194
    Keehi 72
    Lahaina 71, 98
    Makena 71
    Paliku 136-137
    Wailuku 2, 12, 31, 57, 71, 78-79, 137
    West Maui 98
Island of Molokai 18, 108
Island of Oahu xiv, passim
    Ahuimanu 49-50, 101-102, 104, 160
    Aiea 227-228, 230
    Aiea/Pearl City 234
    Aina Haina 61-63, 79, 105, 107
    Ala Moana 82
    Ala Wai Canal 178
    Ala Wai Harbor 142
    Central Oahu 185-186, 226, 230
    Diamond Head 63, 239, 242
    East Honolulu 61, 234
    Enchanted Lakes 239
    Ewa Plain 265
    Foster Village 238
    Ft. Shafter 186
    Haleiwa 3, 185, 226
    Hauula 264
    Hawaii Kai 180, 238-239
    Heeia 102, 239
    Honolulu xiii, passim
    Honolulu Harbor 50
    Iwilei 49
    Kaena Point 185
    Kahala 99, 238
    Kahaluu 49-500, 101-102, 144
    Kahekili Highway 101, 104
    Kahuku Point 184-185
    Kailua 71, 144. 234, 238, 239

Kalanianaole Highway 62
Kamehameha Highway 101
Kamiloiki 238
Kamilonui 238
Kaneohe 101, 234, 276
Kaonohi (Pearl) Ridge 239
Kawela Bay 186
Koolau Mountains 184, 264
Kualoa 212
Laie 264
Likelike Highway 101
Makaha 80
Makapuu Point 184-185, 264
Makiki 2, 181
Manoa 178-179
McCully 178
Mokuleia 226
Moiliili 178, 241
Niu Valley 239
North Shore 101, 185, 188, 226, 247, 264, 266
Nuuanu Pali 184-185
Palehua Ridge 185
Pali Highway 101
Palolo 178
Pearl Harbor 24, 41, 48, 71
Point Panic 194
Portlock 232, 236-237
Pupukea 185
Puu Kainapuaa 264
Sandy Beach 194
Schofield Barracks 185
Tantalus 150-151
Turtle Bay 184-185
Wahiawa 185-186, 226
Waialae Iki 187, 239
Waialae Kahala 235
Waialae Nui Valley 180
Waialae Nui 239
Waialua 185, 226, 230

Waianae Mountains 185
Waikiki 4, 70,-71, 73, 82, 98, 102, 139-141, 148, 178, 209, 229, 241
Wailupe 61
Waimea 226, 229, 264-269
Whitmore Village 226
Wilson Tunnel 101
Windward Oahu 49, 101, 185, 212, 239
Iwilei (Dole) Cannery 26

J

Janion, Green & Company 150
Jardine Matheson 156, 212-213
Marty Jaskot 213
Monica Jennings 108
Willis C. Jennings 62-63, 105-108
J.H. Pomeroy 85-86
Gerritt P. Judd 212

K

Kaanapali Beach Resort 98
Kahala View Estates 180
Duke Kahanamoku 141
Richard Kageyama 102-104
Kahala Beach Apartments 242
Kahala Community Association 232, 235-236, 238
Kahala Hilton 242
Henry Kaiser 141
Kaiwiki Sugar 212, 219
Samuel Kamakau 282
Kamehameha the Great 264, 271
Kaneohe Yacht Club 276
Kansas City, Missouri 6
Kaohsiung, Taiwan 173
Kauai Electric Light Company 158, 160-164, 183, 260, 262-263
Kauai Inn 72, 75, 95-96
Kauai Island Utility Cooperative (KIUC) 164
Kauai Surf 95, 130, 139-140, 144, 148, 158, 208-210
Kau Electric 67
Kau Sugar 224, 226

Keauhou Resort 144
Kelley Family 70
Dr. Richard Kelley 140, 198
Roy and Estelle Kelley 139, 141
Roy Kelley 140
Key West, Florida 4
Baird Kidwell 103
Joe Kiefer 247
Kilauea Sugar 162, 224
Kimball Family 96-97
King Kalakaua 24
Samuel P. King 233
King Sugar 23-24, 212, 221
Kinney and Ballou 2, 20
Bert Kobayashi Sr. 206
Karl Kobayashi 199, 245, 276
Fred Koehnen 78-79
Fritz Koehnen 78
Helie Koehnen 78-79
Koehnens Store 78-80
Koele Lodge 72
Kohala Electric 67
Koloa Sugar Company 8, 23
Kona Light and Power 67
Kona Hilton (Royal Kona Resort) 144
Kona Inn 72-73, 75-76, 93-94, 128, 139, 144
Kona Surf 143-144, 146-148, 202, 208-210
Koolau Center 104
KPMG 60
Kualoa Ranch 110, 212, 215-217
Alan Kugle 272, 274
Kuilima Resort 247
Kuomintang 169
Kuwait 85-87, 121, 152-154

L

Ladd & Company 23
Lake Quivera, Missouri 6
Laupahoehoe Sugar 212

Lehman Brothers 210
Dudley Lewis 75
Peter Lewis 69, 75
Lihue Grammar School 3
Lihue Hotel 71-72
Lihue Plantation 96, 162
Elizabeth Lindsey 253, 256
Lishan, Taiwan 173
Liverpool, England 150
London, England 152-155, 213
Long Beach, California 3, 6, 249
Los Angeles, California 6, 82, 195, 246-249
Kent Lucien 251, 272-273
Tan Tek Lum 178, 241
Lum Yip Kee 178
Lum Yip Kee, Ltd. 178, 241
Martin Luna 194

M

Ray Mabus 193
MacFarms of Hawaii 106, 181, 254-255
Bob MacGregor 94, 140-141, 208, 210
William (Bill) Mackenzie 65, 68
Mao Zedong 169
Magoon Brothers 113
David Malo 232
Frank Manaut 229
Marriott 210
Masaji Marumoto 206
Maui Land and Pineapple Co., Ltd. 194, 257
Matson Lines 70-71, 209
Maui Surf 141-144, 146-148, 202, 208-210
Mauna Kea Beach Hotel 144
Mauna Kea Sugar 224
Mauna Loa Macadamia Nuts 106
Mauna Loa Macadamia Nut Corporation 223-224, 250-252, 254-255
Mauna Loa Macadamia Partners, L.P 181, 250-255, 257-259, 271, 273
Mauna Loa Resources Inc. 250-251, 255, 257-258
Bill Maxeiner 86, 121

McBryde Sugar Co. 23
Bill McCorriston 267, 269
Melville Corporation dba Thom McCann 82-84
Mexico City, Mexico 248
Miami, Florida 4, 6
Frank E. Midkiff 233
Robert R. (Bob) Midkiff 99, 233
Bill Mills 230
Moana Hotel 70
Moana Surfrider 209
Ernest Moore 206
David Morgan 216
Francis Swanzy (Frannie) Morgan 110, 204, 212-219, 220-222, 227, 231
John Morgan 216
Margo Morgan 216
Alexander (Bill) Morriss 108, 111
Patricia Jennings Morriss 108
Mukai, Ichiki, Raffetto & MacMillan 245, 247
Frank Mukai 245, 267
Stanley Mukai 245, 267
Bill Mullahey 141
David H. Murdock 226-227, 229-230
Tony Murray 249

N

Bert Nakano 39
Naniloa Hotel 73, 75, 93, 139, 147-148, 208-211
National Labor Relations Act of 1935 39
New Haven, Connecticut 5
New York City, New York 6, 82
Luman Nevels 10
Richard Nixon 171, 176
Norfolk, Virginia 4, 6
Northwestern Law School 20

O

Oahu Railway and Land Company 48, 50, 52
Oahu Sugar 226-227, 230

Ocean View Inn 71
Dennis O'Connor 206
Sandra Day O'Connor 113
Onomea Sugar Company 24
Alan Oshima 163, 247
Lloyd Osborne 67
Terry O'Toole 195, 246-247, 249
Outrigger Canoe Club 139
Outrigger Reef Waikiki Beach Resort 139
Outrigger Hotels 70, 198-199, 209
Outrigger Waikiki Beach Resort 139-140

P

Paauhau Sugar 212, 224
Pacific Gas & Electric 159-160
Pacific Trade Center 168
Pan American World Airways 141
Papaikou Plantation 24
Parker Ranch 113
Bill Paty 228
Peat, Marwick, Mitchell 60, 177-178, 181-182
Lucy Pence 91-92
Martin Pence 90-92
Pepeekeo Plantation 24, 45
Rudy Peterson 94, 99-100
Pflueger Trust 239
Herman Phleger 38
Charles Pietsch III 264, 266
Pillsbury Madison & Sutro 10
Pioneer Mill 98
Jack Poppe 216
Patricia Morgan Poppe 216
Portlock (Maunalua Beach) Community Association 236
C. Dudley Pratt, Sr. 7-8. 10, 206
C. Dudley Pratt, Jr. 162
Pratt, Tavares & Cassidy 7-8, 10-11, 62, 90
Price Waterhouse 272
Princeton University 223, 250, 272-273
Princess Kaiulani Hotel 209

Princess Ruth Keelikolani 96
Providence, Rhode Island 109
Bob Pulley 148
Puna Geothermal Venture 260, 263
Punahou Cliffs 181
Punahou School 2-4, 7-8, 13, 19, 58, 65, 93, 98, 108, 110, 151, 181, 212, 228, 236
Puu o Hoku Ranch 108
Puuwaawaa Ranch 61, 119, 166

Q

Queen Emma Estate/Foundation 139, 238

R

Reciprocity Treaty 24
William Rehnquist 113
Art Reinwald 206
Charles Rice 96, 113
William Hyde Rice 96
Anita Rodiek 120
Frank S. Roberts 97
John Roberts 193
Carl E. Rohner 78-79
Richard Rosenthal 159, 163
Randall Roth 233
Royal Hawaiian Hotel (Downtown) 70
Royal Hawaiian Hotel (Waikiki) 11, 70, 178, 209
Royal Iolani 148
Jack Russell 83

S

Saipan 194, 245
San Clemente Island, California 4-6, 186
San Diego, California 6
San Francisco, California 10, 66, 253-254
Schofield Barracks 3, 185
Fred Schutte 206
Sea Life Park 264
Shansby Group 254-255

George Shattauer 108
Leonard Shea 82-84
Sally Shea 82, 84
Hugh Shearer 253
Dennis Simonis 254, 256, 258
Sheikh of Kuwait 85-86, 154
Sheraton 99, 141, 209
Sheraton Maui Beach Resort 99, 141
Fred Simms 177-178, 180
Ernie Smith 162
Smith Wild Beebe & Cades 7-8, 41
O. P. Soares 206
Harold Somerset 227-229
Southern California Edison 159
SS Hualalai 71
SS Humuula 71
SS Waialeale 71
Standard Oil Company of California 189, 191
Stanford Law School 9, 25, 34-35, 80, 113, 135, 165, 193, 195
Stanford University 9, 20, 34, 36, 59, 112-113, 135
Bruce Stark 148
Peter Starn 193, 199, 244, 246, 249
Staunton Military Academy 2
James Steiner 73
Stewards of Waimea Valley 268
Jimmy Stewart 109
St. Louis, Missouri 6, 108
Suez Canal, Egypt 85
Sugar Act of 1934 37, 53
Jerry Sumida 192, 260
Sun Moon Lake, Taiwan 173
Supreme Court of Hawaii 19, 21, 25, 80, 103
Francis Swanzy 212
Myer Symonds 206
Sydney, Australia 180

T

Jim Tabor 151-152, 154-155
Taipei, Taiwan 169-170, 173, 175

Taiwan 88, 169-176
Taroko Gorge, Taiwan 173, 174
Nils Tavares 206
Hugh Tennent 59
Madge Tennent 59
Val Tennent 59
Marv Tilker 223-226, 251
Boyd Townsley 162-163
The Hawaii Corporation 151
Theo H. Davies & Co. (Davies) 24-25, 110, 150-152, 154-156, 212, 223
The Ritz 152-153, 155
Topeka, Kansas 2
Tradewind Tours 94, 140, 208, 210
Laurence Tribe 237-238
Paul Trousdale 102-104
Trust for Public Land 269
Wellington Tsao 172-173, 175
Tucson, Arizona 4, 6
Twin Trees Land Company 241

U

United Technologies 188-191
University of California, Berkeley 36
University of California, Los Angeles 3
University of Hawaii 3, 11, 15, 106, 122, 251, 268
University of Michigan Law School 19
U.S. Administration on Aging 275
U.S. Alien Custodial Property Board 41
U.S. Army 4, 41, 184-187, 191, 264, 269
U.S. Army Corps of Engineers 4
U.S. Army Intelligence Corps 165
U.S. Army Reserve Officers' Training Corps 165
U. S. Department of Agriculture 53-54
U.S. Department of Justice 73
U.S. Securities and Exchange Commission 10, 66, 98, 137, 253
U.S. Senior Mens' Amateur Golf Championship 36
U.S. Supreme Court 113, 232-235, 237-238, 266
U.S. Navy 4-5, 24, 82, 108-109, 163, 183

USS Heyliger 4, 5, 14

V

Valley of the Temples Memorial Park 102-104
Wayne Van Dyck 183-184, 190
Bill Vannatta 58
Charles Vannatta 58
Tom Van Winkle 58, 135, 165-167, 193, 195, 199, 201, 239, 244, 247, 249, 252
Ted Vierra 97
Volcano House 70, 72-73

W

Tom Waddoups 206
Waiaka Lodge 76-77
Waiakea Mill Company 25
Waialua Sugar Company 188, 226-231
Wailana 148
Waimea Valley Adventure Park 265
Susan Walker 247
Warren Commission 248
Washington, D.C. 38, 72, 161, 249, 275
Waterhouse Estate 113
Wellesley College 6, 11
Western Farm Credit Bank 213-214, 217-218, 220-221
Western Pacific 5, 14, 233, 244, 249, 276
C.H. Wetmore 24
Hod White 102-104
Charles Rice (Charlie) Wichman 96, 113-114, 116, 119, 131, 135, 151-152, 155, 194-195, 199, 203, 208, 229, 244, 247
Jeanne Wichman 208
Gaylord Wilcox 7-8, 74
George Norton (G.N.) Wilcox 3, 7, 74
Urban Wild 8
Williams College 4-5, 18, 69, 80, 82, 109
Don Williams 194
Johnny Wilson 20
Wimberly Allison Tong & Goo 178, 180
George Wimberly 178

Windfarms, Ltd. 183, 187-191, 260
Sir Charles Percival Law Whishaw 86, 152-154, 157
Herbert E. Wolff 185, 187
Christian Wolffer 266-267, 269
Art Woolaway 210
Harold Wright 8
Jim Wriston, Jr. 229

Y

Yacht Harbor Towers 142, 148
Yale Law School 5
Yale University 7
Eric Yeaman 241-242
Yushan, Taiwan 173

Made in the USA
San Bernardino, CA
17 January 2019